BACKSTREETS
SPRINGSTEEN
THE MAN AND HIS MUSIC
FIRST PAPERBACK EDITION

Charles R. Cross and the Editors of **Backstreets** *Magazine*

. . . . .

With Contributions by Erik Flannigan, Robert Santelli, Robert Hilburn,

Mary Schuh, Andy Reid, Ed Sciaky, Paul Williams, Arlen Schumer,

Ken Viola, Marcello Villella, Chuck Bauerlein, Ruth Atherly, Steven Allan,

and the Asbury Park Rock 'n' Roll Museum

. . . . .

HARMONY BOOKS

. . . . .

New York

Photographs by Phil Ceccola, Lynn Goldsmith, David Gahr, Eric Meola, Barbara Pyle, Joel Bernstein, David DuBois, Debra L. Rothenberg, Rex Rystedt, James Shive, Watt M. Casey, Jr., A.J. Pantsios, Mike D'Adamo, Kathie Maniaci, Steve Zuckerman, Jeff Albertson, Paul Johnson, Robert Minkin, Kenny Barr, the Asbury Park Rock 'n' Roll Museum, Peter Philbin, Ron Delany, Vinnie Zuffante, Brooks Kraft, Chuck Jackson, Franck Stromme, Joanne Jefferson, John C. DeSantis, Jim O'Laughlin, Mary Alfieri, Larry Busacca, Pete Kuhns, and Todd Kaplan.

Editorial Assistance: Jonathan B. Pont • Production by Dale Yarger • Type by RocketType

Most of the contents of this book were originally published in *Backstreets* magazine.
The following articles are reprinted by permission of the authors:

"Out in the Streets" by Robert Hilburn. Originally published in the *Los Angeles Times*.
"Lost in the Flood" by Paul Williams. Copyright © 1988 by Paul Williams.
"Bruce Has the Fever" by Ed Sciaky. Copyright © 1978 by Ed Sciaky.

Published by Harmony Books, a division of Crown Publishers, Inc.,
201 East 50th Street, New York, New York 10022.
Member of the Crown Publishing Group.
Originally published in hardcover by Harmony Books in 1989.

HARMONY and colophon are trademarks of Crown Publishers, Inc.

Manufactured in Japan

Library of Congress Cataloging-in-Publication Data

Backstreets: Springsteen • The Man and His Music/Charles Cross and the
editors of Backstreets, with Erik Flannigan, Mary Schuh, and Robert
Santelli; contributions by Andy Reid...[et al.].
p. cm.
Discography: p.
1. Springsteen, Bruce. 2. Springsteen, Bruce—Interviews.
3. Rock musicians—United States—Interviews. I. Cross, Charles.
II. Backstreets
ML420.s77s7 1989
784.5'4'00924—dc19   89-1882

ISBN 0-517-58929-X

10 9 8 7 6 5 4 3 2

CONTENTS
· · · · · · · ·

REASON TO BELIEVE

An Introduction to Backstreets *Magazine and This Book*

Have You Heard the News?   *by Charles R. Cross*   11

GROWIN' UP

Asbury Park, Freehold, and the Jersey Shore Music Scene

Twenty Years Burning Down the Road   *by Robert Santelli*   23

The E Street Band Family Tree   *Artwork by Andy Reid*   32

George Theiss   *Interview by Robert Santelli*   34

Remembering the Upstage   *by Robert Santelli*   36

Southside Johnny   *Interview by Charles R. Cross*   41

Tour Guide for Asbury Park, New Jersey   *by Robert Santelli*   45

Tour Guide for Freehold, New Jersey   *by Robert Santelli*   50

TALK TO ME

Interviews with the Man and the Band

Lost in the Flood   *Bruce Springsteen Interview by Paul Williams*   57

Bruce Has the Fever   *Bruce Springsteen Interview by Ed Sciaky*   67

Out in the Streets   *Bruce Springsteen Interview by Robert Hilburn*   77

Max Weinberg   *Interview by Charles R. Cross*   83

Little Steven Van Zandt   *Interviews by Charles R. Cross and Marcello Villella*   87

Clarence Clemons   *Interview by Marcello Villella*   93

Danny Federici   *Interview by Robert Santelli*   97

Mike Appel   *Interview by Charles R. Cross*   107

Cover Me: Behind the Design of *Born in the USA*   *by Arlen Schumer*   131

CONTENTS
· · · · · · · ·

SPARE PARTS
Springsteen's Studio Sessions, 1966-92

143

PROVE IT ALL NIGHT
Springsteen's Performances, 1963-92

167

RESOURCES AND PHOTO CREDITS

223

*Bruce Springsteen eating a Big Mac
at a New Orleans McDonald's, September 7, 1975.* ▶

REASON TO BELIEVE

Have You Heard the News?

Running into the Darkness: Seattle, Wash., December 20, 1978.

REASON TO BELIEVE

An Introduction to Backstreets *Magazine and This Book*

"Have you heard the news? There's good rockin' tonight." That's the line I thought I heard Bruce Springsteen shout out at ten minutes before eight on October 24, 1980, and hearing it sent panic through my bones. Listening now to tapes of that night, I'm sure that's what Springsteen said — but at the time I could barely make out Springsteen's gruff mumble before the E Street Band kicked in behind him. Though there was a front-row-center seat inside the hall with my name on it, I was still standing outside the coliseum when those first chords came pounding out.

Now, almost ten years later, you hold in your hands one culmination of that tardiness. Rather than hear the news that night, I was outside passing out my own version of the news — the very first issue of my own Springsteen fanzine, a four-page tab called *Backstreets*. Little did I know at the time that a decade later the damn thing would still be around as a quarterly magazine and be called by some "the world's greatest fanzine." As I write this, more than 30 issues of *Backstreets* have been published, and in the magazine industry (where 90 percent of all new titles fail within the first three years) that's a lifetime. Add all those issues together and you get over 1,000 pages of Bruce Springsteen news and comment, making *Backstreets* the single largest source for Springsteen information anywhere — bigger, more complete, and, perhaps, with even more continuing impact than any of the many biographies written about the Boss.

Backstreets was, is, and probably always will be a nutty idea: an entire magazine devoted exclusively to one performer. While there have been numerous other fanzines about popular performers through the years, most have been either photocopied labors of love devoted to cult artists or publications created by performers' press agents as vehicles for pin-up pictures. *Backstreets* has never sought to be a pin-up forum, nor have we ever been photocopied. Our timing has been such that we never had the opportunity to write about Springsteen as a cult figure; by the time we began, he was already a certified superstar.

We did have one model, a Springsteen fanzine called *Thunder Road* that broke some ground when it first appeared in 1978, while Bruce was still a cult artist. It had its problems, though. Only six issues were published in seven years, and its mix — half official and approved of, and half fan-oriented — didn't take. But following that lead, and fueled by a desire to spread the gospel of Bruce Springsteen, I decided to publish my own Springsteen fanzine. I had already written numerous stories about Springsteen for my college newspaper, of which I was the editor, but undertaking my own magazine called for a leap of faith. And I think a leap of faith was exactly what I was looking for.

Getting ready for that jump meant dropping the objective, distanced stance taught me by my college journalism instructors. I had never felt that the Associated Press inverted-pyramid style of news reporting was appropriate for rock 'n' roll, and it certainly made no sense as applied to Bruce Springsteen. That's not to say one *can't* be objective about Springsteen, as I once wrote an objective, AP-style story about Springsteen with little of my personal emotion in it. This was back in 1975, when Springsteen performed his Seattle debut only a week after the *Time* and *Newsweek* Springsteen covers hit newsstands. I wrote a factual piece that described Springsteen's background, listed the songs played and the manner in which they were performed, and left the hyperbole out. I turned the article in to the paper's editor, who completely ignored my story (though he used my background facts) and wrote his own "rip job" illustrated by the word "HYPE," which he'd spelled out by cutting those letters from the *Time* and *Newsweek* covers. The headline read, in part, "Bruce Springsteen, 'the biggest hype since Frankie Avalon.'" So much for the virtues of objectivity. I get a little satisfaction by looking at that clipping and realizing that collectors pay upwards of $100 for a mint *Time* or *Newsweek* from that week. That editor not only made one of the biggest critical miscues in history, but he also cut up a $400 nest egg in the process.

I'd first seen Bruce Springsteen play in the summer of 1974 at the Bottom Line in New York City. Though it was a legendary show, it's hard for me to remember too much about it, as I was completely unfamiliar with him or his music that night. Springsteen ended up playing a guitar solo standing atop my table, and as he dripped sweat on me that hot summer night, I imagine I was baptized in some alien way. I came out of the theater a changed sixteen-year-old (I'd snuck in on a fake ID). I lived on the East Coast at the time, so I caught as many Bruce shows as I could after that, seeing some incendiary shows at halls like the Mosque in Richmond, Virginia, my hometown.

Those were early days of wild romance, late-night drives, summers at the beach — both for me in my life, and in Springsteen's songs at the time. I enjoyed seeing Bruce live more than any other performer. But you couldn't have called me a Bruce Tramp yet. That happened on December 20, 1978, at the show I chose to write about in the first issue of *Backstreets*.

The hall was the Seattle Center Arena, which held about 5,000 spectators. The Seattle date was less than a week after the legendary Winterland concerts and broadcasts, but for my taste it was an infinitely better show. Springsteen performed "Pretty Flamingo" for the first time in years, and unreleased versions of songs like "The Ties That Bind," "Rendezvous" and "The Fever." "Prove It All Night" ripped like a chainsaw from hell, and during the guitar solo Bruce broke two strings, yet he never hesitated or changed guitars, he simply continued playing, and what the song lacked in dynamic range he made up in dynamite. He did both his "Mona/She's the One/Gloria" medley and the touching "Backstreets/Drive All Night" segue. There was also an early version of "Independence Day" and the classic romantic barn-burner "Fire." Of the 26 songs played that night, 15 were either entirely unavailable on record or not available in the versions performed that night.

Yeah, it was great; it was magic; it was *something*. When Springsteen ended his third and seemingly final encore with "Quarter to Three," declaring himself "just a prisoner of rock 'n' roll," I remember distinctly thinking to myself, "This is the best concert I've ever seen in my life." By three encores I don't mean three *songs* as part of an encore set, I mean he left the stage on three separate occasions, only to be drawn back out by the applause. For the Winterland broadcast, Springsteen had also stunned the crowd, the announcers, and the radio audience by doing three encores (stunned them so completely that the final song "Quarter to Three" was cut off the broadcast). In Seattle, "Quarter to Three" ended about one in the morning, with Bruce stomping on my fingers while Clarence dripped about a gallon of sweat onto my already sopping head. If I'd gone to Clarence's house that night, I'm sure his dogs would have greeted me like family.

I was sitting in my chair completely exhausted. (It wasn't my chair, but I'd rushed the stage about three hours earlier and hadn't seen my chair since then, so who cared?) I'd been on 20-mile runs that had left me with more energy. My knuckles were bleeding, my ears were ringing like an errant auto alarm, and I was so hoarse from shouting that I sounded like Sally Kellerman with a head cold. I wasn't doing too much talking, though — my friends and I just sat there staring at each other, and there was nothing to say. There were about 200 people left in the hall at this point, and all of us seemed too confused or too tired to know what to do with the rest of the evening, maybe with the rest of our lives. I imagine we were all asking the same questions of ourselves: Just what do you do to follow this experience? Is there an encore in life that matches what we'd just seen Bruce Springsteen accomplish? We sat and pondered the answers while the roadies ripped down the speakers. I was lucky enough to grab the set list from the front of Springsteen's monitor — the set he'd drawn up had ended about two hours earlier, and the rest had been uncharted. The hall was silent as I read, since all the applause had ended ten full minutes earlier. Those of us who remained were just too tired to leave, so we sat and watched fat guys rip wires out of sockets and drop speaker cabinets.

Then it happened. It was such a strange thing to see that I at first actually wiped my eyes to make

Holmdel, N.J., 1978 ▶

Tacoma Dome, Tacoma, Wash., October 19, 1984.

sure it wasn't some apparition. From stage left, with a towel around his neck and carrying a guitar, Bruce Springsteen was running onstage. When I said before that there was no applause left, I meant there was absolutely no applause at all (almost everyone had left) when Springsteen came running onstage. He wasn't walking or sauntering, either, the way most performers would go onstage for an encore; he ran as if in some mad dash, like the character in the movie *D.O.A.* in a desperate search to locate an antidote that would be the only thing to save him from certain death. Not only did the sight of him stun me, but the whole audience watched in disbelief. I think they, like myself, were half expecting him to go up to the mike and announce that some horrible national tragedy had occurred, or that maybe he'd say, "The building is on fire, get the hell out of here!" But when he ran up to the only remaining mike stand, the one usually reserved for Steve Van Zandt, he started yelling and strumming his guitar. He wasn't yelling anything about a fire, though. He was unamplified, but I could hear him yell "Rave on!"

Around this time the rest of the band started to waltz back onstage, and maybe 20 people in the crowd started politely clapping. Springsteen was already into the second verse at this point, which was a little strange since he had no amp for his guitar and "Rave On" is not exactly "This Land Is Your Land" when it comes to intimacy. Finally, Bruce pulled up and waited as the roadies madly dashed to get equipment plugged back in. Everyone — the band, the audience, the roadies — just sort of stood there for a while, looking at Bruce. And there he was, with a big grin. After three years of nasty lawsuits; after a time he described even ten years later as his own season of hell; after a three-hour concert that had exhausted even the hot-dog vendors; after it seemed he'd already said everything that could or should be said about rock 'n' roll; after all that, Bruce Springsteen just stood there with that stupid gap between his teeth, looking for all the world like the Cheshire Cat. It was one of the handful of times in your life — like your first kiss with the woman you'll eventually marry — when you know you are experiencing a moment that you will never forget. I've never forgotten that grin. I never will.

Springsteen played "Rave On" and "Twist and Shout" and finished it up. There had been about

200 people left in the hall, but when the sound became amplified, anyone within hearing distance charged back into the arena and maybe another 200 made it, knocking over security guards in the process. When Springsteen finished "Twist and Shout" and left the stage again, it was with confusion as much as appreciation that the crowd responded. The tape I have of the show is fascinating — you can hear the remaining members of the crowd trying to come to terms with what they'd just seen (and you can hear me in the background, shouting "BROOOOOCE!" like a loon). "I thought it was all over," says one guy standing right next to the tape recorder. "I kind of got caught off guard. Half the people had already left." "Yeah," chirps in another. "Wild, isn't it?" Wild and innocent.

At this point, nobody was leaving the building until the security guards threw us out — I mean, who was to say that Bruce wouldn't come back one more time? Finally, all the lights were turned off, which meant that the remaining crowd had to find their way out in the dark.

When we did leave the building, we found a chilly December night and a full moon. The temperature had dropped a good 20 degrees in the five hours since we'd entered the hall, and it was so late that the Monorail (the main method of transportation between the Seattle Center and downtown) had shut down. With my friends, I walked the 20 blocks to the core of the city in silence, and it actually started to snow — a rare occurrence in Seattle, even in December. I made it home at 15 minutes after four on the morning of December 21. It had never felt more like Christmas.

· · · · ·

That December 20 show may not be the single best Springsteen concert ever (that honor may be held by Berkeley Community Theater 1978 or L.A. Sports Arena 1981 or maybe the Main Point 1973) but it was surely the best show *I* ever saw, and it planted a seed that urged me to start *Backstreets*. I felt like a man on a mission, and when Springsteen came around two years later with the *River* tour, I was ready to ride.

I persuaded a local radio station to pay for some of the printing costs in exchange for an ad; a friend of mine donated typesetting; another offered photos from the Arena show; I put up a couple of hundred bucks and soon I had 10,000 copies of a four-page tabloid. I called it *Backstreets* after my

favorite song, and subtitled it "Seattle's Bruce Springsteen Fanzine." The front-page story was about the December 20 show, illustrated by some great pictures from that night. The center spread was a poster, and there were three small stories on the back page about collecting. My girlfriend, her sister, and I spent the two hours before the show handing them out free to everyone standing in line, which was why I missed "Good Rockin' Tonight." I never gave any thought to charging for the magazine — do the Gideons charge for hotel Bibles? — though I was a bit disappointed after the show to see so many copies trashed beneath people's seats. Anyone who trashed the mag made a mistake, but I made the biggest mistake of all by not saving a few thousand; I now own only one copy albeit an autographed one.

Serious collectors now will pay upwards of $100 for copies of that first issue of *Backstreets*. And though there are probably not 10,000 people who would put out that sort of dough for something so small, if there *were*, you could say I gave away a million dollars' worth of fanzine that night. It was worth every cent, no matter what it cost me, because it has paid off with friends, with the ties that bind over the years. That was the genesis of the magazine, and from that point it has grown into something far greater than it was that night, something far greater than I could ever have imagined it becoming. And finally, when we realized we'd written about five books' worth of material about Bruce Springsteen, we decided to create this book.

Our growth was slow, however. The magazine was around for four years before the number of subscribers passed 1,000, and even today more people see Springsteen at a single coliseum-sized concert than subscribe to *Backstreets*. Eventually we added color printing, slick paper, and the sort of graphics that make us look like any other magazine on the newsstand. But it was seven years before the magazine could afford to move the office out of my basement, and it has never been a financial success (I've always worked other full-time jobs to support myself). But remember — since the magazine was fueled by passion rather than entrepreneurial drive, we don't judge our success on a business scale.

The major impact of the magazine has been on the hearts and minds of the people who read it. Every day we get letters from Bruce Tramps (many in far-off places around the globe) who tell us they

thought they were "the only one in the world" who felt this way about Springsteen, until they read *Backstreets*. Every subscriber I've ever spoken with has admitted to reading the magazine from cover to cover on the day it arrives, which is not something you can say about *Rolling Stone* or *Time*.

Considering that *Backstreets* has always counted my personal fanaticism as its major (and sometimes its only) resource, we have accomplished some surprising things. It was in an interview with *Backstreets* that Steve Van Zandt first announced he was leaving the E Street Band for his solo career; it was *Backstreets* that dug up Suki Lahav, former E Street Band violinist, for her first interview with the press in more than ten years; and it was *Backstreets* that led the pack in first reporting on the upcoming releases of the *Born in the USA* and *Live* records. That's all in addition to having the most complete coverage of the *Born in the USA* and *Tunnel of Love* tours anywhere, including *Backstreets'* tradition of running song lists from every Springsteen performance. We've also tracked and reported on every individual Springsteen record release from the United Kingdom to Uruguay. At least two couples have met and married through the pen-pal classifieds in the back of the magazine (probably to the tune of Bruce's "I Wanna Marry You").

If you're noticing that I'm not boasting about *Backstreets* being the first to break the news of Springsteen's marriage (or divorce) or any of the other developments in his personal life, there's a good reason for that; *Backstreets* is about Bruce Springsteen's performing and recording career, *not* about his personal life. We surely would have sold more copies of the magazine if we covered that stuff (Bruce's personal life has been hot copy these past few years), but that idea is contradictory to everything we are about. When I saw Bruce that night in December of 1978, it wasn't who he was sleeping with that impressed me. Reporters are constantly asking me questions about Springsteen's life, and when I choose to tell them nothing but the obvious, they seem offended; it is as if, in this celebrity-driven media circus, my neutral position offends people. They seem to think that all public figures deserve to be dragged through the lion's den, and anyone who doesn't agree with that concept is some sort of heretic. Springsteen fans, for the most part, are concerned with who Spanish

Johnny is sleeping with, but not Bruce himself.

In this respect, *Backstreets* might seem to take the company line on Bruce Springsteen. But before you start thinking of this magazine as some extension of a publicity machine, consider that the magazine has also been highly critical of some of Springsteen's career moves (playing stadiums, doing funk remixes, and, in general, the gross over-commercialization of his career around the time of *Born in the USA*). Though I have yet to hear a Springsteen song I dislike, many of the machinations that go on around those songs are open to debate in *Backstreets*. This occasional criticism, and the very fact that we have an independent viewpoint on Springsteen that doesn't have anything to do with selling his records, has led to mixed relations with his management company.

As I've said many times before in the magazine, *Backstreets* is not so much a magazine *about* Bruce Springsteen as it is *for* Bruce Springsteen *fans*. That may sound like a minor point, but it is indeed a large distinction. *Backstreets* does not even necessarily have a whole hell of a lot to do with Springsteen *the man*, while it has everything to do with Springsteen's *work*.

It's ironic to consider that Springsteen himself doesn't examine his own work as closely as his fans do. He's very aware of his image and he considers his art carefully. (He said prior to the *Tunnel of Love* tour that that album was his personal favorite. He says that every time he starts a tour, but you get the feeling he really means it.) I think he finds fans like me, who collect and catalog all his work, including unreleased studio outtakes and rare one-time-only concert performances, to be a little off the deep end. As I understand his composition process, it's the material he's currently writing, the new songs for the *next* record, that concerns him — not the unreleased version of "Loose Ends" recorded in 1979 that I think stands as his best unreleased work. He probably hasn't listened to that song in years.

So what does Bruce Springsteen think about *Backstreets*? I've asked him on more than one occasion, and the best I've ever gotten out of him was a response like, "Everybody's sure talking about it." Even if he liked it, I couldn't much imagine him saying so publicly, since he's very careful with any sort of public endorsement. He reads it, I know, since on at least two occasions in concert he's referred to information only published in *Backstreets*. And I know he read my review of *Born in the USA* because in 1984 he autographed my copy of it and said he thought my discussion of western imagery was more appropriate for *Nebraska*. That autograph on my review in that *Backstreets* is my most prized possession — owning Elvis's gold lame suit wouldn't mean more to me.

When I was younger and caught up in the hysteria surrounding the *Born in the USA* tour, I probably was guilty of being a pain-in-the-ass fan. Whenever I ran into him I bugged him about playing some unreleased song or I tried to gain some B-side release info. A typical exchange follows:

Cross: Bruce, when are you going to release 'Roulette'? It's your best song.

Springsteen: We don't know that one.

Cross: Yeah, you know it. I'll even write down the words for you.

Springsteen: Nah, the band doesn't know it.

Cross: They do, they told me they want to play it.

Springsteen: Ah, Charley, could you just leave me alone? Can't you see I'm trying to swim laps here?

Springsteen did finally release "Roulette" in 1988 as a B-side, but one would have to figure it was be-

cause he ran out of finished studio outtakes from *Tunnel of Love* and not out of a desire to see my wish finally come true. Nonetheless, when it was first announced that it would be the new B-side, there was more screaming in our office than you'd hear if the actual incident the song is about (the Three Mile Island nuclear accident) was happening right across the street.

Despite being an unofficial publication, and without the benefit of late-night phone calls from Bruce himself (Bruce: you can call collect), *Backstreets* has continued to exist because there are many people within the organization, within the band, and within the music business who believe in the concept of a magazine that is nonexploitative and who basically think *Backstreets* is an honor to Bruce Springsteen, whether he sees it that way or not. Occasionally we've made the wrong call or

gotten information wrong, but considering our situation we've done better than one might have expected. On the last two tours, *Backstreets* covered the shows more extensively than any historian could have, listing sets from every single stop, be it Indianapolis, Indiana, or New Delhi, India. We have our sources, but again they are people who provide us with information on songs and shows and the like, not personal dirt.

We make an effort to make sure that everything we do in *Backstreets* magazine, and everything we've done in this book, reflects the enthusiasm we feel every time those opening chords to "Rosalita" come cranking out. Though we cater to the collector mentality, we try not to be elitist — many of Springsteen's present fans didn't have a chance to see him in small clubs like I did. Still, this is probably not the book for the casual Springsteen fan. The other contributors and I are the type of fans who find almost every bit of information about Springsteen's work important and illuminating. For example, how many people who bought the *Born to Run* album would care to know that nine different titles were considered for the album — including *Sometimes at Night* and *War and Roses* — and that "Thunder Road" was at one point planned to open and close the record? Probably not many, but for those people, *Backstreets* is the *Encyclopedia Britannica* of the Boss. It's an obsession and a passion, and after you look through the concert listings here (detailing every single public performance known to have been played by Springsteen in the last 20 years), you might agree.

This book collects the best pieces we've run in the magazine over the years — interviews, history, behind-the-scenes details about what goes into making Springsteen's music. Also, we've assembled some of the raw data we've collected over the years — on collecting, on Springsteen's recording sessions, and on the aforementioned concert listing. It's a lot, and it's my hope that you'll find every bit of it useful or entertaining.

When reading this material, do consider the time frame; *Backstreets* didn't even begin until after *The River* was released, so most of these stories center around the recent part of Springsteen's career. Though we have included plenty of historical articles, we didn't have the opportunity to review *The Wild, the Innocent and the E Street Shuffle* when it came out. (If we had reviewed it, I'd have given it 11 on a scale of 10 — it's my favorite Springsteen

Philadelphia, Pa., July 19, 1981.

record.) We've also compiled exclusive original material that even hard-core *Backstreets* subscribers will find enlightening and new.

Back during the early years of Springsteen's career, when he was doing lots of interviews (Springsteen even spent his birthday in 1979 driving around all day with a reporter from an obscure New Jersey tabloid), one of the questions he was most frequently asked concerned what drove him to perform with the intensity he exhibits onstage. I think most reporters asked this because sometimes onstage Springsteen is positively otherworldly, and describing even that can get difficult. And, of course, Bruce had no answer for them. He has always been the way he is. Like the heir to a royal throne, he was born the King.

So Bruce usually took the question and turned it around to talk about what he thought about on-stage and where he directed his show. His line was that he put the show on, played the guitar solos, wrote the songs, did the whole thing for "that kid in the tenth row." "I go out every night," he once said, "and I try to think about that kid in the tenth row. If I can reach him, then I know I've done my job."

Ironically, when I walked into the Seattle Center Arena in December of 1978, my seat was nowhere near the tenth row; I was in the rafters, since I'd been out of town when tickets first went on sale. But it didn't matter where I sat, because the tenth row Bruce Springsteen was playing to that night wasn't a physical place — it was a state of mind.

This book is about sitting in that tenth row, and if you can find that place inside yourself, perhaps one day you'll see four encores, one of them ten minutes after all the applause has ended.

—Charles R. Cross

GROWIN' UP

Asbury Park, Freehold,
and the Jersey Shore
Music Scene

Wasted in the Heat: Child, Long Branch, N.J., June 1969.

Twenty Years Burning Down the Road

The Complete History of Jersey Shore Rock 'n' Roll

Mention the English city of Liverpool to the average soul on the street, and chances are the first vision that will pass through his or her mind is that of four mop-topped lads called the Beatles. Try it sometime. Ask your mom or dad, or your boss. Ask the postperson, or the middle-aged woman in the supermarket.

Liverpool isn't known or remembered as an important prewar seaport, which it was, or for its soccer team. It's known to the world as the city where the Beatles originated. It's practically impossible to separate this glum, working-class city from the legacy of the Beatles, and vice versa.

Mention Asbury Park, New Jersey, to that same person, and it's a good bet that they'll say something like "Asbury Park? Yeah, that's the place where Bruce Springsteen comes from." Granted, that's not entirely accurate, because Springsteen was, of course, born and raised in nearby Freehold (although at times in the late sixties and early seventies, he did reside in Asbury Park, and he certainly spent much time playing the city's clubs and bars).

Nonetheless, because of Bruce Springsteen, Asbury Park has earned a secure place in rock history books. The city's rich past as a prewar seaside resort, with once-beautiful beaches and a bustling boardwalk, and the nationally reported race riots that tore through the city and devastated its downtown shopping district in 1970 are both, historically speaking, secondary to the city's relationship to the man they call the Boss. The fact is, Asbury Park is inextricably linked with Bruce Springsteen, and vice versa.

There are other similarities that, in a way, make Liverpool and Asbury Park sister cities. Each is a city whose past is brighter than its present. In each, unemployment remains high, decay is dominant, and the landscape can best be painted in shades of gray. True, there is much talk about a renaissance or rebirth of Asbury Park. And over the past couple of years the city has striven hard to initiate a massive facelift and implement a more positive image. Yet, sadly, Asbury Park largely remains the same Asbury Park that Bruce Springsteen pinpointed so forcefully in his early music.

Interestingly, ever since Springsteen came to prominence, the media have possessed a somewhat morbid fascination with Asbury Park. To many journalists, photographers, TV reporters and filmmakers, Asbury Park has routinely symbolized a particular slice of America's underbelly, a place just brimming with the kinds of stark, gloomy images from which great works of art, literature — and music — originate.

The idea was always that if you could understand the environment (Asbury Park and the rest of the Jersey Shore) of the artist (Springsteen) — namely, the seaside bars and blue-collar beer joints, the boardwalk amusements and pizza parlors, the lonely streets and broken dreams — then you'd appreciate more fully the artist's art (Springsteen's songs). To a large degree, this is true. Few American songwriters have been able to take such detailed images of the American Dream, as well as the tales of hardship and disappointment that accompany them, and imbue them with the universality that Bruce Springsteen has. Springsteen took from all around him. He transformed the characters that hung out in Asbury Park's bars and boardwalk into song personalities that symbolized life's struggle. He worked his impressions of Asbury Park and the rest of the Jersey Shore into his lyrics in such a way that the songs weren't about Asbury or Jersey, but about America and about you and me.

"It was natural right from the beginning that when people wanted to learn more about Bruce, that they came to Asbury," said one local. "It's not much to look at, I know, but for rock 'n' roll it's a

Widner College, Chester, Pa., February 6, 1975 with Suki Lahav on violin.

great place. It's a rock 'n' roll town if there ever was one. And it's really pretty spiritual. I mean, you don't go visiting the town where Jackson Browne came from, do you?"

Actually, the media fascination with Asbury Park began more than a decade ago — in 1975, to be precise. And it started with the biggest of bangs. What longtime Springsteen fan can ever forget that amazing week in October when the covers of both *Time* and *Newsweek* were graced with the face of Bruce Springsteen? Before that came the cover story on Bruce in the now defunct but at the time critically praised magazine *Crawdaddy*. And there were others. It was part hype and part intrigue, but all of a sudden Asbury Park was being touted the same way Liverpool was some ten years earlier.

"It was really weird," said Southside Johnny in an interview a few years ago. "You had photographers and reporters poking their heads into clubs and looking for God knows what. Nobody ever paid attention to Asbury Park or the musicians who played there and lived there before. Some people never got the hang of it."

The world found out about Bruce Springsteen's roots and about Asbury Park. And in the process, some of the more astute observers discovered a music scene that was vibrant and rich with bands. There was Southside Johnny and the Asbury Jukes. There was Cahoots. There was Lord Gunner, the Shakes, and Cold, Blast, and Steel. They were the local stars in the local clubs. Few of them had ever ventured beyond the Jersey Shore with their guitars and amps. It was strictly a home-grown rock scene. While popular music in the mid-seventies began flirting with disco, and rock was caught with a bad case of the blahs, the music heard in Asbury Park clubs — like the Stone Pony — revolved around rhythm and blues and sixties soul. Outside the scene, such influences were considered dated and passe. But in Asbury Park, R&B-based rock was hot and sassy.

Also, blues was big, especially in the late sixties, just as it was in San Francisco and England. It was an easily adaptable style of music, and it lent itself to jamming. Jamming was what Asbury Park's legendary club, the Upstage, was all about. In fact, if any one element was (and still is) most representative of the Jersey Shore music scene in general and Asbury Park's in particular, it was the concept of late-night jams and sitting in. It began at house parties, moved to the Upstage in the late sixties and later to the Stone Pony as well as a whole slew of other clubs such as the Student Prince, the Fast Lane, Mrs. Jay's, and the High Tide Cafe.

Right from the very beginning, there were some bands that began overshadowing the others. Down around Asbury Park, Sonny and the Starfires ruled. Sonny Kenn, a guitarist influenced by the likes of Link Wray and Lonnie Mack, was the bandleader and frontman. The Starfires' backbeat was kept by a self-taught drummer named Vini Lopez. Out in the Freehold area, it was the Motifs, the band that came closest to turning professional and reaching beyond the Jersey Shore, and the Castiles, which included two respected guitarists, George Theiss and Bruce Springsteen. Up in Red Bank, The Source, led by Steve Van Zandt, was making itself known by playing in local battle-of-the-bands contests and playing high school dances.

To take advantage of the wealth of young rock talent at the Shore in the mid-sixties and of the seemingly insatiable appetite of kids there for live rock 'n' roll, a host of nonalcoholic teen clubs sprouted throughout the area. The Hullabaloo chain of teen clubs was especially popular. Sonny and the Starfires became regulars at the Asbury Park Hullabaloo club. Here is how Sonny Kenn remembers those days:

"We wore gold lame suits and fancy boots, and we had Ampeg and Fender amplifiers. We'd get up there onstage at around 8 P.M., and we'd play 55 minutes with a five-minute break. Then we'd go back and play again. It was just enough time to have a cigarette and a soda. We played there all summer and gained a tremendous amount of experience. By this time Vini [Lopez] had introduced me to this kid from Garden Grove, Johnny Lyon [later known as Southside Johnny], and he started coming to all our gigs and practice sessions. Whenever we played at Hullabaloo or a school dance or something, he'd go out in the audience to make sure our amps were turned up high enough."

The competition between bands at the Jersey Shore in the mid-sixties was certainly keen, but it was not cutthroat. Instead, there was a subtle yet strong bond between musicians that later made the Upstage experience such a valuable one for them.

Despite the occasional squabble, such camaraderie allowed for the frequent trading of ideas and riffs, and enabled musicians and bands to grow.

Even though the mid-sixties saw the rise of a large number of bands at the Shore, few groups played anywhere but the Shore. What with teen clubs, high school and CYO dances, and battles of the bands, of which there were many, there were plenty of places to perform locally without having to venture to New York.

One group, the Castiles, had more drive than most. It also had a manager, Tex Vinyard, who took it upon himself to push the group musically and force it to seek brighter horizons. Because of him, the Castiles were one of the few mid-sixties Shore bands to make a record (a self-produced, self-recorded single, "That's What You Get" backed with "Baby I"). Vinyard also worked the Castiles into a regular set of gigs at New York's legendary club, the Cafe Wha?, where groups like the Blues Project and artists such as Jimi Hendrix and Bill Cosby got their start.

"Tex was a big ego builder," George Theiss remembers. "He would sit there and tell you how the girls were going crazy over you. At 16 or 17, that's just what you wanted to hear. He made sure we were confident."

Confidence. That's the key word. Vinyard instilled a sense of sureness in the Castiles, especially Springsteen, that never really left them. Vinyard also exposed the group to a whole new level of rock in New York City that most other Shore bands missed during this era. Such things enabled Springsteen to leave the Castiles when the Jersey Shore music scene was about to enter a new stage in the late sixties and to form his own bands fueled by his own rock visions.

From this point on, it was Springsteen who set the pace, who broke the most new ground, and, as Theiss says, who acted "as if he already had a plan . . . and knew exactly where he was heading."

. . . .

Much has been written about the Upstage. "It was really a unique place, the Upstage," said Van Zandt. "I've never ever run across another club like it anywhere else in the world."

"Everybody went there 'cause it was open later than the regular clubs and because between one and five in the morning you could play pretty much whatever you wanted, and if you were good enough, you could choose the guys you wanted to play with," wrote Springsteen in the liner notes for *I Don't Want to Go Home,* the debut album of Southside Johnny and the Asbury Jukes.

"It was like going to school," recalled Sonny Kenn a few years ago. "Upstage, when you think about it, really was a school. Better yet, for those of us who used to play at Hullabaloo and the teen clubs, it was almost a college of sorts."

The entire Jersey Shore music scene revolved around the Upstage for the two years or so in the late sixties that it was open. Run by Tom and Margaret Potter, it was a meeting place, a proving ground, and a musical laboratory all in one. More groups were formed there, and more groups broke up there, than anywhere else.

Musicians at the Upstage were part of a large pecking order. The best — Springsteen, Van Zandt, and other guitar players like Billy Ryan, Ricky DeSarno, and Sonny Kenn, drummers such as Vini Lopez and Big Bobby Williams, harp players like Southside Johnny, and keyboard players such as David Sancious — had first dibs on stage time. Other musicians worked their way onstage when they were good enough to play with the first team.

The Upstage acted as a springboard for what was to follow at the Jersey Shore in the 1970s. No one could ever have deliberately planned a club so crucial to the development of so many musicians. The incredible thing is that it worked. The informality, the competition, Tom Potter's zany, slapstick-like organizational skills, and the madness that never really surfaced long enough to blow the whole thing out of control, all created an atmosphere of intense apprenticeship.

It was during this time that Bill Chinnock's Downtown Tangiers Band gained notoriety and respect as far north as New York, that Maelstrom (Southside on bass and harp, Kenn on guitar, and Ronnie Romano on drums) practically became the house band at the downstairs coffeehouse section of the Upstage, and that Steel Mill, the first of the truly great Shore bands, was born.

· · · · ·

Steel Mill's best lineup was Springsteen on guitar and vocals, Steve Van Zandt on bass, Danny Federici on organ, and Vini Lopez on drums. On a bad night Steel Mill was still the best outfit on the Shore, perhaps in all of Jersey. On a good night, the band was, well, simply amazing.

I remember going to see the band in concert at Ocean County College in Toms River, New Jersey. It was a typically hot and humid night at the Shore. I think it was August 1970. The gymnasium was packed with sweaty, anxious souls. The word had spread about Steel Mill. Anticipation filled the air. Even though Springsteen had briefly attended Ocean County College, and Toms River is part of the Jersey Shore, it wasn't part of Steel Mill's true stomping grounds. Many people in the audience that night had only heard about how good the band was supposed to be.

For the two hours or so that Steel Mill played, Springsteen and company simply overwhelmed everyone on the other side of the stage. Had his brand of blues-rock been available on record at the time, or had that concert been somehow made into a live album and rushed to radio stations and record stores, it would have rivaled Led Zeppelin's best, I swear.

People who had seen Steel Mill for the first time walked out of that show as if they had participated in a mystical musical experience. Springsteen's manager, Jon Landau, saw the future of rock 'n' roll four years later in 1974. A lot of us at the Shore saw it that night.

There were other fine bands at the Shore during this time. Southern Conspiracy was one. Sunny Jim was another. Both opened for Steel Mill on a regular basis. It was an era of shared apartments and skimpy meals, and of free outdoor concerts at local parks and at Monmouth College in West Long Branch, when the weather was good.

It was also an era of restlessness. Steel Mill made a trip to California and played the Fillmore West. Afterwards, rock impresario Bill Graham offered the band free recording time. They recorded three songs for him but turned down his contract offer. Back in Jersey a few months later, Springsteen formed Dr. Zoom and the Sonic Boom, which represented a classic case of musical absurdity and was the result of wild experimentation never before seen at the Shore.

Musicians came and went. Garry Tallent, David Sancious, Southside Johnny, and others left Asbury Park and headed to Richmond, Virginia, a town that became a home away from home for Asbury Park players. Others split for California, Colorado, and New England. Springsteen's restlessness is well documented. He broke up Steel Mill. He formed the Bruce Springsteen Band. He broke up the Bruce Springsteen Band. He became a folk-

The E Street Band, August 1973 (L to R): Danny, Vini, Bruce, Garry, Clarence, and David Sancious.

singer. He commuted to New York's Greenwich Village and played the clubs there. And then he got a recording contract.

· · · ·

Springsteen's signing with Columbia Records was enough of an event to bring most everyone back to Asbury Park in 1972 and 1973. The scene, which had become disjointed and lost its purpose, was about to be righted.

"Bruce needed a band to make *Greetings from Asbury Park, N.J.* with," recalled Garry Tallent. "So the word went out and people came home." A new version of the Bruce Springsteen Band was formed, the record was made, and the boys hit the road to promote it.

"It was an interesting time," remembers Big Danny Gallagher, who acted as the band's road manager. "We played all these weird places and drove hundreds of miles to do it again the next

night. Nobody saw much in the way of money. We practically starved."

Back home, musicians, caught up in the enthusiasm of one of their own actually making a record and going on tour, formed new bands and hoped to follow in Springsteen's footsteps. One such group was the Blackberry Booze Band.

"The kind of music we played was blues," says David Meyers, the Booze Band's bass player. "Steve [Van Zandt] was in the band and so was Southside. We played the kind of stuff that might have been heard during the Upstage days, but we did it with more polish, I think. We also played a lot of material that no one else had ever heard before. We were a band rather than a bunch of musicians that simply showed up and jammed, although at times that did happen when friends asked to sit in."

By this time a new club had opened up on Ocean

Avenue in Asbury Park, called the Stone Pony. Its owners were looking for a house band that would draw locals to the club on a regular basis. Using some of the ideas worked out in the Blackberry Booze Band, Miami Steve Van Zandt and Southside Johnny formed just the group the Pony was searching for, Southside Johnny and the Asbury Jukes.

Van Zandt, who had toured with the Dovells after Steel Mill broke up, and who had always been infatuated with black music, formed the Asbury Jukes around a horn section and a pepper-hot rhythm section. Not prepared to take center stage himself, he gave that task to Southside. Armed with a blazing harp and an encyclopedic knowledge of blues and R&B, Johnny sang and moved like his heroes — Jackie Wilson, Otis Redding, Sam Cooke, and Ray Charles — and the Pony began to fill up.

When Springsteen and his band came off the road, they found the Stone Pony the place to hang out. Gradually, the club became the unofficial meeting place of Jersey Shore musicians, especially those with strong links to Asbury Park.

"It filled a gap," says Kevin Kavanaugh, an original member of the Asbury Jukes who still plays keyboards in the band. "When the Upstage closed, there was really no place where you knew you could go on a given night and find plenty of musicians. The Pony became that place."

· · · · ·

It was in 1976 that the music scene of the Jersey Shore, particularly in Asbury Park, had matured into one worthy of national attention. Springsteen's *Born to Run*, released the year before, had been critically acclaimed in virtually every nook and cranny of the rock media. The *Time* and *Newsweek* stories had introduced him to mainstream America. All the hype that surrounded Springsteen nearly destroyed his career, but it did wonders for Asbury Park and the Stone Pony.

When record company executives came looking for another Springsteen in the back alleys and beer joints of Asbury, they almost certainly wound up at the Pony, where they were introduced to the Asbury Jukes. Springsteen praised the band and helped open important doors at Epic Records. Soon Southside and the Jukes had a record deal. On Memorial Day 1976 they celebrated the release of *I*

◄ *Atlantic Highlands, N.J., September 11, 1970.*

Don't Want to Go Home with a Stone Pony concert broadcast live on the radio.

David Sancious, who had left the E Street Band, along with drummer Boom Carter, to start a solo career as a jazz-rock fusion artist, also scored a record deal. His album, *Forest of Feelings*, although not nearly as commercially popular as *I Don't Want to Go Home*, scored high critical marks nonetheless.

Other Asbury Park-based bands such as the Shakes, Cold, Blast and Steel, Lord Gunner and the Cahoots scrambled to be the next in line. None ever did land a contract, but they came close. All this added up to what many locals consider the heyday of Jersey Shore music. Asbury Park was, in a word, music-rich. It was primarily a rock-R&B blend that one heard echoing out of area clubs, flavored with the sounds of a saxophone and the gritty vocals of a lead singer well versed in soul and Motown. Black leather jackets, newsboy caps, and earrings were in. Bands like Paul Whistler and the Wheels and the Shots kept the musical momentum strong.

Eventually the scene diversified enough to allow bands such as Kinderhook Creek, with deep-seated ties to country and Southern rock; Salty Dog, the Shore's answer to heavy metal; and Sam the Band, perhaps the area's best Top 40 bar band, to develop large, devoted followings.

One would have thought, though, that with all the musical energy coming out of the Shore and with the large number of bands — and good bands at that — vying for a chance at stardom, at least one or two other outfits would have signed their names on record contracts.

"You have to take into consideration the 'Springsteen curse,'" says one prominent Shore musician who asked to remain anonymous. "As much as Bruce was good for the local scene, he was also bad for it. Every band that was worthy of a recording contract in the late seventies was branded a Springsteen clone, it seemed. That's why nobody got signed in those years. Record companies heard you were from Asbury Park and right away they shut their doors. The hype was over. A lot of good bands were denied their chance to get a deal because of the whole Springsteen bit. Now don't get me wrong. I ain't saying it was his fault. It just happened that way."

Consider the case of Billy Chinnock. An Upstage veteran and longtime member of the Shore music scene, it was Chinnock's bad luck to be

Bryn Mawr, Pa., February 26, 1974.

labeled an Asbury Park artist with an R&B-styled sound that closely resembled Springsteen's. Chinnock even looked and sounded like Springsteen at times. But worse, even though he was one of the precious few to sign a recording contract in the late seventies (with Atlantic), what did he call his debut album? *Badlands*.

"I had no idea Bruce had a song with the same name," said Chinnock in an interview. "I couldn't help it that I sort of have the same features as he does. And we came from the same roots, so why should my music sound all that different from his?

"It was like no matter what I did or where I turned, there was this Bruce-ghost following me. I knew I'd never get the proper attention in Jersey, so I moved to New York, then Maine, then back to Jersey, and finally to Nashville. It was there that I got a record company (CBS Associates) to take another look at my songs. It took a long time and a lot of running."

Gradually, disappointment and frustration began to take a toll in Asbury Park. Bands broke up. Some musicians turned away from music altogether. Disco was hot elsewhere in America, so many club owners sought out DJs or Top 40 dance bands to fill the dance floors on the Shore. Even the Stone Pony began booking cover bands.

What saved the scene was the opening of a new club in Asbury Park, the Fast Lane. Its booking agent and manager, Jim Giantonio, sought out national acts when no one else would, and hired local bands which played original music to open for them. Almost overnight it became the Shore's premier club. Not only did acts like Joe Jackson, the Ramones, Robert Gordon, and seemingly countless New Wave bands from Britain play the club in the early eighties, but "honorary" Shore groups such as Beaver Brown and Norman Nardini and the Tigers developed strong followings.

Giantonio actively encouraged area bands to

focus on original music. He was, for example, responsible for pushing a band called The Rest, which included a lead singer named John Bongiovi (later to be known as Jon Bon Jovi), to deal seriously with its image and stage presence as well as its original songs. The result? The Rest became the best on the Shore in the early eighties.

The success of the Fast Lane prompted the Stone Pony to change gears and revert to its old policy of featuring original music bands. Another club, Big Man's West, owned by E Street band member Clarence Clemons, opened in nearby Red Bank. A whole new generation of Shore bands filled these clubs: Clarence Clemons and the Red Bank Rockers, Sonny Kenn and the Wild Ideas, Hot Romance, Cats on a Smooth Surface, Junior Smoots and the Disturbers. At the Pony, E Street Band members were back hanging out, and Springsteen would routinely show up on Sunday nights to sit in with Cats on a Smooth Surface. Suddenly the Shore music scene was back on its feet.

· · · ·

Sidenote: While all this was happening in Asbury Park and Red Bank, a hardcore punk offshoot of the Shore music scene sprouted in nearby Long Branch. The host club was the Brighton Bar. It permitted slamdancing and gave the rowdiest punk bands a place to perform.

"Hardcore at the Shore is just a violent reaction to all the hype that surrounds Asbury Park and the bands that play there," said The Mutha, owner of Long Branch's Mutha Records and a leader of the local punk movement a couple of years ago. "We don't want any part of that crap." Brighton bands openly resented bands that played the Asbury Park/Red Bank circuit and repudiated the R&B roots of the area in grand fashion.

Yet there were ties. John Eddie played the Brighton as much as he played Big Man's West. So did Sonny Kenn. Little Steven was even known to sign in at the Brighton when he was at the Shore. And some very good bands came out of the scene, bands that, with the proper guidance, could have gone much farther than they did. One such group was Secret Syde. Another was the Wallbangers.

· · · ·

All this brings us to the present. The Fast Lane is gone, as is Big Man's West. The Stone Pony has reclaimed its right to be called the Shore's most prestigious rock club, though redevelopment plans for Asbury Park will probably mean the demolition

Bryn Mawr, Pa., October 31, 1973.

of the club's Ocean Avenue site. The Brighton Bar lives on. And there are some new clubs — the Deck House in Asbury Park, the Green Parrot in Neptune, Jasons in South Belmar — that regularly book the best local bands and carry on the tradition of the Jersey Shore music scene.

There is yet another generation of artists and bands worth noting, too. John Eddie is at the top of the list, and right behind him is Glen Burtnick. Then there are the Cruisers and LaBamba and the Hubcaps, two bands with strong links to R&B; the Fairlanes, the Shore's best blues act; and new entries like Mike Wells and the Wage, Big Danny and the Boppers, Beyond the Blue, Baby Boom, and the World.

"The Shore music scene is still something special," says Stone Pony DJ Lee Mrowicki. "Overall, the quality of bands is quite good, and you'll never know who might jam on any given night. It's a tight scene, too, just like it's always been. Maybe that's what makes it so special. If you play in a Shore band, I think you feel like you belong to something bigger than the three or four guys in your group. You feel like you're part of a legacy or a tradition. Few other scenes have that. And I know most of us are pretty proud of it."

—Robert Santelli

RESEARCH: ASBURY PARK ROCK 'N ROLL MUSEUM
ARTWORK: ANDY REID © 1988 BACKSTREETS MAG.

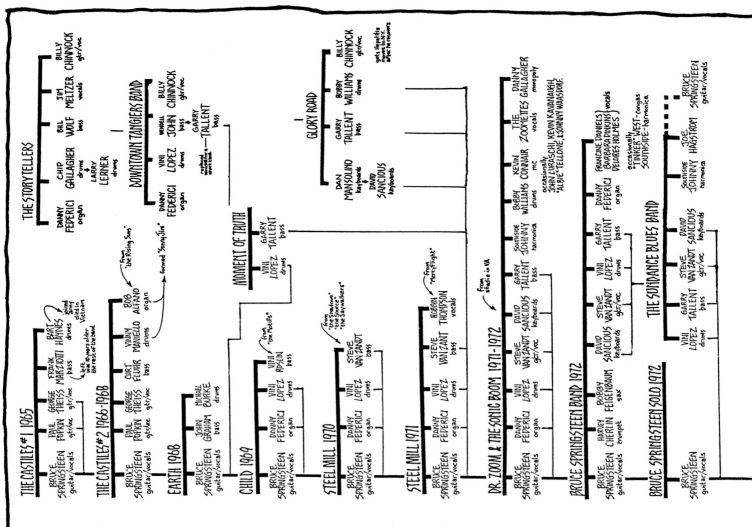

THE CASTILES were formed in 1965 in Freehold, NJ and they were managed by Gordon "Tex" Vinyard. The members at the time were George Theiss (vocals and guitar), Bart Haynes (drums), Frank Marziotti (bass), and Paul Popkin (tambourine, guitar, vocals). They soon added a young guitar player named Bruce Springsteen who also sang occasional vocals. The first change in the band came in 1966 when Bart Haynes went off to Vietnam (he later was killed in action). Next Frank Marziotti left the band — he was ten years older than the rest of the guys and couldn't afford to be in a band that was still struggling. Frank was replaced by Curt Fluhr and Haynes was replaced by Vinny "Skibotts" Maniello. It was this line-up that recorded the single "Baby I" on May 16, 1966 in the Bricktown Studio. Later Bob Alfano (from the Rising Suns) was added on organ. The band broke up by 1968. Theiss went off to form a band called the Rusty Chain while Alfano and Maniello formed a band called Sunny Jim.

Bruce met John Graham and Michael Burke while enrolled at Ocean County College in 1968. Together they formed **EARTH** (Bruce played guitar and sang vocals, Burke played drums and Graham played bass). They were a power trio and were managed by Fran Duffy and Rick "Spanky" Spachter, who called themselves "Ooze and Oz Productions." They played on the Shore throughout 1968.

That summer Bruce began to frequent the Upstage, a new club on Cookman Avenue in Asbury Park. From the instant he arrived he gained a reputation for being a fast guitarist. Vini Lopez was also hanging around the Upstage at the time and was looking to start a new band. Lopez had previously played with Moment of Truth (along with Garry Tallent) and with the Downtown Tangiers Band (with Dan Federici and Billy Chinnock). Lopez approached the new guitar whiz and together they formed **CHILD**. The line-up featured Bruce on guitar and vocals, Lopez on drums, Federici on organ and Vini Roslin (formerly of the Motifs) on bass. Child played regularly throughout 1969 calling "Pandemonium (an Ocean Township club) their home. Advertisements for some of their shows read "Pandemonium gives birth to Child," and "It's a Birthquake with Child." Their shows included a gig opening for blues great James Cotton.

After hearing of another band from Long Island named Child also, they changed their name to **STEEL MILL**. The name came about one day when Bruce, their manager Carl "Tinker" West and a friend named Chuck Dillon were sitting in a bar called the Inkwell in Monmouth County thinking up new names for the band. Dillon suggested the name Steel Mill. Bruce liked the name and it stuck. Not long after switching to the new name, Roslin left to be replaced by Steve Van Zandt (formerly of the Shadows and the Source from Middletown, and the Jaywalkers from Asbury Park).

Steel Mill played the Shore during 1970 and were the top local band of the time. They also found a second home in Richmond, Virginia and even considered relocating there at one point. Tinker booked them on a tour of California and they went out to San Francisco where their Matrix show received rave reviews and interested Bill Graham. Graham recorded three of their songs in his studio and made them an offer (he now cites it as the biggest mistake of his career not to sign them at any cost). Manager West turned it down and the band returned to New Jersey. Back in New Jersey the band continued as a popular Shore band sometimes playing to crowds over 10,000. They added Robbin Thompson as a second vocalist (he'd come from the band Mercy Flight in Richmond) and their draw continued strong. The band eventually broke up in January of 1971 after playing a series of "final" shows at the Upstage. They never released a record.

Springsteen decided to go off in a more R&B direction and called it **DR. ZOOM AND THE SONIC BOOM.** The Zoom Band consisted of a rotating line-up including Vini Lopez and "Big Bad" Bobby Williams on drums, Garry Tallent on bass and tuba, Bruce and Steve Van Zandt sharing guitar and vocals, Southside Johnny on harmonica, David Sancious on keyboards, and a female vocalist section known as the "Zoomettes." "Kevin "Bird" Connair served as the MC and other local musicians such as "Big" Danny Gallagher, John Luraschi, Kevin Kavanaugh (eventually of the Jukes), "Albie" Tellone and Johnny "Hot Keys" Waasdorp joined the band occasionally playing everything from vibraphones to monopoly on stage.

The Zoom band was too large to ever make any money or to play regularly (most members had other band projects on the outside). Bruce formed a slimmed-down version of the band and called it **THE BRUCE SPRINGSTEEN BAND**. Shows, however, were done under such names as The Bruce Springsteen Blues Band and Bruce Springsteen and the Friendly Enemies. This band featured Lopez on drums, Tallent on bass, Van Zandt on guitar, Sancious on keyboards, Harvey Cherlin on trumpet, and Francine Daniels, Barbara Dinkins and Delores Holmes on vocals. Manager West even occasionally played congas and Southside Johnny played harp whenever he was available.

THE E STREET BAND FAMILY TREE

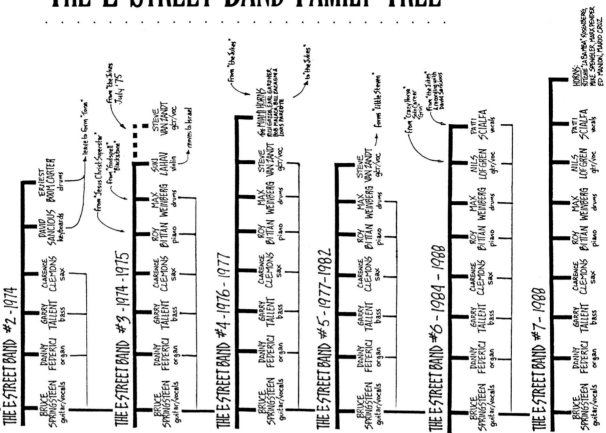

At the same time across town, Southside, Lopez, Van Zandt, Tallent and Joe Hagstrom were in a group called the **SUNDANCE BLUES BAND**. It was the first band where Southside really made a name for himself. Springsteen was an occasional member of this outfit, joining in on vocals.

Even the scaled down Bruce Springsteen Band had trouble finding work and making money so **BRUCE SPRINGSTEEN** went off **SOLO** and played throughout 1972 by himself. Tinker West introduced Bruce to Mike Appel who signed on as Bruce's manager. Appel managed to get Springsteen an audition with John Hammond of CBS Records. Hammond liked what he heard and signed Springsteen to CBS with plans for an album. Both Hammond and Appel saw Springsteen at the time as a solo artist, very much in line with the folk scene that was happening at the time. Bruce, however, insisted that he be allowed to form a band. Hammond said he couldn't imagine how Springsteen would be able to pull off such songs as ''Growin' Up'' and ''Saint in the City'' with a full band but he finally allowed Springsteen the chance. Bruce called together his old Asbury Park cohorts including Lopez, Van Zandt, Sancious, Tallent, Federici, and former Joyfull of Noyze sax player Clarence Clemons. They rehearsed in Point Pleasant, NJ before going into the studio to record **Greetings from Asbury Park, NJ.** Van Zandt soon left the E Street Band however to work construction and to tour with the Dovells on the oldies circuit (the band was hardly making any money at the time). The band was called the E Street Band, named after a street in the area near their rehearsal space.

That core formed the **E STREET BAND** from 1973 through 1974. In February of 1974 Vini Lopez became the first E Streeter to leave. Now called ''Mad Dog'' and with a reputation for outlandishness, his personal style clashed with the rest of the band and his drumming style was not the precise machine fueled drums that Springsteen's new material called for. He was sacked in February of 1974. Before Lopez was fired the band had already booked a couple of dates and one of them — at the Starlight in Cooktown, NJ — couldn't be cancelled. So the band needed a drummer and fast. Ernest ''Boom'' Carter, a friend of Davey Sancious, was recruited and with less than two days of rehearsals played his first date with the band on Feb. 23 at the Starlight Lounge. Carter stayed with the band until August of that year when he and Sancious played their last gigs as E Streeters. They left to form Tone, a fusion jazz group (a group that Patti Scialfa would incidentally sing with). Sancious' departure was expected — he had long wanted to go off on his own — but it left the group without a musical core.

The next group of E Streeters were to come from an unusual source — an ad in the Village Voice. Many different players were auditioned though eventually Max Weinberg and Roy Bittan were added to the band. Both had done work on Broadway shows and done stints in rock bands and both were masters at their instruments. Roy, in particular, was a machine on the keyboards able to play ''absolutely anything'' as Mike Appel says. When the band started touring again that September they added Suki Lahav on violin. Lahav stayed through March of 1975 and many still call this the seminal period in E Street history. Bob Dylan's ''I Want You'' was the highlight of the set and many shows started off with ''Incident on 57th Street'' — experimentation was the matter of the day.

After Lahav left, Springsteen decided a guitar attack was in order and added Miami Steve Van Zandt to the band again. Van Zandt took on a Keith Richards-styled rhythm role and had the job of musical arranger whenever something unusual was called for. Steve also directed the Miami Horns who joined the band during their 1976 tour and played over 50 shows with the band. The horn section included Rich Gazda, Earl Gardner, Bob Malach, Bill Zacagni and Louis Parente. Apart from the addition of the horns, the core of the E Street Band remained the same for the longest period of its history — until Steve left in 1982.

In 1984 the E Street Band thought of auditioning guitar players but one special player already stood out — Nils Lofgren. Lofgren had extensive experience as a solo artist, with Neil Young's band Crazy Horse and with his own band, Grin. He took on the Van Zandt slot in 1984. Patti Scialfa also joined the band in 1984 — she had previously toured with the Jukes and had sung with David Sancious. She became only the second female to join the E Street clan. That line-up finished up the lengthy **Born in the USA** tour but for the **Tunnel of Love** tour Bruce again added a horn section — this time around made up of Ritchie ''La Bamba,'' Rosenberg, Ed Manion, Mark Pender, Mike Spengler and Mario Cruz. The E Street Band has remained relatively stable when compared to many other bands that have been around for 15 years, but one would expect further changes are down the road as Bruce adds ideas or concepts to his ever changing body of work.

GEORGE THEISS
· · · · · · · · · · · ·

Interview by Robert Santelli, June 1985

erious fans of Bruce Springsteen know that the very first band he was a member of — and the only one in which he was not the undisputed leader — was the Castiles. This mid-sixties outfit wore matching shirts and vests onstage and played mostly covers by such groups as the Rolling Stones, the Who, and the Doors. It was based in Freehold, Springsteen's hometown.

Managed by the late Tex Vinyard, the Castiles quickly became one of the premier bands on the Jersey Shore in 1965 and 1966. The Castiles played teen dances, band contests, area Hullabaloo clubs, and nonalcoholic coffeehouses like the Left Foot. But unlike other young Shore bands, the Castiles, with Vinyard's guidance, eventually made it up to New York City and on a number of occasions they performed at the Cafe Wha? in Greenwich Village.

The Castiles even made a record — albeit a very amateur one — at a recording booth in Brick Town, New Jersey. It was, however, the very first time Springsteen's voice and guitar were captured on vinyl. Unfortunately, only a couple of copies of the record exist today.

Recently, *Backstreets* had the opportunity to speak with George Theiss, a member of the Castiles back then, and today a respected Shore musician who's in the process of re-forming the acclaimed George Theiss Band. As the lead singer and rhythm guitarist, Theiss's role in the Castiles was an important one. One winter night in Freehold, where he still resides, Theiss recalled the days when the Castiles were, as he put it, "one of the best bands on the Jersey Shore, maybe the best."

· · · · ·

BACKSTREETS: *If I recall correctly, didn't the Castiles sort of evolve out of the Sierras, the band which included you and Vini Roslin, who later played bass in Child and Steel Mill?*

GEORGE THEISS: Yeah, indirectly the Castiles grew out of the Sierras. Both were Freehold bands.
Was Bruce an original member of the group?
No. He came in after the group was formed. At the time I was going out with Bruce's sister, Ginny, so it was very convenient for me to have Bruce in the band. (Laughs.)
Looking back, it seems that much of the credit for the success that the Castiles achieved should go to Tex Vinyard, the group's manager. Would you agree with that?
Oh yes, definitely. The Sierras used to rehearse right next door to Tex's. The drummer lived there. So, naturally, Tex heard us playing. One day he came over, and I guess he felt sorry for us, because from then on, we started rehearsing in his dining room. He and his wife, Marion, did a whole lot for us. They got rid of all their dining room furniture and replaced it with amps and drums. They adopted us. We ate there, hung out there, watched TV there. For a good three years, we were there steady. And it wasn't just the band, it was friends of the band, girlfriends, the whole bit. It must have amounted to about 12 to 15 people on pretty much a regular basis.
How important was Tex's guidance and advice? He certainly did more than simply let you rehearse in his house.
Oh yeah. We definitely wouldn't have gone as far as we did without him, that's for sure. All we wanted to do was play and have a good time. Tex took care of everything else. He was a great manager. He even bought us equipment. Tex also was a big ego builder. He would sit there and tell you how the girls were going crazy over you. At 16 or 17, that's just what you wanted to hear. He made sure we were confident.
What year was the band formed?
I think it was 1965. And it went to about 1968.
What caused the band to break up?
Tex claimed he fired us. But I think it just got to the point where we weren't getting along too well. A couple of the guys were going to go to college. I

The Castiles, 1965: (L to R): Frank Marziotti, Bruce Springsteen, George Theiss, Paul Popkin, Vinny Manneillo.

didn't know what I was going to do. Bruce was already working on his next thing. He was already jamming with the guys he would form Earth with. So, as soon as the Castiles broke up, he just took over what booking we had and went on.

Musically, what was so special about the Castiles?

We went out and played with confidence. We played without being afraid of blowing it. It was the feeling of thinking we were good which was the thing that made us good. We certainly weren't the best musicians around, but often we sounded like we were — because of our confidence.

Where did the name come from?

Shampoo. At the time, that's the kind of shampoo everyone was using. The name also had a nice ring to it, if you know what I mean.

What was the purpose of making a record? Did you actually plan to distribute it? Was it considered a stepping stone to a recording contract with a record company?

Tex just said, "Let's make a record," so we did. We didn't have any idea of distribution or getting signed to a label. We didn't think that collectively, that much I know. Bruce was probably thinking

along those lines, and I know I did at times. But I don't think the other members of the band did. We were too much involved in the present to really think about what could happen in the future.

Onstage, the band certainly had a sharp, polished look, with those vests, white shirts, and black pants.

Yeah. Tex thought it was important to look good, to have that uniform look. In fact, he called them uniforms. It looked real professional to him to have us all look alike up there on the stage. We didn't care. Later on, we got into the Sgt. Pepper look, with boots and jackets. There was a poster we had made. We were all dressed up in long military jackets. We looked great.

Looking back, did it ever occur to you...

That Bruce would become as big as he has become? *Well, yeah.*

Sometimes its hard to believe how big he really is. But there was always something different about Bruce. He always seemed to know something we didn't. It was as if he always had a plan and that he knew exactly where he was heading.

—Robert Santelli

REMEMBERING THE UPSTAGE

Where the Band Was Just Boppin' the Blues

The Upstage: Is there any longtime, serious Springsteen fan who doesn't know about the legendary Asbury Park club where, in the late sixties, the Boss, future E Street Band members, and the Jukes cut their musical teeth?

Much has been written about the Upstage — the all-night jams, the formation of groups such as Springsteen's Steel Mill that resulted from them, and the intense interplay, both onstage and off, of the Shore's best young musicians back then — but those who have told tales of the Upstage are those who have told them time and time again. The same voices, the same stories. The truth is, the Upstage supported a large and varied cast of characters. Some of them, like Springsteen, Steve Van Zandt, Southside Johnny, Garry Tallent, Danny Federici, David Sancious, Kevin Kavanaugh, and Billy Chinnock were fortunate enough to go on to bigger and better things. But there were others, many others, who were indeed integral players in the Upstage experience, but who have not had the chance to look back in print. Here for the first time three of them recall the club and what went down. In their own words, they remember the Upstage.

. . . . .

BIG DANNY GALLAGHER

Big Danny Gallagher is a mountain of a man with a long red beard and eyes like lasers. Friends of his say he was always to be found at the Upstage when the best music was flying. "Danny had a real good sense about that," said one friend. "And if it wasn't happening, he'd be the kind of guy to make it happen."

A pedal steel guitar player and a vocalist with one of the best blues voices this side of the boardwalk, Big Danny these days fronts Big Danny and the Boppers. He's also had a hand in the High Tide Cafe, an Asbury Park club which could well become a modern day Upstage. "The Shore needs another Upstage type club so the younger musicians can

have the same opportunities to jam and learn and experiment as we did. I'm just trying to do my part to make sure that happens."

. . . .

The Upstage started with some of the real old local musicians, guys like Harry the Hat and a lot of Margaret Potter's friends. The word then started to leak out about this place that she and her husband opened. People started coming from all over. The Upstage was the cheapest motel room in town. Two bucks to get in and you could hang out until dawn when you could go to the beach and sleep there all day — legally. Everybody lived for the weekend when the Upstage was open. Things were good. But when Brucie arrived on the scene, they got great. Everybody knew as soon as they heard him play.

Now there were a lot of real good guitar players at the Upstage — there was Billy Ryan, Ricky DeSarno, Stevie Van Zandt. But no one had it together like Brucie did. Brucie used the Upstage as a perch; he hung out there; he formed his bands there; he used it as a rehearsal hall.

At the time of the Upstage, there were only like eight or nine places for bands to play. By the time Brucie signed his recording contract, there were like forty or fifty places to play up and down the Shore.

Some Sufi guy once said that there are three kinds of music: there's the kind that will move you, the kind that will touch your soul, and the kind that will touch your heart. It seemed like Brucie had all three. And you could hear how he developed all three if you were at the Upstage back in those days. He'd play with Vini Lopez, and afterwards I'd ask Vini, I'd say, "Hey man, are you sure you and him didn't rehearse that stuff you just played?" And he'd laugh. He'd say no, and he wasn't lying. It was all spontaneous. That's what made the club special.

There was a lot of blues played. And old rock 'n' roll. Rockabilly, too. Once we had a fifties party at

The Sundance Blues Band, Upstage Club, Asbury Park, N.J., 1970 (L to R): Steven Van Zandt, Joe Hagstrom, Vini Lopez, Southside Johnny Lyon, Garry Tallent.

the club. Margaret made a garbage can full of spaghetti, everybody rolled up their sleeves and greased up and went on stage and played what today you'd call classic rock 'n' roll. That's how the Zoom band started, at one of those parties. Brucie said, "Hey, why don't we just take everybody we know and party on the stage while we're playing." And next up was Dr. Zoom and the Sonic Boom. I was in the band. I played Monopoly and drank wine. That was my part in the band. We tried to get a guy to fix an engine onstage. But he said it was too much of a hassle to do it for just a few songs. We had baton twirlers, an emcee. People were in tuxedos.

There used to be lines at three in the morning to get in the Upstage. People were three and four across, and the line would wrap around the corner. This was in the middle of the night. Fortunately, the police were cool. They knew they had a good thing. Hell, they knew where every kid in the area was every Friday, Saturday, and Sunday night.

Southside, Big Bobby Williams, Van Zandt,

these guys were there all the time, so they kind of ran the stage at the club. You wanted to play, well, you had to see one of them. I had no considerations about playing prime time in those days. I wasn't no great musician. But I took part when I was able to. I enjoyed myself. I contributed. I have good memories of those days that nobody can take away from me.

· · · ·

MARGARET POTTER

It was Margaret Potter and her husband, Tom, who opened the Upstage back in 1968. At the time, she was fronting her own band, Margaret and the Distractions. They became the Upstage house band. Both she and Tom were hairdressers, and they lived and worked two doors down from the Upstage.

After the Upstage closed in 1971, Margaret and Tom separated. Tom moved to Florida. Margaret stayed in Asbury Park and continued to work as a hairdresser. She dropped out of the Asbury Park music circle, however. "I needed to earn a living and try to make my life work," she said. "I loved music just as much as I ever did, but I had to

First show as Dr. Zoom and the Sonic Boom, Sunshine Inn, Asbury Park, N.J., May 14, 1971.

put bread on the table." Little was heard of Margaret Potter until recently, when she joined a band, the Final Cut, which includes original Upstage drummer Big Bobby Williams. "We don't play on a regular basis," said Margaret. "But when we do play, we enjoy it. It kind of reminds me of the old days."

. . . . .

I'm so happy that people want to know about the Upstage almost twenty years after it opened. Those were great days. Lots of people ask me if the club had anything to do with Bruce's success. I don't know. If anyone deserved to make it, Bruce did. He worked so hard. His desire and his straight, right-down-the-line approach to music is what did it, I think. I give the credit to him, not to the club.

Still, the Upstage was special because it was a place for the local musicians — young kids — to find themselves. You can have a bunch of young players playing in their basements, but they can't all meet there. They could at the Upstage.

You know, with the amount of kids we had at the Upstage week in and week out, we never had any real problems. Sure, there were a couple of incidents. Like the time Big Bobby, who was a bouncer at the club when he wasn't playing drums, had a gun put to his head. Thank God nothing

more happened. And there was another time we had a local motorcycle gang show up. Fortunately there were no ugly confrontations. They came, they enjoyed themselves, and then they left, although one of them wanted to take me with him. Other than that, we had no big problems.

We had two sessions at the Upstage. We opened at 9:00 P.M. for minors, kids under 18. That's when my band, Margaret and the Distractions, would usually play, although there were times when we had other bands perform, too, and we had our share of jamming. But at midnight the Upstage closed for an hour. All the minors left and we cleaned up the place. An hour later, at one in the morning, we opened up again. This time you had to be 18 to be let in, although if you had a driver's license, I let you in. I was usually at the door collecting money. The difference between 17 and 18 wasn't so much. We weren't serving alcohol or anything. And this is when the jams were best. You'd get some musicians to come down and jam for the early session, but most came later, and they usually stayed until dawn. Then everybody would go home or to the beach.

One thing unique about the Upstage — and I haven't seen it since — was that you could come all by yourself, whether you were a member of a band or not, and play. You didn't have to bring your instrument. We had house instruments, house equipment. This has become lost here in Asbury Park. It's inhibited the young kids. Some kids today don't even know about the blues. But back then, it was loose, if you know what I mean.

There was a spirit that the musicians had. They respected each other. They knew who was good and who needed to get better. But they worked it out, they really did. It just sort of worked out naturally who got to go onstage this time and who didn't. There was competition, sure, but it was a healthy competition. And it made them all better players.

There's not much else to say other than it's gone now, a part of history. Everybody's grown up. God, when I see some of those kids, well, they're not kids anymore, are they? But we were all like one big happy family. I miss those days, I really do.

· · · · ·

JOHNNY LURASCHI

Johnny Luraschi was one of the youngest of the Upstage regulars (along with David Sancious). "My father and mother died when I was young, so I lived with my older brother," recalls Luraschi. "That meant I was pretty much able to do whatever I wanted at 15 years old." What he did was hang out at the Upstage and learn all he could about rock 'n' roll and the bass. Luraschi played in a number of popular Shore bands over the years, including Cahoots; Cold, Blast and Steel; and Hot Romance.

· · · · ·

This guy Tom Potter, he was a hairdresser. He had this idea to open up a place where musicians could come and hang out and jam, have some coffee and a good time. I first heard about the Upstage from some of the older musicians. I remember they used to rave about this club in Asbury. I was younger than most everybody else, but I knew I had to go to this place they called the Upstage. Everybody was buzzin' about Bruce. Everybody would say, "There's this kid who plays guitar and comes to the Upstage, and he's incredible. You got to check him out." I was living with my older brother, so I got to do what I wanted, you know.

I used to go with my brother Eddie to the Upstage. He used to play a little keyboards, but he was a big guy, so he wound up being a bouncer. But I played all I could. You had to get in on the roster, though. They had these 40-minute jams set up. You'd try to get together with some guys who

you knew were going to get the chance to play. You had to work your way in.

Every once in a while you'd get some New York hippies who came down to play. Leslie West and the Vagrants came down one night, I remember. Members of the Rock 'n' Roll Ensemble would come down. But most of the players were local. If you were too cool to go to the CYO dances and stuff, you came to the Upstage.

Me and Davey Sancious used to walk to the Upstage from Belmar, where we both lived. Later, when I was old enough to drive, I rode my motorcycle there. The whole thing about the Upstage and Asbury Park was timing. Asbury Park was — and still is — in a sort of Bermuda Triangle. You didn't play there for money or anything. You played because it was the thing to do. All of your musician friends were trying to get onstage, so you did the same. Most of the guys came every week. Bruce, Steve, they'd be there all the time. Even back then Bruce had that take-charge ability when he walked onstage. And whenever he played, there was magic at the Upstage. You could feel it, you could touch it. It was all around you. And you could definitely hear it.

It was a wild place to look at, too. I mean, the whole place was painted in psychedelic colors and Day-Glo. There were black lights that made the place cool. It was real easy to have all this happen because all you had to do was bring your instrument. The amps and sound equipment were there. All you had to do was plug in. One complete wall of the place was speakers. So you'd walk up on the stage and plug in.

It's hard to say why the Upstage finally closed. It was around when everybody was going through a real creative period, I guess, and when people moved on to the bars and formed bands, there weren't enough younger players to carry the torch. You couldn't make any money at the Upstage; it wasn't that kind of place. So the musicians, if they wanted to stay musicians, had to look for work. And when they were old enough — when they turned 21 — they moved on to the bars and the Jersey Shore. It was a matter of survival. And even then, a lot of musicians didn't make it. They stopped playing and moved on to other things. After the Upstage, the scene sort of moved to the Student Prince, a bar in Asbury, as well as a club called Pandemonium. But it just wasn't the same afterwards. It couldn't be.   —*Robert Santelli*

SOUTHSIDE JOHNNY

. . . .

Interview by Charles R. Cross, December 1984

When God was dishing out talent to the Asbury Park set, he gave Bruce Springsteen songwriting, Miami Steve producing, and for Southside Johnny Lyon, he saved something very special: *The Voice*. Southside may very well have one of the purest rhythm-and-blues voices this side of Otis Redding. Watching him perform in a small, smoke-filled club with his band, the Jukes, one of the best bar bands in America, is something akin to the second coming of rhythm and blues.

Southside grew up in Ocean Grove, right next to Asbury Park, and he was a seminal figure in that early scene, jamming in countless bands with Bruce, Steve, and a host of other local legends. From his very start in the business, everyone knew he had *The Voice*, so Southside was always the choice when a Shore band needed a singer. He knew the lyrics to over a thousand songs, and his understanding of and appreciation for early R&B is rivaled by few.

Based on the massive popularity of his club shows and the tremendous talent of his band (which included Steve Van Zandt before he joined Bruce's band), Southside was signed to a record deal in the mid-seventies and put out several classic albums — most notably 1978's *Hearts of Stone*. Southside was great at singing, performing, and putting out records. He was admittedly less than great at the business aspects of music, and almost from its very inception, his career has been marked by a nightmarish battle with record companies.

This interview was conducted in early December 1984 over the course of several hours (and several beers), first in a bar, then in a dressing room, and finally on the Jukes' bus.

. . . . .

BACKSTREETS: *Let's start with your roots. It must*

◀ *Southside Johnny, Parker's Ballroom, December 1984.*

have been something growing up near Asbury with the local music scene what it was in those days.

SOUTHSIDE JOHNNY: Yeah, even before I started playing I would go to the clubs. I had this friend, Buzzy Labinski. Buzzy started collecting records and he'd run dances. I worked for him — I would guard his records and help him set up. He'd take me to see all these different bands when I was 14 years old. These were the great local legends. He took me to see James Brown at the Convention Hall, which turned my head around quite nicely.

Speaking of record collecting, I understand you've got quite a collection of James Brown and other early R&B.

Yeah, I don't do it so much anymore. The competition on the East Coast is fierce.

I'm sure collectors of your records wonder if there is much unreleased Jukes material.

Not really. Unlike Bruce, we don't go in and record a whole bunch of songs. Bruce is searching for the pith, I guess, of what he feels like at the time. I just try to pick the ten best songs. We've got a lot of demos we've done on 16-track — we must have 20, 30 songs from the last few years. The only album where we have a real backlog of stuff is the *Hearts of Stone* record. We recorded eight songs and decided we didn't like the direction we were going, so we threw away seven of them. There are some Bruce tunes, a couple of my songs, but they weren't coming out the way we wanted them. One of the reasons *Hearts of Stone* never got the promotion it should have was because we alienated the record company by going over budget and over time.

That's a real shame, since I think that's your best record and should have been a monster hit.

Yeah, it's a shame. When it first came out it was picked up by 125 stations. but I saw a record-company memo that had both Cheap Trick's marketing plan (posters, radio ads, tie-ins, giveaways) and our marketing plan. Our plan said "release album, see what happens." That was the entire promotion for the record.

Your career seems to have been one continuing nightmare of problems with record companies.

Well, we're a difficult proposition for a record company. They want to be on top of the next big thing so they can sell millions of records. And from our very first record we were considered established artists, so they figured if our record didn't immediately sell 300,000 copies it was dead. Instead of treating us like a group that could be promoted, they figured we'd already been promoted. There are a lot of people in the music business who don't know what they're doing.

There were a lot of mistakes that were made, but we made as many as they did by letting them do the things they did to us. There's too much money in the music business now. Now it's the music business, the video business, and *then* music.

But in many ways we've been our own worst enemies. I'm not ambitious to be a rock 'n' roll star. Consequently, I'm not willing to do all the things people do to promote themselves. Those outrageous images are just alien to me. I wouldn't look good as Boy George, Prince, or Dee Snider. It's hurt the sales of the albums, the success of the band but it's the only way I know how to stay sane in this ridiculous nightmare of the music business.

A lot of your longtime fans were really disappointed in Trash It Up. *What's the story behind that record?*

Yeah, I wasn't happy with it either. The story behind that was that after doing the live album and having Mercury completely ignore it, I got pissed off and left. At that point I was so frustrated I never wanted to make another record. It took me a year to get over that feeling. Then Billy [Rush] and I spent a year putting together new material and trying to get another record company that we wanted to work with.

Finally there came a point where if I didn't make another record, my career as a recording artist was going to be in serious jeopardy. And Billy had written a bunch of songs and he'd been listening to the dance charts and he had an idea for a new kind of R&B sound for us. I said yeah, but I didn't want to produce it. Jerry Greenburg played it for Nile Rogers, and Nile said he wanted to produce it. It sounded like a great idea but I think Nile stretched himself a little too thin. He was working on three other projects at the time and doing a new Chic record. And I also get the feeling that Nile doesn't like to work with musicians so much. We like to be in the studio and he likes to do his own thing,

which in its own way is brilliant. So at that point I said he could have complete control — I didn't want anything to do with it. Billy took over my position and I started drinking and a lot of things happened that were unprofessional. Consequently, a lot of things on that album came out less than they could have been.

You seem surprisingly aware of your own limitations.

Well, I learned a lot during those years I took off between the live album and *Trash It Up.* You have to remember too that I started singing almost by accident. I drifted into it. I used to sing on the street with friends, Italian guys. One day Sonny Kenn asked me to join his band and sing and I also played harmonica 'cause I knew a little of that. I just always took things for granted. The things I took for granted most people never get. I've learned that you may have a natural talent, a gift, but sometimes those things aren't enough. Sometimes you have to get in there and start punching.

I think the whole nature of the music business has changed too. There was an optimism back in the seventies in Asbury Park when you were first signed.

They had so much money then. We signed for $35,000, the price of the first album — Steven and I got the money and we used it to pay for the recording of the first record.

In the late seventies the money dried up and a lot of bands like ours, who didn't sell millions of records, weren't taken seriously. And we had the problem of who we were. We don't look like a unified theme. We look like an American band that plays American music and really wants the audience to have a good time. That's not a very marketable idea for a corporate thinker.

I'll always remember something Miami Steve told me. I was in the studio singing "The Fever" when a bunch of executives walked in and Steve told me to stop singing. I don't like to stop singing, so I asked him why. He said, "These guys don't want to see what you do. It just makes them nervous. All they want is the album, the album cover, and the publicity pictures. They never want to meet us. All they want is the product to sell." He's right.

Getting back to your roots, your father was a musician, wasn't he?

My father was a musician and my mother loves music. I was very lucky to have parents that really loved music. There was no Muzak in our house. When they turned it on, they turned it up. I could have been in a lot of trouble if I stayed on the

Southside Johnny, Parker's Ballroom, Seattle, Wash., December 1984.

streets 'cause I was very wild in those days. Without some kind of direction that takes you out of that, you don't escape. You end up working in some shitty job in Asbury Park, getting in trouble on weekends, and before you know it you're 60 years old.

It was almost as if the fates destined me for a musical career, because of my parents and Sonny. I met Bruce and Steven. Other than meeting them, I'd still be in Asbury Park with a very popular band, making a lot of money. They were ambitious and I wasn't.

I've never read an article about you that didn't mention Bruce Springsteen, and I'm falling victim here myself. Do you ever get sick of hearing that connection?

There was a period between the second and third albums when I felt, "Hey, what about me?" I don't care about the analogies as long as you get a chance to see me and the band play. It's an easy linchpin — like last night's review, "Bruce's Friend Puts on a Great Show." It can be bothersome, but it could be a lot worse. If it has to be anybody, I can't think anyone better than Bruce. He's one of the most honest, straightforward guys with the most integ-

rity and he's given me some great songs and some good advice. He's been decent to me all these years, and I'm sure it pisses him off more than it pisses me off.

There was talk that Steven's leaving the Jukes to join Bruce's band left some bad feelings.

That only happened later. Him leaving the band wasn't a problem — we all knew he was. Steven and I talked about it long before it happened. He came and asked me and I said definitely go with Bruce; he had a hit record and we were still trying to get our foot in the door. Plus, Bruce and Steven had been friends for a long time. And Bruce needs friends like that. Bruce doesn't get that close to people, and when he does get close to someone like Steven, it helps him function.

When Steve was leaving the Jukes, unfortunately other businessmen got involved and created some problems which Steven and I have patched up now. In the early days Steven and I even lived together for a number of years in a number of places. We were very close.

Before forming the Jukes, you were in a number of bands with various names and styles. Were any particularly

Southside Johnny, Cleveland, Ohio, 1978.

memorable? And who were your major influences then?
There were a million bands. In Asbury Park, we'd have like "band of the week." Someone would con a bar owner into hiring them for a couple of weeks and we'd run out and get together a band. We'd get Garry on bass, Vini on drums, and me to sing. We'd take three days and learn 25 R&B songs.

We formed hundreds of bands for particular things we'd get interested in. Steven would want to do an Allman Brothers thing, so he'd put together a band. I'd want to do something like Otis Redding or Muddy Waters, so I'd put together a band. Bruce would want to do Van Morrison or Dylan, so we'd try to find musicians who would play that stuff and an outlet to play it in. If we couldn't, we'd do it at the Upstage.

The Upstage is a place of legend in the Asbury Park lore.
Many great stories came out of that place, but the best thing was the musical interaction. It was a situation where you'd be playing with someone you didn't know, so you have to react to them, to this unknown quality. And it gave me an insight into what can happen onstage: great things or terrible things. It made all of us more loose. We learned early in our careers that you could do some oddball stuff and it wouldn't ruin your career.

I'm a big fan of the early Steel Mill stuff — particularly the Allman Brothers sound.
Yeah, that stuff was great. And the Allman Brothers were a big influence then. When Steve and I had the Sundance Blues Band, Bruce came back from California and he wanted to put together a horn band, but he also wanted to get some cash and have some fun, so we made Dr. Zoom and the Sonic Boom. There were 13 musicians plus a chorus, Monopoly game, baton twirlers, announcer.
Back to your present-day career — despite all your frustrations, you still seem to really love performing.
You go on faith in music. You're willing to swallow a lot of garbage to get to do the thing you love the most. For a musician in the business, you've got to put up with a lot of stupid people who don't know what they're doing.

On the one hand, if you don't have success you're frustrated. But on the other hand, if you have success, like Michael Jackson, you've got problems of your own. He's going to have a hell of a time doing anything again. It's become a media circus.
Sometimes I worry that by selling 5 million records Bruce has entered the circus arena whether he likes it or not.
Bruce has the strength to get through anything. He chooses to live in New Jersey — he can't go walk down the streets sometimes. I'm sure he didn't choose that, but he wants to be what he is. And I think that's more important to him than being able to go to the pizzeria. In his case I think you can say that his stance, his lyrics, his music, are all more important to him than his own personal privacy. Anyways, if you're onstage it's okay for 20,000 people to go crazy over you.
Speaking of going crazy — you're crazy about Otis Redding. I know he's one of your favorite performers and one of your great inspirations.
Yeah, "Try a Little Tenderness." I remember the first time I heard that song I was with my friend Chucky Anderson. We were delivering a TV for his father, who owned a TV repair shop. We were riding into Asbury Park and this song came on and we almost drove right into the lake. It was such a dynamite, unbelievably tension-filled performance — it killed us. You can't believe how intense that song is.

That song would scare the shit out of anybody today. If you brought that song in to some record company executive or a radio programmer, he'd throw it out the window he'd be so frightened.
—*Charles R. Cross*

TOUR GUIDE FOR ASBURY PARK, NEW JERSEY

Cruising Down Kingsley

Here on the Jersey Shore, especially in Asbury Park, we see it each summer: Springsteen fans from all over pull into town, wide-eyed and excited and eager to embrace the rich musical tradition of the area. For many, the trip to Asbury Park is the culmination of a rock 'n' roll pilgrimage — it reaffirms their commitment to the message and spirit of Springsteen's songs, and qualifies them as fans of the highest order.

They come to experience first hand the culture and musical climate that continues to inspire much of Springsteen's lyrical imagery. They come, too, with the hope of spotting Springsteen in a local club or, better yet, of catching an impromptu performance by the Boss with one of the area's many local bar bands.

They also come because Asbury Park is not only the mythical home of Springsteen and the E Street Band, but also of Southside Johnny and the Jukes, John Eddie, Little Steven, and a certain kind of

Madam Marie, Asbury Park, N.J.

rock 'n' roll that is as honest and time-tested and as grassroots and distinctively American as the rock 'n' roll you'll find in other regional musical meccas like Macon, Georgia, and Austin, Texas.

If you're a serious Springsteen fan and have thought about visiting Asbury Park, now is the time to do it. The reason? The city is about to undergo a massive renewal that will permanently alter its look, its soul, and, most important, its rock 'n' roll tradition. Soon the Stone Pony, the Shore's flagship club, will be but a memory.

For those who do come to Asbury Park soon, here is a guide to the must-see spots that bear importance to the Springsteen legacy and that have served to make this seaside resort a truly classic rock 'n' roll town.

THE STONE PONY
913 Ocean Avenue

One of the most famous of all American rock 'n' roll clubs, the Stone Pony could be called "the house that Bruce built." Springsteen, however, did not begin his career here, as many think. It opened in 1974. At that time, Springsteen was on tour promoting his second album, *The Wild, the Innocent and the E Street Shuffle.*

But Springsteen has performed at the Pony on countless occasions over the years. During one winter stretch in the early eighties he played practically every Sunday night with the group Cats on a Smooth Surface. Springsteen even launched his now legendary *Born in the USA* tour from the Pony stage in June 1984. He's played more in this club than any other hall.

Southside Johnny and the Asbury Jukes were the Pony's first house band. In 1976 a live broadcast from the club introduced the Jukes and their debut album, *I Don't Want to Go Home*, to rock fans across America. Since then, hundreds of great rockers have played the Pony, including Elvis Costello, Little Steven, and Bon Jovi.

ASBURY PARK ROCK 'N' ROLL MUSEUM
Check phonebook for location

No visit to Asbury Park would be complete without visiting the Asbury Park Rock 'n' Roll Museum. Unfortunately, the museum's location is presently up in the air due to the redevelopment of Asbury Park. Springsteen fans can easily spend a couple of hours looking at the many photos and bits of memorabilia that pack the walls and cases of the museum's collection. So can fans of the Jersey Shore's other favorite rock sons, such as Southside Johnny, Little Steven, Jon Bon Jovi, and an entire cast of lesser-known musicians. The posters alone are worth the price of admission.

Curators Billy Smith and Steve Bumball are experts in Springsteen and Jersey Shore rock history. They almost always take the time to elaborate on the museum's many treasures, and they'll certainly answer your questions. Featured in the museum are rare photos of Steel Mill, Springsteen's most important pre-E Street Band outfit; the psychedelic sign from the Upstage; promo posters; instruments; and relics from a number of area musicians. Among the most prized items on display is one of the only copies known to exist of the Castiles' record, "That's What You Get"/"Baby I." The single was recorded in 1966; only a couple of copies of it are still known to exist.

Check a local phonebook for the museum's current location, or write to P.O. Box 296, Allenhurst, N.J., 07711.

PALACE AMUSEMENTS ARCADE
Cookman and Second avenues

This classic amusement center was partly responsible for the inspiration behind the title track of *Tunnel of Love*. In fact, one of the *Tunnel of Love Express* tour T-shirts for sale at Springsteen concerts had the familiar "Palace face" emblazoned on the front of it. The Palace was well-documented in Springsteen songs and many promo pictures of Springsteen were taken here.

The building is now threatened by redevelopment and its future is in doubt.

CASINO ARENA
Asbury Park boardwalk

Located across from the Palace Amusements Arcade at the southern end of the Asbury Park boardwalk is the Casino Arena. During the early seventies New Jersey rock promoter John Scher regularly featured major concerts here from June through September. More recently, Springsteen filmed his "Tunnel of Love" video in the Casino Arena. Unfortunately, the venue is in desperate need of repair. Whether it will be spared the wrecking ball remains to be seen.

At one time there were rumors that a renovated, remodeled Casino Arena would house a "new" Stone Pony, an expanded Asbury Park Rock 'n' Roll Museum, a Hard Rock Cafe, and perhaps even a state-of-the-art recording studio. Time will tell what the future holds for the Casino Arena.

THE WONDER BAR
1213 Ocean Avenue

Speaking of Springsteen videos, it was at the Wonder Bar that Bruce filmed his "One Step Up" video. When it comes to classic Asbury Park beer joints, the Wonder Bar fits the description perfectly. Over the years a number of Asbury Park musicians have played the bar, including Springsteen, former E Street Band drummer Vini Lopez, former Dr. Zoom Monopoly player Big Danny Gallagher and many more. These days the Wonder Bar rarely features big-name local bands — what you'll hear instead are copy bands, if that. But you've got to grab a beer or two at the Wonder Bar just for the experience. Here's another club that probably won't be around once the renovation of Asbury Park's beachfront begins in earnest.

THE CIRCUIT
Ocean and Kingsley avenues

"The Circuit" comprises Ocean and Kingsley avenues; together they form a long loop around Asbury Park's beachfront area. During the summer, and on Saturday nights the rest of the year, Ocean Avenue, which parallels the boardwalk, is alive with fast cars and Harley-Davidsons. You'll find the Wonder Bar and the Stone Pony on Ocean Avenue, as well as Mrs. Jay's, known as a biker bar and a place where some of the best bar bands play. Kingsley is one block west of Ocean Avenue. You'll find rock clubs on this street, too, including Dimples and Club Xanadu, where Springsteen first performed "Dancing in the Dark" live. He played it with the local group Bystander. Springsteen mentioned the Circuit in his songs "Night"

The Stone Pony, Asbury Park, N.J.

and "Fourth of July, Asbury Park (Sandy)," to name but two. For years the Circuit was the place to be seen and to see others — especially if you had a hot set of wheels. You can't do it too fast — the traffic lights are tuned to stop speeding.

ASBURY PARK BOARDWALK
One block over from Ocean Avenue

Any visitor to Asbury Park has to take at least one stroll on this famed boardwalk. The seedy shops, the sausage stands, the pizza parlors, and the amusement rides are all destined for destruction soon. In their place will rise — you guessed it — condos and walkways. There's a lot of Asbury Park musical history embedded in these boards. Numerous Springsteen and the E Street Band photo sessions took place here — you might recognize some of the settings. Southside Johnny and the Asbury Jukes used it, too, as did many other local bands. Boardwalk images and themes swirl about early Springsteen songs. Perhaps his best known

boardwalk tune is "Fourth of July, Asbury Park (Sandy)."

MADAM MARIE'S
Boardwalk and Fourth Avenue

This small fortune-teller's stand is also mentioned in "Fourth of July, Asbury Park (Sandy)." It's not any more important than the other Asbury Park landmarks mentioned in Springsteen songs. It's just more obvious. It also makes an excellent backdrop for a photograph. Madam Marie still works the tourists, too.

CONVENTION HALL
Boardwalk, between Fifth and Sunset avenues

This is the largest venue on the Jersey Shore, excluding the Garden State Arts Center in Holmdel Township. Back in the 1960s, impresario Moe Septee presented such bands as the Rolling Stones, the Who, the Jefferson Airplane, and the Doors at

St. Rose of Lima School, Freehold, N.J.

Convention Hall. Southside Johnny and the Jukes performed here a number of times over the years.

· · · ·

PARAMOUNT THEATRE
Boardwalk and Fifth Avenue

Soundwise, the Paramount has always had it over Convention Hall by leaps and bounds. Many concerts were held here, too. There are plans to refurbish the theater in the near future. Springsteen and the E Street Band rehearsed here before setting out on their 1978 tour to promote *Darkness*.

· · · ·

DIMPLES
911 Kingsley Avenue

Years ago, Dimples was called the Student Prince. A popular hangout for Monmouth College students during the late sixties and early seventies, the Student Prince regularly featured Springsteen and his various pre-E Street Bands. It was at the Student Prince, as legend has it, that Springsteen first met up with Clarence Clemons.

· · · ·

PARKING LOT
Kingsley and 1st avenues

Here once stood the Hullabaloo, a mid-sixties teen club where many of the area's young musicians performed in groups like the Motifs, Sonny and the Starfires, and the Castiles, Springsteen's first group. Later on, the Hullabaloo became the Sunshine Inn. Springsteen performed in this sleazy yet popular venue on many occasions. Perhaps the most memorable show he did at the Sunshine Inn was with the short-lived group Dr. Zoom and the Sonic Boom. Like Convention Hall, the Sunshine Inn featured many up-and-coming bands that would later rise to superstardom, including Kiss and the Allman Brothers Band.

· · · ·

UPSTAGE
702 Cookman Avenue

The Upstage ranks with the Stone Pony as the most popular and most important club, historically speaking, of all the Asbury Park and Jersey Shore clubs. It was located atop a Thom McAn's shoe store; today it's OK Shoes. From 1968 through 1970, the Upstage was where not only Springsteen but such members of the E Street Band as Garry Tallent and Danny Federici, plus former E Streeters Davey Sancious, Vini Lopez, and Miami Steve Van Zandt (Little Steven) jammed until dawn each weekend. Southside Johnny, members of the old Asbury Jukes, Billy Chinnock, and dozens of other talented but lesser-known area musicians also hung out and performed here. The Upstage gave local musicians valuable stage experience and sparked the formation of numerous bands, including Steel Mill, Springsteen's heavy-metal blues outfit.

· · · ·

FAST LANE
206 Fourth Avenue

Like the Upstage, the Fast Lane is but a memory. In the late seventies and early eighties, when the Fast Lane was the most popular club in town, groups like Beaver Brown and the Rest, Jon Bon Jovi's early band, performed there regularly. Springsteen frequently hung out at the club and often jumped onstage to jam with visiting and local bands. Many of the best English New Wave bands of the era played the Fast Lane. Joe Jackson even began one of his American tours at the club.

—Robert Santelli

Stone Pony, Asbury Park, N.J., August 21, 1987. ▶

Tour Guide for Freehold, New Jersey

My Hometown, U.S.A.

For years, Asbury Park has gotten most of the spotlight as the symbolic home and stomping grounds of Bruce Springsteen. A lot of fans actually think he was born there. Some fans who are really dancing in the dark believe he lives there now.

Even those fans with only cursory knowledge of Springsteen's past know it was Freehold and not Asbury Park where the Boss grew up and first discovered rock 'n' roll. He was actually born in Long Branch, at Monmouth Medical Center, about ten miles away. But until he graduated from high school in 1967, Bruce Springsteen lived in Freehold, an old town that, at one time, was better known for its Revolutionary War lore (Molly Pitcher and the Battle of Monmouth) and its racetrack (Freehold Raceway) than for its special place in rock 'n' roll history.

It was in Freehold, for instance, that Springsteen's first band, the Castiles, was based. All those tales Springsteen has told from the stage — touching vignettes about his relationship with his father, about his neighbors, about learning to play his guitar — have a Freehold setting. In 1985, when the 3M Company announced that it would lay off 360 workers, and when Springsteen came to their aid with money and moral support, the plant where the jobs were lost was in Freehold. And of course the main inspiration for one of Springsteen's most deeply felt songs, "My Hometown," is Freehold, too.

Without doubt, Freehold has played as much a role in Springsteen's life and music as has Asbury Park. Fans who come to the Jersey Shore to take in Asbury's rock 'n' roll sights should then drive to Freehold to complete their tour of Springsteen's Jersey Shore.

·　　·　　·　　·

Bruce Springsteen's childhood was spent in three Freehold homes, two of which are still standing.

When Adele and Douglas Springsteen brought their new son home from the hospital in September 1949, they brought him to 87 Randolph Street. It was here where, in 1957, Springsteen saw Elvis Presley on "The Ed Sullivan Show" and begged his mother to buy him a guitar.

The Springsteens resided on Randolph Street, with little Bruce's grandparents on his father's side, until he was eight or nine years old. Unfortunately, the house was torn down years ago. In its place is a driveway that leads to St. Rose of Lima Church.

The Springsteens then moved to 39½ Institute Street. The blue and white house with the cozy front porch was, back then, located in a typical middle-class neighborhood. The sycamore tree on the side of the house is the one against which Springsteen is leaning in the photo on the lyric sheet of *Born in the USA*.

A few years later, Springsteen's parents made their last Freehold move before leaving the town for good and starting a new life in northern California. (Bruce, of course, remained in New Jersey.) The house they moved into, at 68 South Street, still stands. From a historical perspective, it is the most important house of the three, since it was here that Springsteen learned to play his guitar by listening to songs on the radio, and became, as one longtime friend put it, "obsessed" with rock 'n' roll. (Today the houses that Springsteen grew up in are inhabited by new families. Please be courteous and respectful of their property and privacy when you visit Freehold.)

Springsteen attended grammar school at St. Rose of Lima, located at the corner of South and Lincoln streets, just a short distance from Springsteen's South Street house. The Catholic school experience was not a pleasant one for him. In fact, scattered through a number of his early songs are lyrics that bitterly depict the difficulty he had with Catholic education and unbending nuns.

After graduating from St. Rose, Springsteen

The house Bruce Springsteen grew up in, corner of Institute and South streets, Freehold, N.J.

attended Freehold High School, on Broadway and Robertville Road, from 1963 to 1967. During his sophomore year he joined the Castiles and spent most of the time he wasn't in school hanging out at Tex Vinyard's house on Center Street, which has since been demolished. Vinyard was the Castiles' manager and practically a second father to Springsteen. Under Vinyard's guidance, the Castiles went on to become one of the most popular Freehold bands in the mid-sixties.

The Castiles played in front of an audience for the very first time in 1965. The place was the Woodhaven Swim Club, on East Freehold Road in the neighboring town of Freehold Township. The Swim Club is no longer around, either. Today its buildings are occupied by the local YMCA chapter.

In an interview with Springsteen's biographer, Dave Marsh, Vinyard recalled more than a decade ago that the band received $35 for its first gig. "It was a suck-ass job to get," Vinyard said. "George [Theiss, the Castiles' lead singer and rhythm guitarist] knew somebody who knew somebody who knew the principal. We got the last open gig of the season."

The Castiles went on to play a number of other venues in and around the Freehold area. Teen

clubs were popular at the Jersey Shore in the mid-sixties, and the Castiles played them. But the band also played school and CYO (Catholic Youth Organization) dances, battle-of-the-band contests, YMCA functions, and private parties.

In the late sixties, three things occurred that prompted Springsteen to leave Freehold: he graduated from high school, his family moved to California, and the Castiles broke up. Since Springsteen had tried unsuccessfully to pursue a college education — he briefly attended Ocean County College, on Hooper Avenue in Toms River — he had turned to what he loved and knew best: music.

By this time he had made friends with a number of other Shore musicians, many of whom lived east of Freehold and closer to the beach, in towns like Neptune, Long Branch, and, of course, Asbury Park. So that was where he drifted and where his next two bands, Child and Earth, mostly played.

Once he was on his own, Springsteen was rarely in a house or apartment long enough to call it home. When he was broke, he'd return to the Vinyards' house in Freehold. But mostly he roomed with friends in cheap, seedy apartments in Asbury and Long Branch, or close to Monmouth College in West Long Branch.

It made sense for Springsteen to live in this section of the Jersey Shore rather than in Freehold. Most of the clubs and coffee houses that featured live music were located there, including the Upstage, and a real music scene was actually beginning to develop there. To complete your Springsteen tour of the Jersey Shore, there are a few other landmarks worth visiting, not located in either Asbury Park or Freehold.

· · · ·

BIG MAN'S WEST
129 Monmouth Street, Red Bank

Today you'll find the World Gym in the building that once was home to Big Man's West, the club opened by E Street Band member Clarence Clemons in 1981. "I want the club to feature the best local and national talent and become a hangout for Shore musicians," said the Big Man himself after he, Springsteen, and the rest of the E Street Band opened the club on a steamy summer night

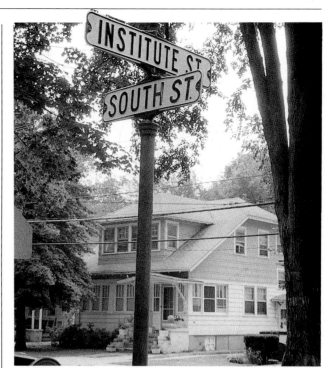

Institute and South streets, Freehold, N.J.

eight years ago. It became just what Clemons hoped it would become. The club also helped the Shore music scene rebound from a particularly low period in the late seventies. During the two-and-a-half-year existence of Big Man's West, Springsteen jammed there a number of times. John Eddie got his start at the club.

· · · ·

CHALLENGER EAST SURFBOARD FACTORY
3505 Sunset Avenue, Ocean Township

During the days of Steel Mill, Springsteen's most successful pre-E Street band, he and Mill members Danny Federici and Vini Lopez lived here. The band also rehearsed in the building. Tinker West, a local surfboard manufacturer, was also Steel Mill's manager.

· · · ·

ROUTES 9, 88, AND 33

These main Jersey Shore roads figure in the Springsteen legacy. Route 88, which runs through the Ocean County towns of Point Pleasant, Brick Township, and Lakewood, is represented in the song "Spirit in the Night." Route (or Highway) 9, a main Monmouth County artery that goes through Freehold, appears in "Born to Run." And Route 33 links Freehold to Asbury Park and other beach towns. Springsteen undoubtedly logged many hours on it. —Robert Santelli

TALK TO ME

Interviews with the Man and the Band

Walk like the Heroes: The E Street Band, 1975 (L to R): Clarence Clemons, Max Weinberg, Roy Bittan, Bruce Springsteen, Garry Tallent, Miami Steve Van Zandt and Danny Federici.

LOST IN THE FLOOD

Bruce Springsteen Interview by Paul Williams, October 1974

Paul Williams is credited with starting the very first rock magazine, *Crawdaddy*, back in January 1966. Under his leadership it predated *Rolling Stone* and literally helped mold the form of rock journalism — it was the first of its kind and, some argue, the best. One thing is certain: *Crawdaddy*'s persistent coverage of an unknown singer-songwriter from New Jersey played an essential role in establishing Bruce Springsteen's credentials; there are those who suggest that without promotion from *Crawdaddy* and other rock magazines of the sort, CBS might have dumped the Boss before *Born to Run* ever came out. Williams, and the editor who followed him, Peter Knobler, used *Crawdaddy* to spread the word on Bruce. *Crawdaddy* also was the one rock magazine Springsteen said, at the time, that he always read.

In 1973 and 1974, Williams followed the Springsteen tour for weeks, working on a story for *New Times* magazine. Researching the piece, he conducted an interview with Springsteen on October 13, 1974, less than a month after Max Weinberg and Roy Bittan joined the E Street Band. The interview was conducted the day after a show at Princeton University and a week before Bruce would heat up the Passaic Capitol Theater with the first of his many legendary shows there. Williams interviewed Bruce one evening at Bruce's apartment in Long Branch; Max Weinberg was also there in the background and can be heard pounding his drumsticks on a chair throughout the entire interview.

At the time of the interview, Springsteen was still writing most of the songs that would eventually appear on *Born to Run*. He was still working on the lyrics to "Jungleland," and Williams remembers writing down the lyrics for Dave Marsh, who at the time had just gotten into Bruce and was await-

ing the new album, due for release in 1975.

Williams's interview, however, was never used by *New Times*; they first put it off because they "weren't sure anybody would be interested in Bruce," Williams says. Soon afterwards, *New Times* folded. Williams did write a piece on Bruce for *Gallery*, a skin magazine, which CBS liked enough that they sent out photocopies with the script cover album. He also penned a story in the *Soho Weekly News* titled "You Don't Know Him, But You Will . . . ."

. . . . .

PAUL WILLIAMS: *What Dylan influenced you musically?*

BRUCE SPRINGSTEEN: In 1968 I was into *John Wesley Harding.* I never listened to anything after *John Wesley Harding.* I listened to *Bringing It All Back Home, Highway 61, Blonde on Blonde.* That's it. I never had his early albums and to this day I don't have them, and I never had his later albums. I might have heard them once, though. There was only a short period of time when I related, there was only that period when he was important to me, you know, where he was giving me what I needed. That was it.

That was really true for a lot of people.

Yeah, it was the big three. I never was really into him until I heard "Like a Rolling Stone" on the radio, because it was a hit. FM radio at the time was just beginning, but even if there was no FM at the time, I never had an FM radio. In 1965 I was like 15 and there were no kids 15 who were into folk music. There had been a folk boom, but it was generally a college thing. There was really no way of knowing because AM radio was really an incredible must in those days. The one thing I dug about those albums was — I was never really into the folk or acoustic music thing — I dug the sound. Before I listened to what was happening in the song, you had the chorus and you had the band and it had incredible sound and that was what got me.

What about the Stones?

Yeah, I was into the Stones. I dug the first few Stones albums, the first three or four maybe. After that I haven't heard any of it lately except the singles, "Tumbling Dice" and stuff like that — it was great. There was *December's Children* and *Aftermath*. . .

And Between the Buttons *and*. . .

Between the Buttons was when I started to lose contact with the Stones. It was right around there.

What came after *Between the Buttons?*

First Their Satanic Majesties, *then* Let it Bleed. . . See, I never had a record player for years and years. It was a space from when my parents moved out west and I started to live by myself, from when I was 17 until I was 24, and I never had a record player. So it was like I never heard any albums that came out after, like, '67. (Laughs.) And I was never a social person who went over to other people's houses and got loaded and listened to records — I never did that. And I didn't have an FM radio, so I never heard anything. From that time on, from around '67, until just recently when I got a record player. I lived with Diane [Rosito] and she had an old beat-up one that only old records sounded good on. So that's all I played. Those old Fats Domino records, they sounded great on it. If they were trashed, they sounded terrific. A lot of those acts lost what was important after they could really be heard — it just didn't hold. They didn't seem to be able to go further and further. They made their statement. They'd make the same statement every record, basically, without elaborating that much on it.

How about the Yardbirds? Did you listen to them?

Oh yeah. I listened to the Yardbirds' first two albums. And the Zombies, all those groups. And Them.

That's funny for the people who talk about your Van Morrison influence, that it really came from the Them records.

Yeah, that was the stuff I liked. There's some great stuff on those records. When he was doing stuff like "Out-A-Sight James Brown."

But mostly your contact has been through jukeboxes and AM radio?

I guess, yeah. I stopped listening to AM radio, too, because it got really trashy and I didn't have a car. I got a classic example right here (*reaches down and picks up a record.*) You've got your Andy Kim records.

And you've got stuff like "The Night Chicago Died." Those are the same guys who wrote "Billy, Don't Be a Hero."

Oh God. If somebody shot those guys, there's not a jury in the land, there's not a jury in the land that would find them guilty. (Laughs.)

But it was like that in the sixties prior to the Beach Boys.

Yeah, a wasteland.

Union, N.J., September 22, 1974.

Yeah, "Poetry in Motion." But maybe there's hope. It's all cyclical. I sometimes wonder, though, if what the record business is like these days could stop things from happening. I mean at least on the radio.

Only to a certain degree. I don't want to get into specifics because I know some things that have been done to me. I don't want to sound like — I don't want to whine — but at least to a degree they can't stop you from going out there and playing every night. They can't stop you from being good if you've got it. They *can* keep it off the radio. They *can* make sure it gets little airplay, or no airplay, which, really, it hurts you.

Like look at us: we've been going for two years and the second record is at 70,000. That's nothing.

Trenton, N.J., November 30, 1974. ►

That really is nothing. That's zero. It depends on who they're dealing with, who they're messing with. It depends on the person. It's like anything — some people can be stopped and other people can't be stopped. It's just like me — I can't stop, they can't make me stop ever, because I can't stop. It's like once you stop, that's it — I don't know what I'd do. But it's like that, though — if you're dealing with people who say, "Ah hell, I gotta go back to hanging wallpaper," or who say, "Ah, I'm gonna go back to college and forget this stuff" — that's what people always say — "I don't know if I want to play or if I want to get married." If you have to decide, then the answer is don't do it. If you have a choice, then the answer is no. I like to use the term "the record company" because they always get painted as the bad guys. But the pressures of the business are powerless in the face of what is real.

It's like what happens when they push you to make a hit single. Then you get a hit and they push you to go on the road because now you can make $10,000 a night and you might only be able to make $10 a night five years from now. It happens to a lot of people, most people. Then you get out on the road and you can't write anymore and then you can't figure out what the hell else is happening besides.

What happens is there are certain realities that force you into things right now. We got a band; we got a blue bus; we got a sound man; we got an office in New York. Those are the sort of things that influence my decisions. We have to play, because if we don't, everything falls apart. We don't make any money off records. We have to go out and play every week, as much as we can. If not, nobody gets paid. In order to maintain and raise the quality of what we're doing, we gotta play all the time.

At this point you're on salary?
Yeah.
And is that it? Does everything else go back into it?
Everything else pays for the blue bus and everything else.
And you got debts, I bet?
Oh, we owe like a mint.
Some people don't realize that the economic remuneration at this point is like working in an office.
At best. Diane came in and said "Oh, this is terrific. I just got a raise working at my newspaper job in Boston." She said, "Now I'll be getting this

◄ *Philadelphia, Pa., December 30, 1975.*

much." And I realized that was how much I was making. There's no money saved at all. You can't sell 80,000 records and have any money saved. Unless you're totally by yourself and you're your own manager. Then you can make a thousand dollars and stick it all in your own pocket and go home and put some in the bank. But when you're trying to do what we're trying to do, there's no way.

The thing that bothers me, that you seem to have gotten around, is that there seems to be nowhere to play except big arenas, new acts or old acts.

What you gotta do is, like...I did the Chicago tour. I did that tour because I had never played big places. And I said, "I ain't gonna say no because I don't know what they're like." So we went and played it, about 14 nights in a row. I went crazy — I went insane during that tour. It was the worst state of mind I've ever been in, I think, and just because of the playing conditions for our band. The best part of the tour was the guys in Chicago — they are great guys. They are really, really real. But I couldn't play those big places. It had nothing to do with anything, but I couldn't do it. It had nothing to do with anything that had anything to do with me, those big arenas. So I won't go to those places again. That was it. Usually we won't play anyplace over 3,000 — that's the highest we want to do. We don't want to get any bigger. And that's even too big.

The challenge comes when you get more popular, which is inevitable.

But there's no way. I'm always disappointed in acts that go out and play those places. I don't know how the band can go out and play like that. I don't know how Joni Mitchell can do it. You can't. You can't effectively do it.

But then there's the Who. They announce they're playing Madison Square Garden and it sells out in an hour. So I'd guess they'd have to book a week, a whole week.

You gotta do that. And if you get that big, you gotta realize that some people who want to see you ain't gonna see you. I'm not in that position and I don't know if I'll ever be in that position. All I know is that those big coliseums ain't where it's supposed to be. There's always something else going on all over the room. You go to the back row, you can't see the stage, talk about what's on it. You see a blot of light. You better bring your binocs.

I guess people go for the event.

What happens is you go to those places and it turns into something else that it ain't. It becomes an

New York, N.Y., 1975. An outtake from the "Born to Run" album cover sessions.

event. It's hard to play. That's where everybody is playing, though. I don't know how they do it. I don't know what people expect you to do in a place like that. Especially our band — it would be impossible to reach out there the way we try to do. Forget it!

Listen, I got the word from somebody in New York that you're a real sex star now.

Who?

Well, a girl who works at the newspaper. She's 26. I guess 26-year-old women haven't found anything for years that they could get off on.

That's interesting.

And like, pow, they went to your show at the Bottom Line and Schaffer and it's natural because it's all part of the thing. It was a big thrill for them.

Well, we do some pretty heavy things onstage sometimes. There's lots of different currents, lots of different types of energy going on in each song, and that current is very strong. But that's interesting.

I tried to get her to describe why. I made notes as she was talking over the phone. She said it's like "he knows that you know that he knows what he's doing." She said certain

circles are really aware of what a joke it is because it's done really totally seriously. But she also says she'll sit there and laugh her ass off.

There's so many different conflicts and tensions going on in each tune. It can affect people in totally different ways. That's what a lot of the act is based on — it's setting up certain conflicts and tensions. We're going for the moment and then, there'll be no . . . release.

And you'll say, "We'll be back next time."

Really. And that's the way this life is. Next, next, next, next. No matter how heavy one thing hits you, no matter how intense any experience is, there's always, like, next. And that's the way some things we do are structured, for there never to be any resolve, for there never to be a way out, or an answer, or a way in, anything! It's like a constant motion in a circle.

And the two-hour sets are a manifestation of that, needing room to build?

That's a lot. Right now that's the utmost amount we could ever do. It could work better than it's been. It's just a question of finding the right spot

for everything, where things make more sense than other things, what's just the right place. When we were playing the Bottom Line we'd do an hour and a half. And those were long. We'd do an oldie, we'd do "Saint in the City." we'd do "Jungleland," we'd do "Kitty's Back," we'd do "New York City," we'd do "Rosalita" sometimes. We'd do like ten things. Now we're doing like . . . one . . . two . . . we're doing "Lost in the Flood," we haven't been doing that . . . we're doing that new song "She's the One" and a few other things. We're going about two hours. I think the longest we did was Avery Fisher, which was about two-twenty.

Most acts will do that with an intermission.

An intermission might be a smart idea just because it will set up a reference point where people can collect their thoughts. At clubs I never expect people to order alcohol because they're too tired. I know I'm pooped, I figure they're dead. There's outlets for a lot of different things in our shows, a lot of different emotions. It runs the gamut, from violence to anything. It runs through a lot of different outlets. We try to make people as close to it as they want to get.

There are a couple of songs on the first album, "Growin' Up," and "For You," that are more personal.

Well, we were doing "For You" for a while with the new band a few weeks ago, but there's just no time. You gotta realize there's just no time.

Also, I feel the new songs have been more towards archetypes and away from . . .

Yeah, to a degree. I think what happened is I'm using a slightly different language to express the same thing. The songs haven't gotten any less personal — probably just more and more.

They're not as first-personal. On those songs on the first record, you identified with the singer.

I find that if it gets too personal, people get too high. So you've got to use this second person. I tend to be more direct. I'm just getting down there, you know. I think it gets harder to do if you want to continue reaching out there, if you don't want to fall back and play it safe.

I like "Jungleland" a lot.

That's been coming along. There's a verse that's not really finished. It goes . . . there's a chorus that goes . . . "The street's alive with tough kid jets in nova light machines."

Tough kids in nova light machines?

"Boys flash guitars like bayonets, and rip holes in their jeans. The hungry and the hunted explode into rock 'n' roll bands that face off against each other in the street, down in jungleland."

Then the band plays. And what goes next . . . uh . . . I think the next part is the slow part. It goes "beneath the city, two hearts beat, soul engines warm and tender, in a bedroom locked, silent whispers soft refusal and then surrender. In the tunnel machine, the rat chases his dreams on a forever lasting night. Till the barefoot girl brings him to bed, shakes her head and with a sigh turns out the light."

Tunnel machines?

Yeah. (Sings/talks.) "Outside the street's on fire in a real death waltz, between what's flesh and what's fantasy. The poets down here don't write nothing at all, they just sit back and let it be. In the quick of the night, they reach for their moment and try to make an honest stand. But they wind up wounded and not even dead. Tonight in jungleland." Those are some of the words. There's a new verse and some that's not done, but that's the slow part.

"In the quick of the night, they reach for their moment."

Yeah. That's it.

Jungleland. That makes a nice title. It's a nice word.

Yeah, it resolves.

You could call the whole album that because it fits all your songs.

I thought of that. I'm thinking of titles for the next album, that was my initial thought. That's one of them.

It fits. It makes sense.

Yeah, but I usually change them. I work a lot on the lyrics before we record a song. I get self-conscious about them. So I change them. It's the same with a lot of the old songs. I notice them so even on some of the old songs I add new bits. There's a bit on "E Street" and that one on "New York City." It's done differently.

And I like the violin.

Yeah, it's great.

Well, I better call a taxi.

Yeah, what time is it?

BRUCE HAS THE FEVER

. . . .

Bruce Springsteen Interview by Ed Sciaky, August 1978

Ed Sciaky is one of the original Boss Jocks — along with Kid Leo in Cleveland, his early support of Bruce Springsteen was essential to the band's survival during the lean years when most radio stations wouldn't even consider playing a Bruce Springsteen record. Sciaky not only played Bruce, but helped to develop the loyal Philadelphia audience that to this day is the most fervent of all Springsteen crowds. He also introduced many of the early shows and did several on-air interviews with Bruce. During his years at WMMR and later WIOQ, he also always made it clear that he was a "fan," and his radio support has always had an enthusiastic flavor not found in other jocks.

The following interview was conducted in the early-morning hours of August 19, 1978, after Springsteen's show at the Philadelphia Spectrum. An edited version of the interview was broadcast later in the day on station WIOQ. The full, unedited version of the interview follows.

. . . . .

ED SCIAKY: *I'm beat, I have nothing to say.*
BRUCE SPRINGSTEEN: Well, Eddie, you did a hell of a show — that's why. No wonder you're tired.
Well, I was a little far back tonight. I was about seventh row, and I like to be a little closer.
Must have been murder.
Tonight was the most high-energy show I can ever remember at the Spectrum. I rate them, you know, and I'd put this in the top five. Do you rate them like that?
Sometimes. There's ones that you can say, "Wow, this one's really up there; that one was, like, way up there; this one was really something." But this one tonight was pretty wild. It just felt right — it felt good.

◀ *With Ed Sciaky, Philadelphia, Pa., 1978.*

I was just blown away. There were certain highlights and certain changes from the last time you were here, like "Because the Night" which you didn't do last time.
Last time we were here, it was the third show on the tour, and we weren't doing "Darkness on the Edge of Town," we didn't do "Factory," we didn't do "Because the Night," we didn't do "The Fever."
Wait a minute — you didn't do "Fever" for about five years. Now why is "Fever" back?
It was just a surprise, you know. We'd done it two or three times and the tape had gotten out through someone's help whose name I won't mention. So we did it a few times and we had to do it here. I used to have kids run up on stage and yell in my ear, "BRUCE! 'FEVER'!" That was always a request.
You used to say you didn't like the song, and a lot of people think it's one of your best.
I don't know. It was just something that I wrote so long ago. It was just an older song and never a real favorite of mine. I liked it, I always liked it. But just for myself. I liked Johnny's version — I liked what he did with it a lot. But we wanted to have something extra, so we pulled it out.
I saw you down in Washington the other night, and I thought you'd do something for Elvis, like "Wear My Ring," for his anniversary.
I had a song we were gonna do, but in the end we didn't learn it in time. I wanted to do — what's the song from *Blue Hawaii*? It was his theme song. One which everyone relates to his Las Vegas period: "I Can't Help Falling in Love with You." Which I think is a great song. But everyone relates to it as being Las Vegas-y, but I don't think it is. I wanted to do that one. But we just didn't get a chance to run it down before the show. It was something because when we went down to Memphis, Bruce Jackson, the fellow that does our sound, did sound for Elvis for a long, long time, and I went up to Graceland there.
This was recently?

Yeah, it was a couple of weeks ago.

Is it true what you said in Rolling Stone *about the time you tried to sneak in there?*

Oh, that time, yeah, that was two years before then. It was just real late at night and we were looking for something to do. And we got in the cab with this guy and we said — it was me and Miami Steve — and we said, "Listen, we wanna get something to eat." And this guys says, "I know, I'll take you to Fridays." And we said, "We don't want, like a hangout — we want a place where we can go and eat." So he says, "There's a place out by Elvis's house." We said [snaps his fingers], "You mean there's a place out by Elvis's house?" And he said, "Yeah," and I said, "Take me to Elvis's right now." He says, "You guys celebrities?" We say, "Yeah, yeah, we're celebrities." So he says, "Oh." We tell him who we were and he says, "Can I tell my dispatcher that I got some celebrities in the cab?" We said, "Sure, sure." So he gets on the thing and says, "Joe, Joe, I got some celebrities in my cab." And Joe says, "Yeah, who ya got there?" And into it he says, "I got, I got . . ." Then he shoves the mike right in my face because he doesn't know who we are, and I say, "Bruce Springsteen and the E Street Band, we're from New Jersey, blah, blah, blah." And the cabdriver says, "Yeah, I got them and we're going out to Elvis's." The dispatcher says, "Damn." He thinks we're, like, going out to have coffee with Elvis or something.

So we get out there and I'm standing up and looking at those gates — he's got a big, long driveway and I saw a light on. And I say, "I gotta find out if he's home, Steve." And I said, "I can't stand here — I gotta find out if he's home." So I jumped over the wall, a stone wall. And the cabdriver is going, "Man, there's dogs in there. You're gonna get it. You're gonna be in trouble." But I gotta find out, so I ran up the driveway and there was nobody. And I ran up to the front door. And I got to the front door and I knocked. And I knocked . . . And then, from out of the woods, I see somebody watching me. And I figure I'm just going to go over and I'm going to say hello and tell this guy I just came to see Elvis or whatever. So I walk over towards the woods and out comes this security guy. And he says, "What are you doing?" I said "Well, I came to see Elvis. I'm in a band. I play the guitar." "Well," he says, "Elvis ain't home. Elvis is in Lake Tahoe." And I say, "Are you sure?" And he said,

"Yeah, yeah." I said, "Well, if he comes back, tell him Bruce Springsteen . . ." And he didn't know me from nobody, you know from Joe Schmo. I said, "Listen, I was on *Time*, I was on *Newsweek*." He said, "Ah, sure, buddy. Well, listen, you gotta go outside now." So he took me on down to the gate and just dumped me out, back onto the street.

What if he had been home, would you have gone in?

I tried, that's why I went up there.

You saw him at the Spectrum once, remember, and you didn't try to meet him.

It was different then. It was a funny kind of thing. I never liked, you know, going backstage and stuff. I just feel uncomfortable when that happens — I don't know why. But if I could have snuck in and saw him, it would have been different — it woulda just been different.

So you can dig people that want to break into your house and all?

(Laughs.) They want to break into my house?

You know, people that follow you around and all, and people who want to relate to you the way you relate to Elvis.

It's hard for me to put it together like that. Sometimes kids come up and say "Hi" or something. It's hard for me to relate to it the same way. It's different — it just seems different to me on some level, though I guess maybe it isn't. I could just never put it together. I still feel like more the fan than the other thing — the performer. It's like I can't relate. I relate easier from that viewpoint than the other.

I think I've lately seen a change in how you relate to people. You're dealing a little more with the press and the realities of the record business and all that kind of stuff, sort of getting to be the "rock star." I mean dealing with all the different aspects rather than just going out and having the fun of playing.

The *Born to Run* thing — I just got blown away by that particular side of it. I was just too raw and green about it or stupid. And this time I was a little more prepared for people writing stories about [me] and things like that. Plus I was really interested in, and I believed in, the record a lot. I was interested in it getting out there. I thought it was a more difficult record to get into than *Born to Run* was. It was something that I spent 11 months doing and I was just glad I did it. I liked it. I loved playing all the songs from it — it's the most fun of the night. So I said to myself, "Hey, I'm going to get on out there and hustle it." Ya got to get it out to people for people to hear it. I used to think that being on *Time* and *Newsweek* was bad — that's bad

New York, N.Y., 1975. Outtake from the "Born to Run" album cover sessions.

for *me*. It made me feel funny. I just felt funny about it. Then later I looked back on it and thought it was good because maybe somebody read a story and bought the record and it meant something to them and that was good. What was bad was the way I let it get to me on certain levels. And that was my own fault.

It was an unusual situation. Nobody usually goes through that.

Yeah, it was unusual. So this time out I was interested. I said, "Hey, I wanna get it out to as many as I can."

You've had some criticism about the record — some of it mixed — that it was intense, with no "Rosalita"-type songs on it. You said that doing the new LP is the most fun part of the night for you, more fun than the oldies and "Rosalita," the fun songs?

It's a different kind of fun. It's more fulfilling. I don't mean they're fuller. There's this stretch where we go from "Darkness" to "Thunder Road," a stretch of songs that we do basically in the same order every night because there's this continuity thing that happens. It makes connections and it

gives the rest of the show resonance. So then we can blow it out on "Rosalita." Or we got this new song we're doing, called "Sherry Darling."

You've always been praised as a performer first. That's the main thing people say about you — that you're an incredible performer, which you are. But it seems to me now that you're talking about you the songwriter. You're more serious about the songwriting on this album. It seems to me you're very proud of the songs and of the concept of the album.

I'm not more serious about it. It's just different things at different times. Like "Rosalita"...well ...they just mirror the particular perspectives I have at that moment. The next album will be different again.

Was the intensity of this album, as most people are assuming, the result of your being down about the legal hassles?

I don't know. I wasn't really down about it. It was a funny sort of thing — there were only a few days where I got down about the legal thing. This is stuff that matters but it doesn't matter. It's like as much as all this stuff is in the world, like all this stuff — all of it — they can take this away, they can take that, they can take the rights to this, or

money, or whatever, but the one thing that is truly mine, the one thing I value the most, is the ability to create a moment where everything is alive, or it happened. There's no papers or stuff that can take that kind of stuff from ya. You do it one place or you do it another, whether you do it in a club or a concert. But there were a lot of different sides to it. At the bottom, I always felt that way. That was always real consoling. And on the other side, I said I wrote "Born to Run," and the money from that song, maybe that belongs to somebody else, maybe somebody else is responsible for the money that that song made. Maybe that's true. But that song, that song belongs to *me*. Because that's just mine. So that was sorta my attitude about it. I was interested in those things during the lawsuit, but I knew that no matter how many times they sue you or you sue them, or it goes to court or you're doing a record and you get held up doing that, or they try to attach the box office, or this or that. . .no matter how much of that went down, there was always the reason that I felt I could so something that can't get touched by that stuff in a certain kind of way.

So you're glad it's all over.

Yeah, it's all by the boards, it's finished, it's done, and it worked out for the best, in my mind. The whole thing with Mike, who was my old manager, like everybody painted him as the monster, this is the "good guy" and this is the "bad guy," it was like a big misunderstanding. He worked real hard for me for a long time — he did, he really believed in what me and the guys, what everybody was doing. So he got painted as being a little too much of a monster, I think sometimes, which he never was to me. I had a lot of great times with him. You get to a point with two grown men where they disagree or there's a misunderstanding that can't be resolved. And you have those things. It's like growing up.

You used to say you were writing about characters, not really you, not even people you knew, but people you thought existed or you made up. And now there's a little more personal you, a song for your father, more of the personal part of you, rather than fictional characters. Is that right?

A little bit. You're always writing about you. You're talking to yourself — that's essentially what you're doing when you write — and to other people at the same time. There's a little more of it — I don't know what you call it, the first person or second

person — and a little more directness. On this album I didn't write about the city as much because I grew up, basically, in a smaller town. I guess in a way this album was a little more real for me than some of the other ones.

Would you call it your favorite album?

I don't know. I have favorite songs and stuff.

How about "Because the Night." Tell us a little bit about how it happened that Patti Smith did it?

We were in the same studio and Jimmy — Jimmy Iovine — was producing her and he was engineering for us. And we were in a couple of nights at the same time and we had a different engineer or something. I had a tape of one song that I gave to her and he gave her the "Because the Night" tape. A long time ago he asked me if I was going to put it on the album and all. And she said she liked it. I said I don't have all the words done or anything and she said, "Oh," and she wrote the words. And that's pretty much how it went down.

Were you happy with it?

Yeah, yeah.

You're doing it now and it's unbelievable.

We didn't do it for a while and we just started doing it.

And of course you're not doing "Fire" anymore, which is the Robert Gordon thing.

We did that at first.

That reminds me: another major change over the last couple of years is that you're playing guitar so much now it's incredible. You had sort of gotten away from that. I remember the old days at the Main Point when you used to play a lot of guitar. That was before you got Steve in the band, I guess.

I used to play a lot. There was a period when the main thing that was important to me was the arrangement and the song; for a long time that was what mattered to me the most. For a long time I don't think I played any guitar, I mean lead guitar. And this tour there was just a couple of songs where I said, "Oh, I can take some solos here and there." And the guitar fit a little better into the tone of *Darkness* than the saxophone did this time. So there was a little more on the album, and in the show there was a little more than in the album.

That goes back to the old days, when you used to play a lot more lead guitar with your other bands, didn't you?

I used to be just a guitar player. I was never a singer.

What possessed you to say, "I'm not just going to be a guitar player, I'm going to write and I'm going to perform and do something else"?

There were so many guitar players. There were a

Springsteen and Karen Darbin, his girlfriend in 1975. From "Born to Run" cover sessions.

lot. I felt there were the Jeff Becks and the Eric Claptons, there were guys with personal styles, Jimi Hendrix. Guys who were great. I guess on the guitar I never felt I had enough personal style to pursue being just a guitarist. And when I started to write songs I seemed to have something; it was just something where I was communicating a little better. It wasn't a real choice, it just sort of fell that way.

At one time you wrote your first song?

Well, I did that since I started playing the guitar.

What was the first one? Do you remember?

I don't remember. It was some old song.

You've been listening to a lot of Buddy Holly lately?

I did when I was in California more. I go through lots of people. What I've been listening to now, which is funny, is a lot of Hank Williams.

I notice that there's a little hint of country on the record, like on "Factory."

But that was before I started listening to him. He was fantastic. God, he's just incredible. It's hard to describe.

You've always liked Sam and Dave and Chuck Berry, and I guess Elvis. Those were some of your influences.

The rockabilly guys. I listened to a lot of rockabilly this tour. We opened with "Summertime Blues" tonight. I listen to a lot of other stuff.

Is there a performer that you've seen live that does to you what people tell you you do to them? That magic experience live. I've always felt sorry that you couldn't see yourself live sometimes, because you'd love "you." You do something to people and I'm not sure if you know what that is, and I don't know if you've seen that in another performer.

I haven't seen that many shows.

Well, we know it wasn't Led Zeppelin. We know at least that much.

I've seen a lot of good bands. I'm trying to think who I've seen live.

Elvis didn't impress you? That was sort of the end for him? What did you think of the show?

That wasn't a good night. I saw him at Madison Square Garden and he was really great. I saw him the first time he went to New York, and he was really good — he was great. And then on the '68 special, he was just the greatest. It's a shame — he was so good on that 1968 TV special. He was only

Philadelphia, Pa., October 25, 1976. ►

about 32 at the time, and man, he was good.

It was also a very honest show.

I just loved that show.

You ever thinking about doing TV or movies now?

No, I haven't thought about that much. We were gonna do a TV commercial because there's places, like down South and in the Midwest, where we're not very well known. It's getting better, though. This time we're not super well known, but . . . We were gonna do us playing or something for 30 seconds. That's about as close to TV as I guess I'm gonna get. And another thing is because of the lawsuit, I'm a little behind. I got records I gotta make. I got a lot of songs I want to get out, and big allegiance to music. That's what I do — that's my job. The other stuff — if it was something that was really good and I had the time. But I've always got a lot of stuff to do and I have a lot of catching up to do.

Well, do you have a final word to all the people who remember you from the moldy oldie days?

I just want to say the crowd was fantastic tonight — it was great. I was thinking that because this was summertime and all, it was going to be a letdown. And tomorrow night, if those girls would not jump up and kiss me when I'm singing. It sounds funny and all, but it's sorta true because you can't sing when somebody jumps up and kisses ya and does all that stuff. So if you can sorta just stay down, off the stage, it would be appreciated. I don't like to have security in front of there and stuff, so I just depend on the fans to be okay. So less kissing would be appreciated.

We're going to set you up in a little booth in the lobby, and you're gonna kiss all the girls, okay?

I don't know about that.

Does it freak you out when they get up and do that?

It's funny, you know. It's fun. But what happens is, when a whole mess do it, you can't play. You gotta stop singing. And these security guys, I guess they think this 15-year-old girl is gonna knock me out or something.

Does it happen everywhere, or just in Philadelphia?

No, it was much more tonight than ever before. There was never that many.

Do you remember that guy who called me up on the air?

Oh, that was funny.

Remember, he was the guy who called me up and said he screamed "Bruce" during a quiet part of a song. And I asked him why he did that and he said, "During the quiet part is the only time when I can establish one-to-one communication with Bruce."

He had a good reason. He had a good answer.

And that's what running onstage is about, isn't it? That's one-to-one.

That's about as one-to-one as you're gonna get. But it does make it hard to play and stuff, and I'm always worried. It makes it difficult. And I don't like people getting hustled off and stuff.

Do you have any fond memories of the old days at the Main Point? Was that typical for you, too? You've played lots of small clubs around the country, but to me that was special because I saw that and I didn't see those other places.

We played a lot of great nights there. I'll always remember Travis Shook.

Yeah, you opened for them in 1973.

They were nice people.

I remember you also opened in 1973 for Chicago, and that was a bad experience.

That was one of the worst shows we ever did.

And then you said you'd never play the big places, but now you're doing it and you're doing it well.

What happened on the Chicago tour was that at the time we were not known, and it was difficult to come out and go on. We went on at eight-thirty and we'd be off by nine every night. The guys in Chicago were great — they were some of the nicest people that I ever met. I had fun on the tour like that, but it sort of put me off bigger places. And this [the Spectrum] was the first big place we played after that because there were so many people who wanted to come. And after that it just felt so good. It's been good experiences.

We thank you, Bruce, and we'll see you again Saturday night at the Spectrum.

I'll be there, Eddie.

I hope so. And the Shockmobile did make it tonight. Got 94,000 miles on it.

It did? What was that, a Rambler? A Rambler. The Shockmobile. Well, good luck with that thing, Eddie.

◄ *Philadelphia, Pa., October 27, 1976.*

OUT IN THE STREETS

. . . .

Bruce Springsteen Interview by Robert Hilburn, October 1980

Though Dave Marsh is the journalist most usually associated with Bruce Springsteen, *Los Angeles Times* critic Robert Hilburn has probably interviewed Springsteen more than any other journalist. *LA Times* readers know that Springsteen has been a popular subject with Hilburn through the years and Hilburn put together material from his many interviews with lavish photos for his 1985 book *Springsteen.*

At the start of *The River* tour back in 1980, after seeing a concert in Cleveland, Ohio, Hilburn wrote one of the best pieces on Springsteen from that period. He described Springsteen at the time as "a blending of Presley's dynamics and Dylan's inspiring vision."

Hilburn interviewed Springsteen in Bruce's hotel that night. Springsteen spoke in detail about *The River* album, which had just been released, about his rock idealism and the public image of rock's destructive life style. The text of the interview follows.

. . . .

ROBERT HILBURN: *What about the destructiveness? All the deaths, including now Led Zeppelin's John Bonham, must make you worry at times about the demands on you.*
BRUCE SPRINGSTEEN: Rock has never been a destructive thing for me. In fact, it was the first thing that gave me self-respect and strength. But I totally understand how it can be destructive to people. There was a point when I felt very low after *Born to Run.* I felt bad for two, three, maybe four months. Before that, it had been me and the band and we'd go out and play. We'd sleep where we could and drive to the next show. All of a sudden I became a person who could make money for other people, and that brings new forces and distractions into your life.

◄ *New York, N.Y., September 22, 1979.*

What does that do to you?
Two things happen. Either you are seduced by the distractions of success and fame and money or you're not. Look at all the examples of people in rock and what happened to them — people who once played great but don't play great anymore, people who once wrote great songs but don't write great songs anymore. It's like they got distracted by *things.* You can get hooked on things as much as you can on drugs.
What led to your confusion?
I felt like I had lost a certain control of myself. There was all the publicity and all the backlash. I felt the thing I wanted most in my life — my music — being swept away and I didn't know if I could do anything about it. I remember during that period that someone wrote, "If Bruce Springsteen didn't exist, rock critics would invent him." That bothered me a lot, being perceived as an invention, a ship passing by. I'd been playing for ten years. I knew where I came from, every inch of the way. I knew what I believed and what I wanted.
What was the low point?
One night in Detroit, I didn't want to go onstage. That was the only time in my life — that period — that happened. At that moment I could see how people get into drinking or into drugs, because the one thing you want at a time like that is to be distracted — in a big way. I was lucky. I had my band, which was people I had grown up with. No matter where we went, they were always there for support.
Don't the pressures continue when you get more successful? Do they ever stop?
Yes, it keeps coming, more so. But I'm a different person now. When you're young and vulnerable, you listen to people whose ideas and direction may not be what you want. But you don't know that. You just stepped off the street and walked into the studio. On the first album there's almost no electric guitar. If anyone ever told me I was going to make a record without guitars, I would have flipped out.

Seattle, Wash., December 20, 1978, third encore.

I would not have believed him. But I did make an album like that.

Why do you still work so hard on the stage? Don't most performers tend to ease up as time goes by?

I don't know how people do that — if that's what they do. To me, you do that when you're dead. You don't live anymore. You don't exist. That's what "Point Blank" on the new album is a little about.

There's a lot of idealism and inspiration in your work. What were the things that inspired you?

When you listen to those early rock records or any great rock 'n' roll, or see a great movie, there are human values that are presented. They're important things. I got inspired mainly, I guess, by the records, a certain purity in them.

I just know that when I started to play, it was like a gift. I started to feel alive. It was like some guy

◄ *Austin, Tex., November 9, 1980.*

stumbling down a street and finding a key. Rock 'n' roll was the only thing I ever liked about myself.

On the new album I wrote this song called "Out on the Street." I wasn't gonna put it on the album because it's all idealism. It's about people being together and sharing a certain feeling of joy. I know it's real, but it's hard to see sometimes. You go out in the street and there's a chance you get hit over the head or mugged. The song's not realistic in a way, but there's something very real at the heart of it.

But there's also a lot of struggle in your music.

Life is a struggle. That's basically what the songs are about. It's the fight everyone goes through every day. Some people have more success with it than others. I'm a romantic. To me, the idea of a romantic is someone who sees the reality, lives the reality every day, but knows about the possibilities too. You can't lose sight of the dreams.

That's what great rock is about to me, it makes

the dream seem possible. It's like I felt more dead than alive before I started music. I said that before, but it's true. I go to places and see people all the time, and what they're doing ain't at all livin'. They're dyin'. They're just taking a real long time about it.

I found something in rock that says it doesn't have to be that way. We try to say that to people in the songs, and they say it back to you with their reaction. The greatest part of the show is that they will sing the words back.

I came out the first night of the tour in Ann Arbor to do "Born to Run" and I forgot the words. I knew it was gonna happen. I listened to the song ten times just before the show, but when I walked up to the microphone my mind was blank. I went back to the drums and all of a sudden I heard the words faintly in the back of my mind and I realized the audience was singing. That was a real thrill. It was like a special bond. They weren't just sitting out there; they were really involved.

I started sensing that bond during the last tour. It's more than just that you're successful or a big rock star. There's something else happening. I meet kids in the street and there's something we have in common — something they know and I know, even if we don't talk about it.

On the new album, there's more of a balance between the idealism and the realism than before.

Rock 'n' roll has always been this joy, this certain happiness that is, in its way, the most beautiful thing in life. But rock also is about hardness and coldness and being alone. With *Darkness* it was hard for me to make those things coexist. How could a happy song like "Sherry Darling" coexist with "Point Blank" or "Darkness on the Edge of Town"? I could not face that.

I wasn't ready for some reason within myself to feel those things. It was too confusing, too paradoxical. But I finally got to the place where I realized life had paradoxes, a lot of them, and you've got to live with them.

You talk a lot on the album about dreams, losing them and regaining them.

That's one of the things that happens in life. The great possibilities you have in your early twenties. When you're in your thirties or late thirties, the world is different. At least it looks different. You may not have the same expectations. You're not as open to options. You may have a wife and a kid and a job. It's all you can do to keep those things

straight. You let the possibilities go. What happens to most people is when their first dreams get killed off nothing ever takes its place. The important thing is to keep holding out for possibilities, even if no one really ever makes it. There was a Norman Mailer article that said the one freedom that people want most is the one they can't have: the freedom from dread. That idea is somewhere at the heart of the new album. I know it is.

A lot of the songs on the album talk about marriage, but many are yearning for it and others are racing away from it.

One of the ideas this time was to touch on the feelings that everyone has. People want to be part of a group, yet they also want to disassociate themselves. People go through these conflicts every day in little ways. Do you wanna go to the movies tonight with your friends, or stay home? I wanted to get part of that on the record — the need for community, which is what "Out on the Street" is about. Songs like "Ties That Bind" and "Two Hearts" deal with that too. But there's also the other side, the need to be alone.

You used to say that it was harder to write songs because they got more personal.

That's what writing and growth are all about, I guess. I had an album of 13 songs finished a year ago September, but I didn't put the record out because it wasn't personal enough. This album seems much more personal to me.

In many of your songs you deal with the same images: streets and cars. One of the critical complaints about you is that they become almost cliches.

The songs are always different to me. I became fascinated with John Ford movies in the fact that they were all Westerns. I watched the early ones and the late ones. It was fascinating to me how he'd film the same scene — a dance scene or a confrontation — and make it different in every picture. There was a lot of continuity in his work. I liked that.

Why?

You go back to the previous movie and have a clearer understanding of where he was coming from. What he was saying in this film was changing the shape of what he said in another one.

Why cars and streets?

I always liked those images. That's American, in some ways. If you're outside of the big cities, there's people and there's cars — there's transition. That's why people are moving so much in my songs. They're always going from one place to another, and it seemed the natural place for them. Besides, I

New York, N.Y., September 15, 1978. (L to R): Danny Federici, Garry Tallent, Max Weinberg, Miami Steve Van Zandt, and Roy Bittan.

love the road. I like to get on the bus after the show and ride all night.

Do you like to leave a town after the show?
Yes, I'd rather go on the bus to another city than stay in a hotel. I don't like *staying*. It's funny. It makes me feel uncomfortable.

Why so much night imagery?
I don't know. I think there seem to be more possibilities at night. You look up ahead and you can't see nothin'. You don't know what's there until you get there. And I've been playing in bars since I was 15. I live by night. I was never up during the day. People are alive at night.

Looking ahead, what do you see for yourself over the next five years?
I don't do that. Now is now. Tonight you can do something. I don't count on my tomorrows. I don't like to let myself think about the next night. If you

do that, you begin to plan too much and begin rationing yourself.

What do you mean by "rationing"?
There may be no tomorrow, there may be no next record. If you start rationing, you're living life bit by bit when you can live it all at once. I like the latter. That's what I get the most satisfaction out of: to know that tonight when I go to bed I did my best. It's corny, I guess, but isn't that what living is all about? If you go to the show, the kid has a ticket for tonight. He's got no ticket for the show in L.A. or New York. He doesn't have a ticket for Detroit. He only has a ticket for Cleveland. You can't live on what you did yesterday or plan on what's gonna happen tomorrow. So if you fall into that trap, you don't belong onstage. That's what rock 'n' roll is: a promise, an oath. It's about being as true as you can be at any particular moment.

MAX WEINBERG
· · · · · · · · · · ·

Interview by Charles R. Cross, July 1984

Bruce Springsteen has been called the hardest-working man in show business, and if there's any truth to that, then Max Weinberg, as the E Street Band's drummer, can top that claim. Long ago, Bruce dubbed him Mighty Max, and there is perhaps no other nickname in the band that's as appropriate.

Born in 1951, Weinberg grew up in north Jersey, around Newark and Maplewood. By his early teens he was already playing with several local bands, backing up lounge acts and even working as a drummer for Broadway shows.

In 1974 he saw a classified ad in the *Village Voice* that changed his life — "Drummer (No Jr. Ginger Bakers)," it said, and gave a Columbia Records contact number. Max auditioned (the first song he played was "Let the Four Winds Blow"), and both Weinberg and Springsteen describe it as just short of love at first sight.

Apart from his body of work with the E Street Band, Weinberg has been active during off seasons doing seminal work with Southside Johnny and playing a host of other session dates. In 1984 he turned his talents elsewhere and authored *The Big Beat,* a book of conversations with rock's finest drummers. It is an admirably well-written book, and despite its central focus on drummers, it is of great interest to any fan of rock 'n' roll. Weinberg's theory is that although the drummer is infrequently in the spotlight, he is still an integral part of rock history. And for some reason they always have great stories to tell.

We decided to apply this concept to the E Street Band, and found Max one of the easiest band members to talk to, and truly a nice guy. This interview took place over the course of a couple of

◄ *Max Weinberg, Brooklyn, N.Y., February 1984.*

days in July 1984 in Cleveland, Ohio, first in a hotel room and then backstage after the show, while Weinberg soaked his hands.

BACKSTREETS: *First I wonder if you could clear up some of the rumors I've heard about the recording of* Born in the USA *and* Nebraska. *What kind of stuff didn't make it on the record?*

MAX WEINBERG: Well, we recorded about 80 songs for *Born in the USA.* Some of them are great. "This Hard Land," which didn't make it on the record, is just fantastic. That's probably my favorite song we've done.

I know there are rockabilly versions of most everything on The River, *but is there really an electric* Nebraska?

Yeah, we did a lot of those songs with the band.

One of my personal obsessions is with the River *outtakes, which I happen to think are better than the actual commercial album — songs like "Cindy" and "Roulette." What's the story behind "Roulette"?*

Yeah, that's a great song. That was the very first song we recorded when we went into the studio to do *The River.* I don't know, but for some reason it just never made it on the record.

Tell me about your problems with your hands. I understand there was a chance you might never drum again.

I developed incredibly bad tendonitis in my hands. I had these hand operations. It was very painful, that's why I'm soaking my hands in ice now.

I noticed in your book you thank your doctor.

Yeah, Richard Eaton. He's acknowledged as the greatest hand surgeon in the world. I sat down at the table, my hands spread out like this with a drape. I'm a drummer and I'm giving him my hands and he fixed me up.

Are these shows hard for you? I know your hands are rumored to bleed after most shows.

I've been working out for this — woodshedding for about four months. I got done with *The Big Beat* in March, so from March until when we left, I didn't do much but drum. I've got sort of a studio in my basement and I'd just go down there every day and play until I'm tired. I work out real heavy — I run a lot, I do weights.

Why did you decide to write The Big Beat?

The book came about because I've always been interested in talking to drummers and musicians. *The Big Beat* is a result of my special fascination with the drummers that are in the book and the era in which they played. Ringo and Charlie Watts, Dave Clark of the Dave Clark Five, these are the guys I listened to when I was becoming a drummer, when I was a kid. These are still my favorite drummers. That's not to say that they're the only drummers I listen to. I like Stewart Copeland, Simon Phillips is great, the guy from Talking Heads is great. Strictly speaking in rock, these are my all-time favorites, my heroes more or less.

One thing that surprised me was that you didn't write of any jazz drummers.

Well, I love jazz drummers. Buddy Rich is probably my all-time favorite jazz drummer and all-around drummer but in the book I strictly deal with rock 'n' roll 'cause that's what I play and that's what I know best. It's not a technical book, it's a book that the fan of rock 'n' roll can really gain a lot of information from. It's a tribute, my way of putting the spotlight on these guys and also giving them a chance to tell some of their stories. These guys were eyewitnesses to some of the greatest history in rock 'n' roll. Ringo, Levon Helm, Dino Dannelli with the Young Rascals, D.J. Fontana, who was Elvis Presley's drummer — they all have fascinating stories.

One of the best things about The Big Beat, *I think, is that it really does, as you say, put the spotlight for once on this usually unknown member of the band.*

The drummer's always in the back. And if you're doing your job as a drummer, you're solid but you don't stick out. You're not singing the song, you're not writing the words. The foundation of the band begins with the drummer. You can't build a building without architecture, and the drummer is the main architect if he's doing his job. He can cause it to crumble if he's not doing his job. There's a picture of Ringo in the book that's never been used before. I love this picture because the spotlight's on Ringo, and John, Paul, and George are in silhouette. I thought it was particularly fitting because when I looked at the Beatles I saw Ringo.

It was watching Elvis Presley, wasn't it, that you first became interested in music?

I had two older sisters and a younger sister. They were teenagers at the time, and naturally into Elvis.

I was about five or six and I remember vividly sitting down and dressing up as Elvis with a cardboard guitar and this hair and sideburns, it was very cute. And when he played "Hound Dog," the roll of D. J.'s was what really blew my mind. It got my attention immediately. I guess I was just always keyed into rhythm and percussion, because that made me want to develop my rhythmic sense. About a year or two later I got a little drum. I was really only about six or seven when I got my first drum. I was banging on that thing and I had a little promise. I got my first set, my parents bought me this little Japanese drum set — I think they went into hock, it was this little Japanese drum set that cost $125 — when I was in the end of sixth grade. I first heard of the Beatles in November of '63. By the time they were on Ed Sullivan I already had a drum set and a little band, and then when I saw Ringo, that just changed my life. That just made me want to be Ringo. I just wanted to be in a great rock 'n' roll band, playing for screaming people.

It must just have been a hell of a kick for you to be able to meet these drummers and talk about your craft.

Yeah, it was a total gas. Naturally I was nervous — I've never gotten over my nervousness talking to Ringo. It was great because I got to ask all the millions of questions I had when I was a kid, and these guys were so nice, warm, and engaging, it was a real pleasure. It's great when you have heroes and you come away after meeting them and they're bigger heroes. These guys are still big, big heroes to me. Every time I listen to Russ Kunkel I learn something, and that's what it's all about and I'm proud to be part of the tradition.

Bruce has been called the hardest-working man in show business and that makes you perhaps even harder-working, being the drummer. Playing a song like, let's take "Backstreets" from tonight, that must put some great physical demands on you.

It's emotionally hard. You try to conserve your physical energy as much as possible while at the same time giving a thousand percent. That's what economy of emotion and finesse technique are all about. But the emotional thing, I try to reach a certain emotion when I play, especially a song like "Backstreets," it's so emotional. And I've played that song, shit, I've played that song 500 times and every time I listen to it or play it, I just get choked up. I love that song. That song describes totally a period of my life for three years during the mid-seventies.

"Dancing in the Dark" has a different drum sound. Did you do anything special on that song?

It was just the straight beat. No fills. Bruce played that song in the studio, it was the last song we cut off *Born in the USA.* I've been listening, like everybody else, to a lot of Stewart Copeland and the Police. I was really into the Police and I had just seen the Police two days before we cut that track. They played "Every Breath You Take," and it's just groove and momentum. It's the exact opposite of "Born in the USA," which has its own groove and momentum, but "Born in the USA" is very busy drumming — I love that song. "Dancing in the Dark" — you play what the song dictates, and that's what the song dictates.

How do you consider yourself as a drummer? What do you think of your talents?

I have my moments, but I don't put myself in the same league as any of the guys in the book I wrote. I have my moments — it's about moments, trying to get as many of them as you can. But I don't put myself on the level of a Ringo — not that I'm putting myself down, but I never listen to myself like that. Only on a few things do I sound as good as I want to sound — "Born in the USA," that's how I want to play. I like "Dancing in the Dark," I like "Candy's Room." I play good on "Ramrod" — "Ramrod" is probably one of my favorite pieces of drumming I've done. "Born in the USA," that's really me drumming, you've got the true Max Weinberg, Mighty Max, on "Born in the USA." I hit something out there on that one — it's real pleasing to me.

You've done a weird potpourri of session work. What kind of stuff remains that you want to do?

I'd like to do a lot more session work. I've been doing some movie stuff — I did some stuff for *Streets of Fire,* that song "Nowhere Fast," and I'm on *Sixteen Candles.*

Do you get lots of phone calls and requests to play on records?

No. When you're in a big group, people don't think you do stuff. They never ask who the drummer is unless they want my sound. And that's how I get work — I average a few things a month, but I could be busier. I'm going to be a lot busier. It's a little hard to think about what I'm going to do after this tour; this tour just started and we're going to be out here for a year and a half.

Chicago, Ill., July 17, 1984.

Looking into the future, what do you want to do after the E Street Band?

I don't even think about that. I do play every show like it was the last, though — that's the only way I can get through these shows. I don't think about anything but what's going down right now. Especially for drummers, when you start thinking about that shit, you lose your perspective. My job is to keep it happening like right now. I will always desire to play with Bruce Springsteen. He's the most inspirational, most dedicated, most committed, and most focused artist I've ever seen. I like to be around people like that, and there aren't many people like that. I only think about what I did tonight.

Thinking back to when you first saw D.J. Fontana kick in that great opening of "Hound Dog," did you ever imagine you'd become the drummer in a band like the E Street Band? Did you ever dream you'd be where you are now?

This is a dream come true.

—Charles R. Cross

LITTLE STEVEN VAN ZANDT

Interviews by Charles R. Cross, December 1982,
by Marcello Villella, March 1987

Little Steven Van Zandt has been one of the most seminal figures of the E Street Sound. With his own work with the E Street Band, with Southside Johnny and the Jukes, and with his own solo career, Van Zandt has established himself as a true original — an artist of the highest personal integrity.

Backstreets has interviewed Van Zandt on four occasions. What follows are excerpts from the 1982 interview in which he first discussed his plans to leave the E Street Band, along with excerpts from a 1987 interview conducted by Marcello Villella, following the release of *Freedom, No Compromise.*

· · · · ·

1982

BACKSTREETS: *My description of your music would be "soul with modern touches," at least the music on* Men Without Women. *I'd call it an amalgamation of some great old things and some great new things. I'd say part of your problem with radio is that what you're doing is not what one would call the popular music of the day.*

STEVE VAN ZANDT: The real problem is that whenever you do something that combines elements and just transcends categorization, you're in trouble until people get used to it. I'm not overly concerned — I think by the next record, or the one after that, radio will just get used to me. They'll realize I'm not going to fit into one of those categories. I'm always going to be combining different cultural elements because that's what I do. It's always going to be a combination of things because that's who I am. I hope, sooner or later, I'm going to hit some common ground.

You might feel like you're carrying a torch for soul music.
Well, I don't want to be thought of as carrying the torch for sixties soul music. The only common thread I'm very conscious of keeping is the passion

◀ *Stone Pony, Asbury Park, N.J., August 21, 1987.*

and the emotional side of that music. It basically started in the church and in the sixties was brought into a romantic setting; now I'm bringing it to the next evolution, which is carrying that emotional commitment to one's work, to one's life. I'm really not into being nostalgic or anachronistic about it. I am trying to redefine it. It's going to take a little time.

On completely another track, I was listening to a Steel Mill demo tape the other day, and despite the fact that it was years old, the songs seemed timeless. I think Steel Mill would be very popular today with the heavy metal generation.
Yeah, it was a heavy metal band. It was one of the first before heavy metal really happened, so it had the very, very early elements of it. We had a bit more melody and a bit more to the lyrical side of it than a lot of the hardcore stuff today.

Both through your own work and your work with the E Street Band, you've collected a band of followers who are fanatical, to say the least. They're just nuts.
I think we're different. I know, speaking for myself, the fans understand we're artists concerned with communicating. We're not there to entertain and we're not there to take advantage of anybody or retire next week. We've been there a long time and we're going to be here a lot longer. We're going to be playing forever. We have a certain integrity that comes through. We're not temporary. We're not trying to hustle up some bread and buy a house and fade away. We're gonna be here tomorrow, so we have a relationship with people that's permanent.

Your whole career seems to me to have been one best described as "outlaw." You've broken the rules of rock 'n' roll, the first one being that kids from New Jersey wouldn't get a record contract and wouldn't go on to be important in any way. In 1970, the story of your success and that of the other Jersey musicians would have been a shocker.
That's very true, and it's still true. We're still rebels in the way we do things. That's particularly true with me and my band. The rebellion has also taken

a new turn. It's a more focused rebellion. I know what I want to accomplish. You're not going to accomplish anything by screaming real loud and banging your head against the wall. I think in the next 20 years you're going to see rock 'n' roll get more involved in politics, and I think the rebellion of it is going to take on a very interesting focus. The communication that can exist between people of different countries is going to happen through rock 'n' roll.

From what I know of your early history, growing up around Asbury Park, you guys would hang out together, play Monopoly, and jam together all night long. Comparing the material you wrote back then, which has a sense of you struggling on the street, to the material you're writing today, has there been any sense of a loss of innocence?

The innocence is certainly gone, as it is from America — there's no question about it. On the other hand, I've never stopped being on the street or being the underdog. Nothing's changed. Through fate, or whatever, I haven't changed that much. You get more mature and you get better, but basically I'm still talking about the same things. I think if you look at the lyrics on *Men Without Women*, you get both sides. I still have the same anger. "Lyin' in a Bed of Fire" is as angry as I've ever felt.

Considering the creative freedom you've had, at this point in your career do you feel lucky?

I do feel lucky. I'm glad that I'm able to make a living doing what I want to do. That's the great thing about rock 'n' roll: That you can create your own world. If you're good enough, you can play what you want. I'm not doing this in the short run. The audience knows that — you're not going to compromise if you're doing something long-term. This is the only thing I can do. Rock 'n' roll will always be my life. I've always been a gypsy.

Have you ever considered that the music you've created, and the music Springsteen has created, has changed the entire world for kids growing up in New Jersey? It used to be that New Jersey was a joke — you both have worked to make that no longer so.

That's good. What we accomplished could have been accomplished in any little town in America. I think it's really great that Bruce and I did it for New Jersey. It gave hope to all the Des Moineses of the world.

Steve, the thing most people want to know at the moment is whether or not you'll continue with the E Street Band. To this point you haven't told anyone. Only you and your hairdresser know.

It's not my central focus. Miami has retired really. It's just Little Steven now. When I can I still want to, you know, whatever, help out Bruce or play on a record or do a couple of shows but it's really not my central focus. My central focus and my first priority is my own work now.

Are you saying you've rested the Miami Steve title for good?
Yeah, he's gone pretty much, retired to a condo in Tampa. It's a new band, it's a new day, I want it all to be new and that even includes the people who are going to enjoy it. I don't want them to think it has anything to do with the past because it really doesn't.

If you're saying goodbye to the E Street Band aren't you going to miss occasionally playing all those great songs?
I've played them enough. Really. Once you start playing your own music it becomes a big part of you. It's all encompassing and your focus is changed. And this is not something new for me: It's been coming for a while.   —*Charles R. Cross*

. . . .

1987

BACKSTREETS: *Last time we spoke, you had just released* Sun City *and you expressed a lot of hope for its message, if not its sales. And I think the impact of that message has been very strong. Paul Simon recently credited you with interesting him in the issue. Were you happy with the response to that record?*
LITTLE STEVEN: I'm very, very happy with the record, the video, the full length documentary, and the book. I'm happy with the way it reached people. We accomplished everything we set out to accomplish. Our main goal was to reach our own people — those in the entertainment world. And as far as I know, no major star has played Sun City since the record came out.

We wanted also to increase awareness about the issue and we wanted to give the whole movement a little push. Which finally resulted in what I'll call the "symbolic sanctions" of our government. But as symbolic as they were, they were very significant, because Reagan had said "never." It was important at least to break that wall down.

The other thing that was important was to send a message to the South African people that we care — that even we in America and England care, the two biggest supporters of South Africa.

Your message, it seems, was that not all Americans believe in the official government policy on South Africa.

Washington, D.C., August 1985. ►

Philadelphia, Pa., 1975. The only picture ever published of Steve Van Zandt after he joined the E Street Band without *a hat on.*

Exactly. So that was very good. The problem now is that a lot of people think that because these sanctions have gone through, that's the end. Which is, of course, wrong. These symbolic sanctions are only the beginning. Now we have to find a way to keep the issue alive.

What concerns me is that some people may have the perception that things have changed there and consequently the issue is not such an important one for them.

True, but nothing's changed there — it's just as bad as ever. Right now, nobody knows, but right now somewhere between ten and twenty thousand people are detained. About a third of them are children. Things are very, very bad, and very little of this gets out because they have censored the media.

On to your new record: it seems to me that you are continuing the strong messages that you started with Voice of America. *I saw that album presenting an alternative party, and that party is freedom. And with this record, I see you presenting the platform of that party — freedom around the world.*

I think you have perceived it very well — it is meant to be an extension of *Voice of America*, part of

an evolution. There are some similar themes: one being Latin America. The political party thing I've taken to a more literal place on this record, with "No More Parties." This is an evolution of what I've talked about before: people have more loyalty to their party than to the truth. When we elect politicians, we should elect them because they are the most educated, not because they belong to the same club your father was in. In America, because of the way people are elected, with the economics of politics, we are left with virtually no democracy, just a veneer of democracy. We're not that different from the Soviet Union. We have a little more freedom and we dress it up better, but it's the same thing. We elect people by television commercials — who has the money to pay for that?

Despite the power of your message, many people say — with their own reasons — that they don't want any politics in their music.

I had a record that we're going to release as a B-side — it's called "Vote." It was written for the 1984 election, and the message was we must vote — we must use this democracy we theoretically have in place. If we don't use it, then we're going to continue to be manipulated. The problem now is the right wing, the more conservative element — you can use the word *fascist* if you'd like. They are more organized, just like the left wing was more organized in the sixties.

Bruce, of course, joins you on "Native Americans." I think that perhaps finally with "Sun City" you were able to leave the Springsteen references aside. That probably was liberating for you.

Actually, it was the *Voice of America* record that did that for me. I think "Sun City" was also a help. But *Voice of America* was accepted, I think, as something that was uniquely me, that was not like any other record, really.

Do you remain among the believers?

I think it's an important role for an artist to present ideas. We need to wonder what is the ideal. With each record I try to present one song that shows us some ideals. Some people may call that naive, but I feel we need to show the possibilities. The difficult part is fighting the cynicism within ourselves. It's important to fight that as, in the end, that's all that matters. The day we stop fighting, it's over.

—*Marcello Villella*

Philadelphia, Pa., December 8, 1980. ▶

CLARENCE CLEMONS

Interview by Marcello Villella, February 1986

They call him the Big Man. For years, Clarence Clemons held that nickname just because of his size; he had a physique so imposing that in the E Street Band's early days it was an insurance policy that the band would get paid. But now a much slimmer Clarence (from a strict diet and exercise program) has another reason for the name: his solo career. His second album, *Hero*, was one of the biggest success stories of 1985. Buoyed by a hit video, two singles, and a successful tour of the world, it was a hot record for more than a year.

We caught up with Clarence in Italy at the end of his *Hero* tour in 1986.

. . . .

BACKSTREETS: *Let's start back at the beginning, Clarence, with your hometown. You were born in Norfolk, Virginia. And from there you went on to play football.*
CLARENCE CLEMONS: I left there when I was about 18 years old to go off to college. My father had bought me a saxophone when I was nine.
I remember the story of how you'd asked for a train and instead had gotten a sax....
Yeah. I'd asked for the train and he bought the sax and I've never gotten over it. Anyway, I went off to college and I majored in football, but I always had the sax in my car, looking for what I really wanted to do. I knew that what I was doing wasn't it. College wasn't what I wanted to do, and what they were preparing me for I wasn't really ready to do. I wanted to play music. So I was searching for the missing link in my life. And that came when I met Bruce.
Before you met Bruce, what was the style of music that interested you?
I grew up in a very religious house. We didn't listen to a lot of the radio, so I grew up listening to

◄ *Seattle, Wash., October 24, 1980.*

a church choir. It was music that made you feel good. It was old gospel music, which really was where rock 'n' roll and the blues came from. So when I finally got into rock 'n' roll, it was an easy transition. I grew up listening to the Coasters when I got exposed to music, the stuff with King Curtis on sax, and this is really where my roots are.
That's really the sound that I think one hears on your first album, Rescue. *Sort of like Otis Redding.*
Yeah, that's it man, exactly it. Otis.
In contrast to that, I was very surprised when I first heard Hero; *it's a very different sort of sound and approach. It has a much more modern sound, and more of a commercial orientation.*
I look at it as growth. You move from the unknown to the known. When you start something for the first time, you do what you know best. So that's what I did: I started with my roots. This time I wanted to do my own thing. And the music grew from that and it became more modern. I look at it as "the Big Man moves into the eighties." It's called growin' up.
What happened to the Red Bank Rockers?
The Red Bank Rockers died when my drummer, Wells Kelly, died two years ago. He was the heart and soul of the band. So when I first started thinking about this album I had planned to use him a lot more than just as a drummer — he had a great, great voice and I wanted to use him a lot more vocally. I was starting to write songs around him. With the loss of him, the idea was also lost, so that's when I decided to do it myself.
"You're a Friend of Mine" obviously was written about Springsteen. How was it that Jackson Browne ended up doing the duet with you?
The song was written with Bruce in mind. But he had just gotten married and he was in the middle of the biggest tour in the history of rock 'n' roll, so I had to go find someone else to do it with. So I called Jackson. He was a friend of mine for many years, and he liked it and we decided to do it.

Tacoma, Wash., May 5, 1988.

It's safe to say now — you've got a big hit on your hands with your album and the single. This record also seems to me to be promoted now as a Clarence Clemons record, in contrast to your last album, which seemed to me to always be billed as "Clarence Clemons, from Bruce Springsteen's E Street Band." Did that sort of promo bother you?

I was annoyed last time. This time it's a lot different. But I cannot deny that connection, and I don't really get upset when it's referred to a lot, because these are my roots and this is my background. And you can never get away from that. I'm just happy that this time I'm being considered on my own and my career is solidifying itself. I'm a solid solo artist now.

What's the story behind the addition of Mokshagun to your name? Obviously there's religious significance.

It's a name that was given to me by my guru. It means "liberation fire." He says my whole purpose in life is to bring light into the world, to destroy ignorance, to become a liberated fire, a liberated flame for the people. I've really found myself through meditation. I meditate every day.

Going back to the beginning again — would you recount, just one last time, the great story of how you first met Bruce?

It's just like he tells. He was playing in a bar down the street from where I was playing. And it was a dark and rainy night — it was cold. I walked out on the street and saw him and asked if I could sit in with him. He said "Sure," and the magic started.

Let me pose one last question to you. In the great story that introduces "Growin' Up," Bruce speaks of the gypsy lady who granted any wish you'd ask her. If you were in front of her today, and she had the power to grant any wish you asked, what would you wish for?

I would wish that God's will be done. That's the greatest wish that anyone could have.

—Marcello Villella

Landover, Md., August 24, 1984. ▶

DANNY FEDERICI

. . . .

Interview by Robert Santelli, November 1990

They call him the Phantom — with good reason. Shy and introspective, quiet and reserved, keyboard player Danny Federici has been, without a doubt, the mystery man of the E Street Band. Although he's logged more time with Bruce Springsteen than any other musician, Federici is the least known and certainly the least public of all the band members.

Incredibly, Danny Federici had never done a serious, full-length interview with anyone before this one.

BACKSTREETS: *For years you've shunned interviews and avoided the press. You were in one of the biggest rock bands in the world and yet you led a life that was decidedly anti-celebrity. Why?*

DANNY FEDERICI: In the early days I thought that all that was required of me was to do a good job onstage. As things started to progress, the scene got to be a real clique, with a party-like environment backstage. I didn't go in for that kind of thing. As soon as I got done working, I'd go back to the hotel — for whatever reason. You see, Bruce has himself an organization that is there to protect his situation. I think that when I really wanted, and was willing, to break out and say some things, the opportunity wasn't brought to my attention. So, even though I would have talked sooner, I didn't know I could have. It was a very strange situation.

You've been in a band with Bruce for more than two decades — that's nearly one half of your life. When you look back, what impressions come to your mind first?

It was a funny thing. The E Street Band was someone and no one at the same time. To a certain extent, I liked that very much. I mean, if I wanted to, I could go to the hardware store and not be

◄ *Danny Federici, 1974.*

bothered by people. But, at the same time, I always thought I could have been a little bit more famous than I ended up.

I toured with Dave Edmunds recently. What surprised me was that I had to deal with my ego. I hadn't had to do that in a long time. In the early years I had a situation once where I thought I was bigger than I really was. But that was a long time ago. When I went out with Edmunds, our names were used, Max and I, and I figured that would add some credibility to the shows. There were some people who came to the shows to see me and Max, but there weren't as many as I thought there would be.

It's been a year since Bruce told the E Street Band that he would be working with other musicians. Has that been difficult to deal with?

I had already gone through some tough years. I had a bad marriage. I got into drinking very heavily. I went to two rehab centers. I've been sober for seven years. In those days I don't think I would have been able to handle what went down. But today I can deal with it. If you know who you are, you can deal with it. I mean, I went from a situation which meant traveling around in jets, not listening to the news, not knowing what's going on in the world, to one in which I had to face who I was and determine certain things about my life and my future. It was a tremendous growing experience, I can tell you that. I have my wife to stand by me, and that helps. But I worried about that, too. There's no way to know if your partner is going to be your partner under certain circumstances. You just don't know until the relationship is tested.

How long have you been married to your current wife?

Three years. It doesn't sound like much, but it is a lot for me.

Before Springsteen's rise to stardom, before the formation of the E Street Band, what were your goals as a musician? Did you always plan to build your life around rock 'n' roll?

I planned to go as high as I could go. And I did.

That's why the E Street Band was a hard thing to leave behind. During my drinking binges over the years I must have quit the band three or four times. I was always talked back into it, which I'm grateful for. We started out as a band which turned into a super, giant corporate money-making machine. That was an amazing thing for me to go through as a musician.

When was the first time you met Bruce?

I met Bruce at the Upstage through Vini Lopez. I remember the big thing at the Upstage was that this guy was coming down to play and you wouldn't believe how good he was. The situation at the Upstage was that things happened at three or four o'clock in the morning. After everybody got done playing gigs elsewhere, they'd come to the Upstage and jam. So I went down to hear this guy play. Well, he played and he was unbelievable. I had never seen anyone like him before, and I had been all around New Jersey playing in different bands and doing different gigs. Me and Vini began talking about putting a band together with this guy. Bruce was in the band Earth at the time. Basically, it was Vini's idea to start a band that included Bruce. At the time, Bruce was incredibly energetic. He was writing an unbelievable amount of songs — five or ten a day. And they were epics. We did form a band with Bruce. It was called Child. We had one steady gig — at a place called Pandemonium on the Jersey Shore. I remember we played there the day the astronauts landed on the moon. One of the bartenders brought in a TV set. When the astronauts were getting ready to take their first steps on the moon, we were playing. The whole audience takes its eyes off the band and starts watching the TV. Well, Vini got upset and it cost us the gig. We played a 14-night stretch at the club, doing all original material, and that was that. We only had a couple of areas in which we could play. One was the Jersey Shore; the other was down in Richmond, Virginia. The most amazing thing was that one night, say a Friday, we'd do a 30-song set. The next night, Saturday, we'd do an entirely different 30-song set — all written that week. We rehearsed every day.

Was the band living together?

Some of us were. I lived in Bruce's family house in Freehold for awhile when I was 18 or 19. Eventually we moved out of there and moved in with Tinker West, the band's manager. We stayed at his surfboard factory. He had like three or four bath-rooms in the back. They were fairly large, so we slept in them in sleeping bags. Vini had one bathroom, I had another. When things got a little better for us, we rented a house in Bradley Beach. Bruce had a room on the second floor. We all shared the rent. It was one for all and all for one. It was a collection of togetherness. It was a good time. About the only thing that was bad was the Clearwater incident.

The infamous rock 'n' roll riot in 1970. You were a central figure in that. Let's talk about it for a minute.

I haven't had as much press since that time. That was a crazy thing. Thanks to me, we were known as a rebel band. But I was proud of what happened.

What exactly did happen?

The police set the whole thing up. Tinker had booked us to play the Clearwater Swim Club in Atlantic Highlands. The place was packed. We played at one end of the Olympic-size swimming pool. People were standing on all sides of the pool. The reason why we did this show was because Vini was in jail in Virginia. We had the drummer from a group called Mercy Flight playing with us that gig. Jeez, we sounded like a hell of a band. Anyway, this gig was to raise money to get Vini out of jail. So halfway through the set, I saw the paddy wagons arrive. I saw the riot gear go on. I remember we were playing and the police pulled the plug. Well, a guy that was working for the band at the time was behind the stage trying to plug the P.A. back in so we could calm the crowd down. Three cops started clubbing him to the ground for trying to put that plug back in. It was unbelievable. I saw red and just tossed my amplifiers off the stage onto these cops. I never expected them to get up, but they did. They saw me, I saw them. Half the crowd was on the stage by that time. They started calling the cops pigs. I saw my friend and said we better go. So we got out of there. It was amazing how we got out of there. We went through the crowd, got out to Route 36 and hitched a ride. Someone picked us up in a van and we went and partied for a while.

But you were arrested?

After I turned myself in. They had three warrants out for my arrest. It was funny because after Clearwater, Steel Mill played a couple of gigs. We played Monmouth College and I remember there were cops on the roof of the gymnasium just waiting for me to show up. I was hiding in the back of a car until the show was ready to start. I was a

An early Child promo photo of Federici and Springsteen.

fugitive. At the last second I got out of the car, into the building, onto the stage, and we start playing. I'll never forget that gig because we usually played for a while and then took a break. But during the set Bruce came up to me and said, "We're not taking a break; we'll play straight through. But in the middle of the last song I'm going to come up to you and tell you to get out of here." And I got away without being arrested. That was the second time I was able to do that. We had played a concert before that in which we did pretty much the same thing. But that couldn't go on forever. Sooner or later I had to turn myself in. It's funny because I look at that time in my life and it was definitely my

crazy period. For six months it was really wild. There wasn't anything before that or anything after that, but for that six-month period, it was really crazy.

Why was that?

I don't know. Maybe it was because when I was younger and living at home, I never really had a chance to rebel.

If I recall correctly, early on your mother was very supportive of your interest in rock 'n' roll.

For investment purposes. There was a lot of money spent on music lessons back then.

How did things change after the Clearwater incident?

Well, the band broke up. One day Bruce just said

Child 1970: Springsteen, Federici, Vini Lopez, Vini Roslin.

things were too crazy and that the band was breaking up. A week later the band reformed — without me. The police had arrested like 500 people during the Clearwater thing, and I was the only guy they prosecuted, or tried to prosecute.

Why was that?

Because I was in the band. It was perfect. Get the guy in the band.

We're talking about Steel Mill. A lot of Springsteen fans consider that his greatest pre–E Street band. What are your recollections concerning the band?

We were ahead of our time. It was a wild band. That kind of band came along later. I remember we opened for Grand Funk Railroad once, and the audience didn't want to even hear them after we were done. That was when Grand Funk was a really big band. We did some really cool things with that band. Once we played atop a parking

garage in Richmond, Virginia. Bruce had this song called "The Wind and the Rain." It was a windy night and overcast and it was just perfect.

How do you account for the band's popularity in Richmond, of all places?

I don't know how that happened. But our popularity down there helped us survive back then. It was very tough in those days because we didn't play any cover material. We did 100 percent original material. We couldn't play any of the clubs in Asbury Park because, at the time, bands playing there had to play Top 40 stuff.

You had few gigs and little money, yet you, for one, hung on with Bruce. Why? What was it that gave you hope that someday things might be better?

I just always felt that there was something truly special about Bruce. He had a drive and a determination that was so strong that I believed in what he believed in. He didn't preach or anything; it was just his strength from day to day. I didn't care if I made any money. Sometimes I look back and think it was money that spoiled the whole thing.

One of the more interesting pre-Springsteen bands you were in was the Downtown Tangiers Rockin' Rhythm 'n' Blues Band with Billy Chinnock, Garry Tallent and Vini Lopez.
We also had a lead singer by the name of Wendell John who was a Yale graduate and was very politically active. Once, he and Billy wrote some articles or some lyrics and said some things onstage that really upset some people. Once, we played in Constitution Hall for some Daughters of the American Revolution event. Wendell decided to get into this political thing onstage. Well, we never finished the gig. They just asked us to leave. We had a similar incident in Buffalo, New York. Billy is a cartoonist; well, while up there, Wendell wrote an article called "City of Pigs" and Billy drew a cartoon of this big pig holding black people in one arm and hippies in the other. We got thrown out of Buffalo. They literally showed us the way to the city border after that.

Those must have been some pretty exciting days as were, I'm sure, the early days of the E Street Band, when all of you would get from gig to gig in an old van and station wagon and when the camaraderie was especially strong.
That's true, but one of the things I always regretted about those days was what would happen when someone new came into the band. The original guys had logged so many miles and then David Sancious and Boom Carter came into the band. At the time we were enjoying the chance to fly from the East Coast to California. But these guys never had to make that trip by car. They hadn't paid their dues; they hadn't put in the miles that we had. I think I was a little bit upset by that. (laughs)

When Sancious and Carter left to form their own jazz-rock fusion band, Tone, Max and Roy then joined the band.
Yeah, in fact there was something that I never told Roy about his audition.

What was that?
We had gone through a lot of auditions at the time. It was really up to me and who worked well with me, since I was the only keyboard player in the band at the time. I always thought that if I ever needed to, I would tell Roy that.

Bruce left it up to you as to who would be the second keyboard player in the band after Sancious departed?
Yeah, pretty much. After each audition, Bruce would come up to me and say, "Well, what'd you think of this guy?" and "What about that guy?" We had great guys audition, technically speaking, but they had no feel. There was one guy who was one of the best pianists I ever heard, but he didn't get the job because he had no feel. He called me months later. He wanted to come to my house and have me teach him how to play. I was astonished. I mean, this guy went to Juilliard and he wants me to teach him how to play. He didn't have what I had, and I didn't have what he had. He never did get it. But Roy, when he played, he felt real good. I still think Roy's a great pianist.

You were the only keyboard player in the band until Sancious joined the band. Did his presence in the band bother you? What was your relationship with Davey like?
I never really had a good relationship with Davey. I remember when Davey was playing with Billy Chinnock in the early days. I thought he was a terrible piano player back then. He disappeared from the scene for a few years and then he came back as this unbelievable piano player. He must have never left his house; he must have practiced all the time. Davey was the kind of guy who would always tell me how to play. He'd get up and come over to me and say, "You shouldn't play that, you should play this." That really disturbed me. So we didn't have a good rapport.

What about Roy? Was your relationship better with Roy?
We're like brothers, the whole band is like that. But we don't necessarily have to like each other all the time. If one of us got in trouble, I'm sure we'd all be there for him.

Musically speaking, how much of a say did you and Roy have in creating the parts you played in the studio?
Bruce had a lot to do with the parts we played. He heard a lot of riffs in his head. If anything, we'd probably play too busy, and then Bruce would say, "No, no, no. Simplify it." Bruce got more defined as to what he wanted as the years went on. He knew exactly what he wanted. When Bruce had Mike Appel as a manager, he wanted to treat the band as a separate entity. He wanted to do other things with the band as well as with Bruce. Needless to say, he wasn't around too long.

As a young keyboard player, who were your influences?
As an accordion player I really looked up to Weird Al's father, Frankie Yankcovich. I was really into classical accordion as a kid. My mother was Polish and my father was Italian, so there was a big emphasis on the accordion. When I got into keyboards I really liked Jimmy Smith a lot. I always

wanted a Hammond B-3. As a matter of fact, the first B-3 I ever owned Bruce and I pulled out of a cellar in Trenton. It was for the Pandemonium gig. But I really liked that contemporary jazz organ thing. I really like contemporary jazz today, too. It was strange because as a kid I was a Beatles kind of guy. I wasn't into the Rolling Stones. The Animals were great too. I always wanted a Vox Continental organ, but my mother bought me a Farfisa. When I wanted a mini-bike, I got a go-kart. (laughs)

Do you have any brothers or sisters?

No. I was an only child. I was adopted. I'm actually Irish. It came in handy for drinking. (laughs)

So many of these things I didn't know about you.

Yeah, you know, during the last couple of tours with Bruce and the band, I really wanted to get out there and talk about these things. I thought the time was right. It was funny because I'd meet journalists and they'd say, "You know, we tried to interview you guys." It just never happened.

The image that most of your fans have of you is that you're quite a private guy, one who is introverted and not interested in talking about things. What you seem to be saying is that this particular image might not be all that accurate.

Introverted. That's an interesting word. I think I'm a hell of a guy, to tell you the truth. A lot of people don't know that. I don't know what happened to me early on, but I found out that it was easier to stay away from people and situations. It seemed like a lot of people wanted things from me. It's a weird thing, but the littlest guy in the local hardware store would never ask me for a ticket to a show, he would never take advantage of his friendship for me, and now, when I go in his store, he'll charge me a nickel for a bolt or something because I'm not in the band anymore. It's a weird thing. Just when you think you can let some stuff out to somebody, something happens. I guess I'm just not a good judge of character. I always thought I was. But then I found out later I wasn't. It is real hard for me to open up to people. I have some character defects. I also drank a lot and kept it to myself.

Was drinking a way to not deal with some of these "defects" as you call them?

Sure. I had a lot of things going on in my life. I was in this big band. I had a son who I had custody of, but my folks were taking care of. Everytime I saw him, it was like, "When are you going to take me home?" I remember saying to myself a lot, "Nothing bothers me. I'm as hard as a rock." Today, things are different. I'm probably more

easy to talk to than ever before because I held it all in for so long. When the band was together, I'd meet people and they'd always tell me that they couldn't get over how "human" I was. (laughs) They couldn't believe I was this guy who played the organ in the E Street Band. I think I'm a more likeable guy today than I was yesterday.

Earlier on in this conversation you mentioned how you quit the band more than once. Why?

It was always some kind of management thing of junk that was going down, or someone not listening to me when I needed them to, or being jealous over one person or another. I was always very sensitive. There was one incident at Bruce's house in Holmdel that had to do with a certain song. I thought the part should have been an organ part and Roy started playing it. Bruce let it go on. I pulled Bruce aside and said, "What are you doing?" Now it seems petty, but back then, it wasn't. It was part of my character. I think the key to most any kind of success is being able to endure. I don't think I ever thought about quitting and really meant it.

And each time this happened, it was Bruce who pulled you back into the fold?

No matter what happened or what has gone down, Bruce has stuck by me through thick and thin. He never said a word to anyone about my problems. Once, when he made me aware of my problems, I was so far down, I took up praying. I had curtains on my windows. I hid my cars in my backyard. I wouldn't answer the phone. It seemed as if I had only one friend at the time, and that friend was something I could buy down the street. At that time Bruce sent me an airline ticket to L.A. I got to L.A. and I stayed at a hotel by the airport. I partied in the bar. I never made it to his house. Bruce came looking for me. We had this long discussion all the way to Palm Springs. Two or three hours later, being the chemically addicted alcoholic that I had made myself into, my body started to go crazy without a drink. What started out as "So how's things?" "Oh, everything is fine" went to "Hey Bruce, I need a drink." Bruce was there for laughing and crying. He's a great guy, a special person.

It's been a year since Bruce and the band parted ways. In a way, I guess you're starting the second half of your career and your life. You haven't been wasting time. You've experimented with one new band, Stone Hill, which included Bon Jovi drummer Tico Torres and numerous local Jersey

The E Street Band in Oklahoma City, 1975.

Shore musicians. Now you have another, World Without Walls, that includes your old friend Billy Chinnock as well as musicians and songwriters such as Bobby Berger from the local Shore music scene.

I've been busy. I'm trying to establish something so that I can continue to work and make music. I want to stay active. I feel that I've got a lot of music in me.

Why didn't Stone Hill work out? It seemed like a pretty solid band last summer.

I never quite got the personnel thing right, but the group did get my feet wet. I also did the thing with Dave Edmunds. We did some gigs in the States and then in September went over to Japan and did some more gigs. That was really good for me. Actually, I wish it lasted a little longer because we finally learned how to play together.

What are your expectations for World Without Walls?

I try not to have expectations. I find that doesn't help any. I think this band has more potential than Stone Hill because the guys in the band — Chinnock, Tony Smith on drums, Jesse Rex Stemm on guitar, John Kay on bass, Bobby Berger on bass and vocals — are more my age. They're more mature. They've been around, so they're more professional.

Did you write songs when you were in the E Street Band?

No. It would have been a waste of time.

What prompted you to start now?

The time that I've spent alone in the past year kind of got me going. My biggest problem has always been lyrics. I've even been exercising my vocal chords to see what I sound like. It's like looking in the mirror. You wake up and you think you look good, but you really don't know.

Like packing up your own equipment. I noticed your truck and the U-Haul trailer outside. It's loaded with amps and keyboards and what not...just like the old days. How do you feel about that?

I'm pretty excited, actually. I packed up everything myself for this trip to Maine where World Without Walls had its debut. The only difference this time around is that I know my truck won't break down.

—*Robert Santelli*

MIKE APPEL

· · · · · · · ·

Interview by Charles R. Cross, November 1990

Mike Appel has not worked with a major rock 'n' roll star since 1976, yet he remains one of the best known managers in the history of rock 'n' roll. Appel's reputation comes from the extraordinary time he spent with Bruce Springsteen which began when he helped get a scruffy kid signed to Columbia Records and ended in one of the most famous lawsuits in music business history. Along the way, Appel watched the development of Springsteen from an acoustic coffeehouse songwriter into a powerhouse performer who hit the front covers of *Time* and *Newsweek* simultaneously.

Through it all, Mike Appel has remained a mystery man, and prior to speaking with Charles R. Cross, he had not done an interview with a journalist since the lawsuit was settled in 1977. Though he is presently working on a book about the lawsuit, this remains his most extensive interview to date.

BACKSTREETS: *You've been working on your book on Bruce Springsteen, "Down Thunder Road." Why did you decide to do this book now? Was it to counteract the image of you from Dave Marsh's first book? The only picture of you that appears in Marsh's "Born to Run" is one where you're wearing a Marine hat.*
MIKE APPEL: Exactly right. They wanted to paint the picture of Mike Appel as some militaristic kind of angry, aggressive character. You need to be aggressive, to some extent. Not necessarily angry, but you need to be aggressive in the job that I was put in. It isn't easy handling people's lives and handling an individual who, for a long period of time, for two or three years, was absolutely nobody, then all of sudden he's catapulted to the covers of *Time* and *Newsweek* in the shortest time ever. And nobody's had a chance to even tell that. I mean Bruce Springsteen's salary, after *Born to Run* was platinum and he was on the cover of *Time* and *Newsweek*,

◄ *Mike Appel, New York, N.Y., 1990.*

was $350 a week. That's a fact of life. The success hadn't caught up with anybody yet. It was all too big for all of us to even comprehend. Guys would come along, and no matter what the album was selling, they'd say, "Mike, do you have my check today?" And I'd say, "Yeah, here's your $350." And they went away happy. There was no "Jeez, I should be making two grand this week." There was none of that. We never even got to that point. The litigation suit—we never really got to that. It was never a big-bucks situation until a little afterwards, until the settlement.

Bruce is a major figure and has been for some time. Nobody knows that story. They know the fanzine kind of story from Dave Marsh and "Glory Days" and stuff like that. The litigation is glossed over in some sort of haphazard manner and in a very one-sided manner. I felt this was a chance, to some extent, to clear my name. I think I've been blackballed in the industry. I know I have. I felt this was an opportunity to clear the air there. People think I'm some sort of old bald man with a cigar and when they see me they say, "Jesus, are you Mike Appel?" I've had that happen. They say, "Are you Mike Appel? The guy that was supposed to have screwed Bruce Springsteen?" Yeah, that's right. So jeez, just a picture of Mike Appel in the book will change people's attitude, even if there was no substance to my side of the story.

The impression that most people have about Mike Appel is that because of the lawsuit, you were legally bound not to talk about your court battle with Bruce. As I now understand it, that's not the case, but that perception still continues to this day. Why do you think that idea is so ingrained?

Bruce Springsteen, in those days, was so loved by journalists. I always thought that because he was such a great lyricist that endeared him to journalists. In a way, that's what they are. So he immediately endeared himself overnight. Generally, managers, if somebody had to cast their lot on one side of the fence or the other in a dispute, I guess the whole world would jump on the side of the artist. Everybody likes to feel they are part of or supporting the creative side of things. Managers are generally viewed as business guys that watch over money and that are so close to the money they can't keep their hands out of the cookie jar and they steal. Or they steal from the artist and the artist finds out about it too late and all the money's gone and "Oh, the poor artist." That scenario is a very believable scenario and it's a scenario that most magazines and media in general subscribe to. It's a tacit thing. It's not like it's something you discuss or anything. It's just they generally think that way. So I fell into that category just like that (snaps fingers).

I didn't sue him; he sued me. He filed papers against me. And even though the contracts that we had were rinky dink, they held up—they held up alright. It was more than I could have thought. They were trying to say that I had too many hats, that I was manager, publisher, producer. And look at what they did after the lawsuit. What is Jon Landau? Manager, producer, everything. And he's doing just what they accused me of doing. But it held up in court. It held up alright.

What is your response to Dave Marsh's book "Born to Run"?

I just think it was lopsided and had sins of omission. Nobody's asked me what happened. Not even Bob Hilburn. He writes a book and he's a friend of mine and even he doesn't interview me.

What Marsh writes about Mike Appel is that he's a master of hype and he talks about getting the *Time* and *Newsweek* covers on my birthday. What happened was that I conned the goofball editors into that and backed them into a corner until they had no way out. But it wasn't hype. If there was hype, then what sort of hype is "Born to Run"? What sort of hype is "The Saga of the Architect's Angel"?

What people think of me is because of what Marsh has written, that I'm a combination of Colonel Parker, Brian Epstein and Barnum. What they forget is that I was an artist before I was a manager. I didn't get into this to manage an artist. But people don't know that and I blame Dave for that. He said Mike's message is hype. Dave Marsh, as far as a journalist, wiped me out of this business. He threw a brick through my window.

You've said to me before that you considered a lawsuit after the book came out.

Yeah. I considered an action against *Rolling Stone* as well. My attorney said, "Look, there's been such bad press. If you keep fighting it, it's just going to kill you more and more." He said to just let it die. And I did.

If you felt the story was told so wrongly, why didn't you attempt to tell your side back then and clear your name? Did you consider calling a press conference to answer some of these charges?

Well, maybe I was too stupid to call a press conference. That might have been a good idea. I didn't think of it. Until now.

What I thought I would do is maybe do my own book and explain it. Then I found it very difficult to get a book deal because nobody wanted to hear that side of the story. It wasn't until *New Musical Express* ran that big story that David McGee wrote that Bruce's image got the first hint that there may be trouble in paradise, that all that glitters may not be gold. Then following that up was the *Esquire* article. In fact, I told Jon Landau about the *Esquire* story. He had no idea that it was being written. I told him that a guy had interviewed me for a magazine article and I just wanted Jon to know that I hadn't said anything that would damage my present relationship with either him or Bruce. He said, "What are you talking about?" And I said the *Esquire* article. He said, "What *Esquire* article?" And it was coming out in two days. Jon is a well informed guy, and a very professional guy and he's not at all sloppy in the way that he operates and he's a cautious fellow. How he didn't know this absolutely flabbergasted me. I don't know how he missed that one—he must have been very preoccupied.

I assume from your comments you read both the NME article and the Esquire piece. What do you think about the allegations those articles made?

I did read them. Well, I don't know about the Mike Batlan thing. It's tough to take money from Bruce and then spend it and then come back and say, "You owe me more money than this." What he should have done is asked for more money to start with. So Mike Batlan came back and hit Bruce with a curve ball and it doesn't matter what it costs him.

The *Esquire* article? What aspects of the *Esquire* article in particlular would you like me to address?

I guess the article's main contention is that the Bruce Springsteen myth is created. The writer suggests that Bruce is not what he is made out to be, or what he seems to be, and that he doesn't care what goes on in his name. I guess the main contention —and this is not to say that I personally believe the article —is that Springsteen is a bad boss. The article implies that Bruce doesn't seem to care about his own employees. You've seen that relationship firsthand, so how would you describe it?

I think that Jon Landau inviting critics to listen to Bruce's tapes before they are released to the public is sort of like John Kennedy allowing the press to waltz into the Oval Office whenever they felt like it. Kennedy had this great bridge of communication with the press and it endeared him to them. The guys in the press are

too much attention. But he'll do that occasionally. When Bruce found that out he died, because he wanted the drums on "Born to Run" to be done on a trap case. I said I didn't think it would work. Those are such simplistic figures that it's easy to do on a trap case but it wouldn't have worked. But he was mad because he hadn't done it perfectly, the way Phil Spector would have done it.

The trap case drums would have given "Born to Run" an entirely different feel, one that harkened back even more to old-time rock 'n' roll radio.

Exactly. It would have been nostalgia. Sha Na Na. That's a good point. He didn't understand that. I wish you could have been there to say that to him because it would have saved us a lot of hassle.

Of all the material you were involved with, what are you most proud of? What speaks the best of the Bruce Springsteen/Mike Appel relationship?

Lyrically, the first album. Production wise, the third album. But I'd have to say the third album overall because finally there was that blend of lyrics, and melody, and music, and production, and pomposity, and then the macrocosm and the microcosm, and the emotion of the "Born to Run," "Thunder Road" and "Jungleland," and down to the little "Meeting Across the River." It was just a great album and a blessed event to be able to do those kinds of things all on the same record.

How did the title and concept for the album come together?

We sat on that couch right there and he said, "What do I call the record?" And I said, "It would seem to me you call the record 'Born to Run.'" So he said, "Yeah, but isn't 'Jungleland' a good title?" And I said, "Yeah, 'Jungleland' is a good title, I like 'Jungleland' too. It's a possibility we can call the record 'Jungleland.'" And then I think we talked about "Thunder Road" and we might even have talked about "Backstreets." And we kept talking and talking and I said to him, "I don't know, man. It just seems to come back to this." And he looked at me and he said, "'Born, (hits the table) to (hit) Run (hit)' is it, man." And that was it. And that's just what he did. He said it just like that too.

What prompted the switch from the acoustic John Hammond demos to the material that ended up on the first album where Springsteen was writing songs within a rock 'n' roll context?

It was Bruce and Clive Davis, then head of CBS. Myself and John Hammond believed that the lyrics were so wonderful that Bruce could stand onstage and scrub an acoustic guitar and just blab away and he'd be the biggest star in the world. In my naivety, that's what I thought was the case. So did Hammond. Bruce said, "Mike, I really should have a band." I said, "You think so? It's going to get in the way of those lyrics. Where are they going to play? There's no spots. You've got so many words there's no spots for anyone to play." He said, "Yeah, but I really think the band is something we should deal with. I'll get the band together and why don't you just come down and see them and see what you think?" I said, "Fine, why don't you do one of your acoustic ones with the band?"

I went down to see the band he'd put together. Miami Steve was there, Clarence Clemons, Garry Tallent, Danny Federici, Vini Lopez. Okay, they play, "Hard to Be a Saint in the City," "Does this Bus Stop" and I was offended. I said, "Jeez, that's not adding anything fantastic. It's not like there was room for any riffs." So I said, "They're not adding anything really here." Then Clive got on the phone with me and said, "I hear you're having your differences, you, Hammond, and Springsteen, about whether it should be acoustic or whether it should be with a band. I firmly believe it should be with a band. We're not going to get radio play without it and it's going to lose its commercial appeal." As if it were so commercial when we were using the band anyway? What purists we were. So begrudgingly I went to Hammond and said, "I've been outvoted. My own partner Jimmy doesn't give a shit about the acoustic stuff. Clive tells me to forget it. Bruce told me to forget it. I can't go any further. If you want to hang in there, John, you're by yourself." So he caved in and that was how Bruce became a band act.

Even with the band, what stands out about the first album is the lyrics. Some critics argued, however, that there were too many lyrics in each song, that it was overkill. When you were putting it together did anyone stop and say, "Are there maybe a few too many words in these songs?"

There's no question about it. We did get that. I said to Bruce, "What are you trying to do? I just love all these lyrics. They're fantastic. I've never heard lyrics like this before, which means we're doing something that's unique and different and wonderful and I don't mind having my name next to that." But other people said, "Jesus, God almighty. Just endless stream of consciousness lyrics." Well, I said, "There's more than that. And I like it anyway." I said, "This is where we are right now, this is it for us. We're not capable of doing 'Born to Run' at this date, not on your life." Not on your life.

When the first two singles were released from the first record,

Penn State, February 19, 1975. ►

Asbury Park, N.J., 1974.

"Blinded by the Light" and "Spirit in the Night," they bombed in the record store. So few copies ended up selling in stores that the ones that exist today are valuable collector's items. There are lots of copies of the promos, but almost no copies of the stock 45 in existence. You must have been disappointed about the poor performance of the first singles.

We were terribly disappointed by the sales for "Blinded by the Light." We thought it was going to do much more than it did.

Do you have any idea how many copies it sold?

To say "nothing" would be an exaggeration. We were terribly disappointed. I think it still did slightly better than "Spirit in the Night" though. "Spirit in the Night" escaped. No one knew what that was. "Rosalita" was another one. I don't even know if I saw the single myself.

"Rosalita" was never issued in the U.S. as a single.

Really? I'm pretty sure there was one. It was supposed to be the single. That was a time when CBS and I were really at odds, so it might have been they said, "We're putting the single out, Mike," and I never saw it. I had so many hassles on the album and when I called up the promotion men, nobody would pick up the phone. There was nothing we could do. Then they said they

were going to drop the artist. Forget it. That was a very difficult time.

After the release of the second album, which also had poor sales, didn't you literally have to beg on your knees to convince CBS not to drop Bruce?

I did. I made some kind of interim arrangement that if the record didn't sell "X" amount of copies or something like that, they could get rid of me. Between the second and the third record we needed some kind of advance to keep us going. They could apply it to our account, which they did. At the point *Born to Run* came out, *Wild and the Innocent* had only sold 182,000 units. So it was a reasonable seller. And *Greetings* was around a 100,000. We had built that up from touring ourselves. We had created a little base for *Born to Run* to rest upon.

If we would have been dropped by CBS at the time, which they sort of considered after the second record, we would have gone with either Warners or A&M. At that point Hammond wasn't so big in CBS anymore and Clive Davis had left and there was nobody there who liked us.

We were just stone broke at the time. We were trying to record, so we couldn't do many dates and we needed money desperately. So I had to go see a guy at

CBS and literally beg him to loan us $10,000. And they wouldn't do it. So I had to keep bugging and bugging him. I'm not saying he wasn't the sort of guy you'd want running your corporation—since he made every decision based on the corporate bottom line—but we really needed the money and they knew we were going to deliver a big record. So I called and called him and finally he gave it to us. I think it was more to get me off his back than any other reason.

Things changed when CBS finally decided Bruce was their baby. When they decided that—goodnight. Because we had the goods. We had a seasoned performer who could go out there and kick ass and had already done it in a lot of places. It was a known quantity and there as a readymade market for this record.

But with that promotion we knew that when the "Born to Run" single came off that album, people were going to ask "What else is on this album?" It created this impact that previously was impossible for us to get to. At this point all things built up to that point and it all came together.

We had the goods. They had the bucks and the clout and the power and the *will* to do it. And they did it.

And Bruce did it too by writing his first song that screamed out to be a single.

That's right. "Born to Run" went to number 19 on the charts. I always thought it wasn't going to be anything because he asked me, "You think this is like one of those Beach Boy hits?" I said, "Are you kidding? Those have real poppy melodies those things. This isn't like that. You all of sudden go into minor modes here. Forget it. It's a miracle if this thing makes it as a hit." I never thought "Born to Run" was going to have anything, was going to do anything.

In retrospect, it seems strange that the song didn't go higher on the charts. Its impact has grown so much in the passing years that many people don't realize it didn't even make the top ten.

It's become a classic but it's not a commercial hit in my mind to this day. What it is, is a great artistic hit. It was a great work of art, that little record. And a great deal of effort and smarts and craft went into that record. That record has taken its place in the pantheon of great records in all the polls. Andrew Loog Oldham called me, he was the producer and manager of the Rolling Stones, to say, "I wanted to let you know that *Born to Run* is the greatest record of all time. I never heard a greater record in my life." I said, "I don't know what to tell you since '19th Nervous Breakdown' is one of my favorites." It was very complimentary to get a call from one of your peers telling you that.

Looking back at the Born to Run *album, what would you do differently in retrospect? I know you've said before that the tension between you and Jon Landau was extreme.*

Well, Jon Landau wasn't an impediment to making the record. Not really, because I won my way on things. When he and Bruce would say, "Here's 'Lonely Night in the Park' or 'Linda, Let Me Be the One.'" They came in and they thought that was going to be a commercial song. And I won my way. I said, "These are such dogs and the lyrics are so bad." I said, just go away. I said, these songs aren't staying on the record—over my dead body. I told him this stuff was "shit." And nobody today would talk to him like that. Oh, no, they sure wouldn't.

Let's go through album by album and talk about how each record came together. Were there ever any other titles or cover ideas suggested for the Greetings *album?*

The cover of the first album was Bruce's idea. He walks in one day with the postcard and says, "Wouldn't this be great?" And I said sure. So we took it over to John Berg, the art director at CBS, and they loved the idea. I thought CBS would flip over the idea, so I was surprised. Berg then took us back to his office, opened a drawer in his office and it was filled with postcards. He was a postcard collector and he said he'd always wanted to do an album cover like that. It was a standard policy that every new artist at CBS had to have their picture on the cover of their first record. Everyone followed that rule, even Dylan. But for Bruce we had a postcard. We used the standard CBS cover for the second record.

Rumor has it there are acetates of the first album that include "Visitation at Fort Horn" and leave off "Saint in the City." Can you shed any light on this?

He wanted "Visitation at Fort Horn" on the record, but we thought it was too folky. And "Saint in the City" was so great. I had to convince Bruce of that one. I had to throw a fit to get him to go with that.

I remember the first time I heard "Visitation at Fort Horn" I was sitting in Max's Kansas City and Bruce decided to do it that night. He used Clarence, Vini and Garry as these Sons of the Pioneer–type singers. I was with this guy from Epic and after the song he turned to me and said, "I just don't believe this guy. This is the greatest thing I've ever seen."

It's unclear what songs were considered for the second record but never used. Can you shed some light on that material that was recorded but not released? Was "The Fever" ever close to making it on the record?

I don't know. It was like he'd write a slew of songs. We didn't take that one that seriously as it was just one more that we did a demo of. We'd done a lot of demos over the years that didn't turn into master records. It seemed that Bruce Springsteen never did too many casual things. He never took a relaxed approach to music. He would find some cute little riff or something and he'd end up thinking it wasn't important enough to put on the album. Even though you can say "Rosalita" is a good time song, and it is, those were rare moments. He was more serious than that. It's his nature to be more serious. I could have used more playfulness all over but he's the one. He managed to get enough of it in there to not get me aggravated.

How about the title to the second record? What's the story behind that?

He called me up on the phone one day and said he thought he had the record's name. And he said, "The Wild (pause), The Innocent (pause), and the E Street Shuffle." He said it just like that. And I said it sounds like something with Brando and the fugitive. I said, "That's it for me."

Were any other titles considered?

We might have thought about calling it "The E Street Shuffle." I don't know. We might have considered that, but once he came up with the title that was it.

The genesis of Born to Run *was much more complicated. You've told me before that the cover photo had grease pencil marks on it showing how the album was to fold. Can you explain how that came about?*

I had to fight to get *Born to Run* to be a foldout because it's much more expensive to make a record that way. I met with John Berg and he said they weren't doing fold outs anymore. But when I showed him the pictures, he said this one would be great for the cover. We thought about putting the whole picture on the front of the record but I wasn't so sure we wanted Clarence on there. So finally this picture just fell down on the page and it looked perfect there with Bruce on the front, and Berg flipped over the idea.

Though Born to Run *was clearly the big song on the record, even when it was first coming together, I think many people don't realize that several other titles were seriously considered. You previously showed me a mock-up with* Between Flesh and Fantasy *as the title.*

We were also thinking about "Jungleland." "Jungle-land" was such a great title. But we kicked it around a bunch. We were sitting right here on this sofa and he turned to me and he said, "It's 'Born to Run'" and we both knew that was right.

You've told me before that "Tenth Avenue" was one of the hardest songs on the album to record.

That was an interesting one. I think when he first wrote it he called it something like "The Big Fix" or "Scooter and the Big Man," something else entirely different. But when we went to record it, we never could get the right horns. We needed a Steve Cropper guitar solo and we needed those Stax/Volt kind of horns and we never got them. Bruce and Roy had decided to write the horn section and they went down to the beach to do it, but when they came back it just didn't work. And the Brecker brothers were already there and they were waiting around for us to come up with something.

So then Miami Steve stepped in and took care of everything. He gave the record order. They needed direction and he gave it to them. There was finally a way out. It might have not been the best way, but it was a way out. He didn't bring in tasteful riffs—or at least what in my mind were tasteful riffs—but he got them done.

What bothered me were times like when Bruce came to my office and we worked out a solo on his guitar. I said, "Let's not do a solo on 'Backstreets' like whatever comes off your head because it never comes out good. Let's create a solo that everybody can play." So then we started and we put a tape on and in the office we started to play. So he was working and working it. And finally—I'm real good with guitar players since I'm a guitar player myself—we worked it out. We got it done.

Then when I heard the solo on "Prove It All Night" I thought I died. I said to myself, "What a piece of shit!" I said, "What a terrible song." For the love of God I'll never know why they do certain things. Like the stuff Bruce or Miami does on guitar is very questionable. Those guys are not naturally creative guitar players where they come up with great licks. Roy Bittan is more of a lick guy who comes up with very palatable and commercial riffs on keyboards that really make the difference on a lot of Bruce's records. That's why I worked hard with him on the "Backstreets" solo and it came out very well.

Let me throw out a few names of some of the important figures and why don't you throw out some comments off the top of your head.

They were a raggedy bunch of guys overall. You're not dealing with what I call professional or studio musicians. They were not professional guys.

Clarence Clemons?

Clarence was a great "feel" guy. He's a guy that would come up with solos that fell well in a certain range. His sax parts on "Jungleland" are very unique and different but Bruce sung them to him, and I watched him do it, every note of that solo. So therefore, it wasn't created

Arrival in Stockholm, Sweden, November 20, 1975.

by Clarence, it was created by Bruce. Now, Clarence was a guy who you could not focus on at a session. In other words, what I would do is I'd make the guys do several takes and even though I had the tape already, I'd make believe we were doing another take. And I'd go right over what we had and they'd believe they were doing another take. And I'd be running Clarence again. Because if you took Clarence and ran a solo on him and made all the other band members leave the room, forget it. Dry reeds, squeaky notes all over the place. Forget it. I tried it a few times and I realized we were going nowhere. I realized we can't do that with Clarence. We had to make it seem like it was a party. That was how you got the best with Clarence.

Danny Federici?

Danny Federici was a flawless performer. He never dropped a note as far as I can remember. Not an extremely creative guy, but he served a utilitarian purpose. You know accordion, Hammond B3 organ. He was okay for those years. He could do anything that he was told to do and he could repeat it forever. So he served a utilitarian purpose.

I remember one funny story about Bruce and Danny. We were playing this college, and this was back when we were very small and had no money. Bruce and I drove a car there and we were just getting there and getting out of the car when up comes Danny Federici. Danny shows up in the parking lot with a baseball uniform on with eye make-up on. I mean, he looked like David Bowie and it was so funny that Bruce and I started dying laughing. We were laughing so hard we were rolling around on the ground. And Danny was straight about it. He thought this style had become fashionable and he wanted to be fashionable. He thought that the band needed to adopt this modern cutting-edge look and wearing make-up would help.

Bruce hardly ever acted like a boss with those guys. But this time Bruce felt he had to say something. Before the show he went backstage to talk to Danny and he said something like, "Danny, I make the decisions here and I hate to tell you what to do, but you just can't wear the make-up." So Danny played that night and he had on the baseball outfit but no make-up.

Garry W. Tallent?

Not a great soulful bass player but the right kind of bass player for this raggedy set of musicians. And he was a very obedient low-key kind of guy who never had a problem. It was the same with Danny Federici and even the same with Clarence though Clarence used to get in fights with Vini because Vini was a volatile character. Vini would provoke the other band members into fights.

Did Vini deserve the reputation he had at the time in your opinion? How do you rate him as a drummer?

Vini Lopez. A raggedy little drummer. Time wise he would vary. He certainly couldn't do certain basics. He couldn't do a press roll. We were trying to do a press roll on "Wild Billy's Circus Story" and we couldn't get a press roll out of him. He said, "Man, that's it, that's it." And Bruce was sitting right next to me and I said, "Man, that's not it. You know what a press roll is? It's buzz, buzz, buzz. It's simple. You've heard it a hundred times, I've heard it a hundred times. It's simple." So Bruce says, "Ho, I think we got to do it another day." And Vini got up and just stormed out of the studio. We spent like an hour with Vini trying to do this. And he kept saying "I did it, I did it." And I kept saying "You didn't do it." So we got another drummer to come in there and do it in exactly five minutes flat. It was the simplest thing in the world. He did it and said, "Is that it?" We said, thanks, bye; it was that quick. There was definitely another drummer who did that though I don't know if it's credited.

How do you rate Max as a drummer?

Max is a wonderful guy. He's a very sensitive person. He's not a frilly kind of guy. He's as solid as a rock. He can do the fills. He's perfect for Bruce because he's sort of the fulcrum, the shoulders for these songs to be laid upon. Let Bruce be the wild cat. We don't need Carl Palmer here, just straight solid drums. And that's what Max was for.

It wasn't easy following Bruce onstage either. If you screwed up, he'd make a public embarrassment of you, which he did to Max more than once. You had to watch him every instant and see if he pulled on his ear, you stopped on a dime. I remember more than a few shows where Clarence would show up and he'd have been drinking. And I'd say, "No, not tonight. Bruce is going to go crazy." But for some reason, more than anyone else in the band, Clarence always knew the cues. It was almost like he had a sixth sense and he couldn't go wrong.

We've already addressed Roy Bittan's strength as a performer but how do you compare him to David Sancious?

Roy Bittan was not what you'd call a creative musician like Davey Sancious. Sancious was a real artist. He'll come up with great original things. I'm not saying Roy can't come up with an original riff, because that riff in

"Dancing in the Dark" is an original kind of riff. But he's not as creative as he might be. He's a flawless performer. And he comes up with exactly what you seem to need. But Davey Sancious will supply you with a piece of artwork. You see him and you say that's what art is all about. That guy is a real artist. Left to his own devices, what do I think of Sancious? Forget it, can't stand him. It's just loads of jazz and all. I don't know what it is. Sancious came to me lots of times with his tapes and I told him "What am I going to do with this?"

The first female in the E Street Band was Suki Lahav. How do you evaluate her contribution?

Suki was not a virtuoso on the violin but she was kind of pretty and Bruce liked her presence onstage and so did I. There was this female presence onstage with these ruffians. It was a wonderful blend, it was a wonderful mix. It wasn't predictable stuff. It was like a product of the late '60s, it was an evolving product. And for people who saw those shows back then, they saw a very special event. A good mixture of elements. It was drama. I would get chills watching Bruce Springsteen die at the end of "Jungleland." I don't know how many times I watched that, but it would always give me chills. I'd say, "Jesus, this guy takes himself real seriously." It lends credibility to everything he's been doing all night long. He demonstrates to you physically that this is important. To me this is very special. And when I see him do a *Tunnel of Love* tour or a *Born in the USA* tour, it doesn't have that drama. It can't by the nature of the beast. The songs lyrically aren't that important. I guess if you don't have all that there, why demonstrate it.

What exact day was the lawsuit settled?

I think it was May 31, 1977. It started August of 1976 and went through May of 1977.

Some people have the impression you've never spoken with Springsteen since that time. Can you explain the current status of your relationship with him? There is a public conception that after May 31, 1977, you and Springsteen have not even seen each other.

That's completely false. There was such a nasty lawsuit with so much bad mouthing going on against Mike Appel, I think people felt that after all that negative publicity concerning Bruce and Mike Appel, people thought, how could they ever get back together again? How could they ever talk? But I don't know. There was a point where I just felt it was at odds over such an old conflict. I just felt it was time for me; even if nobody else felt the urgency to bury the hatchet between Bruce

Born to Run *tour rehearsal, July 1975.* ►

and Mike Appel. I decided I would do it, and do it then.

So I did it. I initiated the call to Jon Landau and he was very pleased that I did and he thought that Bruce would be very well disposed to sitting down with me and shooting the shit, so to speak, and he was indeed. And we did.

When was this?

November of 1986, November 20th I believe.

And you hadn't had any contact with him for the nine years prior to that?

Certainly no personal contact. I ran into Jon Landau a few times in between and there certainly were no harsh words between us. It was very cordial. With Bruce it didn't really get underway until November 20, 1986. And since then we've seen each other pretty often. I was out with him a couple of months ago in Los Angeles, we had lunch together. And before that sometime in the winter in Los Angeles again. So we have been seeing each other.

What was it like for you personally to communicate with him again? In addition to your business relationship there was a strange dynamic between the two of you, which Marc Eliot writes about as if it was a relationship between a father and son.

Unfortunately for me, because he had that relationship with his father that might not have been the best. If I ended up being some sort of surrogate father figure, then too bad for Mike Appel. In any case, we had a great evening together. It was though, and it's hard for anyone imagining this to believe it, but it was as though absolutely nothing had transpired. It was like maybe later that evening we'd be going back to the studio and he'd be playing me his new songs. No difference. As though time didn't exist whatsoever. It does prove that relationships and emotions can bridge time and all sorts of what I call mechanical conflicts—outside factors producing events that were never natural. In other words there was never a natural reason for Bruce Springsteen and I to break up, if you know what I mean. It was more like Bruce had to be educated to a world of contracts and if these contracts had to be construed this way and that way and this is the way they are construed and therefore that guy's no good and you should break away from him. But that's all mechanical—that doesn't come from a natural relationship or a breech with me personally. It was a great evening.

When I was in Los Angeles, sometime thereafter, a year later, I told him I wanted to play him something from an artist I was involved in, John Andrew Parks, who I had just finished producing. So he said, "Why don't I pick you up at your place?" So I said alright,

and he picked me up in this black little Budget Rent-a-Car Corvette. He is very sloppy. He has tapes, tons of tapes, all over the floor. I could barely get into the car. And we went to Alice's Restaurant for lunch and he had exactly what you'd expect him to have—a burger, a coke, fries. He doesn't change much. We talked. I played him the John Andrew Parks's tapes which he was fond of. He loved the song "Daddy on the Radio." To quote Bruce, "If that ever gets on the radio, it's a smash."

As I was getting out of the car he said, "Hey, I got something for ya." I said, "What do you mean?" He said, "It's in this bag here." I said alright, and he took it out of the bag and here it is, this leather jacket. And I said, "What's this?" And he said, "It's the leather jacket I wore for the two-year *Born in the USA* tour. I'd like to give it as a gift to your son." I was very touched by that. And he said, "Let the circle be unbroken." Because I had given him my leather jacket back for the *Born to Run* album cover. That's my leather jacket he's wearing. So I guess there's a meaning to all this. And of course, my son's going to have to give it back to Evan James someday.

What's the history of your leather jacket that Bruce wears on the Born to Run *album?*

Jeez, that had been around for years. It went all the way back to 1956. I gave it to Bruce in 1975 when we did the cover.

So he hadn't been wearing that jacket prior to the cover photo sessions?

I don't know how it came to be. I told him I had a great leather jacket and it didn't fit me anymore because I had gained too much weight. But it fit him like a glove. He loved it. And he loved the idea that it was old and it was real. He's a stickler for things that are real. He likes things that have been around, weather-beaten things, and that was a weather-beaten thing. He put it right on and wore it and went over for the photo shoot. And that's why he returned a jacket. When he did, I said, "This isn't my jacket." And he said, "I know. Don't get mad. I gave it to a girl. But if you knew the girl you wouldn't mind."

Was it your Elvis Presley Fan Club button on the jacket or his?

That had to be his.

How do you rate the music that Springsteen has produced since your relationship ended? How do you interpret his musical direction under Jon Landau rather than Mike Appel?

There's a bit of sameness about what Bruce Springsteen does. I thought that *Born to Run* was a great album because there were unique things like "Jungleland,"

"Meeting Across the River," and "Night." It was a sort of odd collection of songs and they were very pompous and they were very bold. And they were really what I guess rock 'n' roll is supposed to be about. I don't even think our earlier albums captured anything like that. They captured portions of it. Maybe even subsequent albums that he did after that, with Jon, captured portions of *Born to Run* but certainly not all of it, certainly not lyrically.

Lyrically he has chosen, or the muses don't listen to him anymore, I don't know, I think he has actually chosen, he's made a concerted effort to speak more plainly, lyrically, more directly. Either because he'd rather have a broader appeal or because he wants to be less poetic. He wants to be more direct. It would seem to me that's why the lyrics today don't have that poetic character to them, or certainly not as they did then.

That stuff like "Factory." It's just "blah, blah, blah." It's so repetitive. I don't know why he did that—he can do better. It just beats it into the listener and makes him seem like this blue-collar hero. But take a song like "Thunder Road" and that takes people away and gives them something to hope for.

Musically, he's done a few things that I think are unique, but most of it seems to fall into, it seems to have a sameness about it. I know he's tried. I think on *Tunnel of Love* he tried to break with some of his past records and maybe even the splitting up or leaving of the E Street Band is a further bit of evidence that he's looking or searching for another piece of growth. And maybe he feels this will be it, it will be one way to gain that. I don't think it's something he's entirely unaware of himself. He might have listened to the entire body of his music one day, or on several days and have said to himself, "You know these songs do sound an awful lot alike." Well of course they do, he's singing all the songs and they all sound a certain kind of way. But I think more than that, a lot of them had a certain sameness about them—they weren't that unique. Of course, that's the struggle of every artist who writes all their own songs. And he's not a guy like Don Henley. You look at Don Henley's latest record and you see ten different writers. Bruce Springsteen places the entire burden on himself.

Even early in his career was there ever talk of having him record songs by other artists?
I don't think so. We may have mentioned it to him once or twice in relationship to something commercial, but I don't remember it being said. It could have been said, but obviously nothing was ever done. Nobody ever said

it and nobody ever got together with him as a writing team.
What did you think when you first heard Darkness?
First off, we would have followed up *Born to Run* with a live album. We were recording all those shows and it probably would have been the Roxy or C. W. Post College. I think we also recorded some shows in Toronto. You think we didn't know that a live record was what we needed? It would have been tremendous.

The first song I heard from *Darkness* was "Prove It All Night" and I really didn't like it at all. I just thought the melody and the chorus were dreadful. The melody and the guitar solo were dreadful. And, the album had a certain sameness about it. It was dark and brooding but it didn't seem to have much glory. "Promised Land" and "Badlands" had some of the pomposity musically of a "Thunder Road," it had a little bit of that. That I did like. But the lyrics then were like, there wasn't enough magic. I was so expecting the lyrics to be how they used to be I could hardly conceive of him writing so directly.
To what do you attribute what you see as that change?
Maybe it was the desire to have a wider audience, although *Born to Run* even at that time was a platinum-plus album, so I don't know why he would be so concerned with widening his audience so quickly. It would seem that it would have been a conscious effort on his part to broaden his audience and to get more sales.
What has he done since then that you like?
I like his little "Brilliant Disguise" thing. And what is it, "One Step Up, Two Steps Back"? There's a few things that I like that he's done. I even liked "Dancing in the Dark." And "Hungry Heart" was a fun thing. Musically "Cadillac Ranch" was another fun thing that I liked. I can't say that I didn't like anything he did since *Born to Run*, since that wouldn't be true.
You told me you saw the Tunnel of Love *tour when it was in New York. What were your impressions?*
I had called up the office and they gave me tickets. I went and I thought it was tremendous.
You probably saw a thousand live Springsteen shows. You saw the infamous Bottom Line shows from 1974 and 1975, and the Roxy shows. Of the dates that you saw, what individual nights stand out as ones where Springsteen's performance soars above all others?
I would have to say that the Bottom Line in 1975 was magical. There were many magical shows, but it just seems that he was devastating in that club. He was so close to you. And those little narrow tables where he came out and danced on those tables. There are damn few guys that can swagger enough to do that and get

away with doing it the way he did, as Bruce Springsteen. And he demonstrated night after night, in front of Paul Simon and Bette Midler; I was sitting with Faye Dunaway, Peter Wolf, and God knows who else, and he just went right on the tables there. One night I was sitting at a table there and he jumped on it and he jumped and sat right on my lap. He was soaking wet. And he said into the mike, "You know the guy sitting here? He's my manager." And everybody clapped and hooted. He was such a live wire.

He just endeared you to him. There was nothing you didn't like about him. Just looking at him, you'd say just look at how much fun this guy is having with this band. He brings out the best in you. It's good for the soul to see an act like that, especially at that time in his career.

One interesting thing though is that the Bruce Springsteen you see onstage is not the same one you meet offstage. To what do you attribute this personality change?

It seems that there's a transition, a metamorphosis if you will. He seems to be thinking all day about something, or brooding about something. You never know what the hell it is. You never know whether he had a fight with a girlfriend. There weren't that many, so you really didn't think that could be the cause. And since you didn't see anything, you'd wonder what is wrong with him. Why is he so moody and blue and brooding and doesn't say much? And then all of a sudden he hits the stage, and he starts kind of slow. He's a man who knows where he's going and just how long it's going to take him and just how much energy he's going to expend getting there. He conserves that energy very well and let's it explode when necessary. He holds it back when he doesn't feel it's necessary. He's got great control that way onstage.

It seems that maybe that brooding nature all day is a conservation of energy. It's almost like the hatred a fighter has to have locked inside him to be unleashed in the killer instinct when he gets inside of that ring. Springsteen had that kind of a brooding nature so that when he went onstage and started in with the music, somehow the music released him from the mental burdens of the day, the psychic load as he would put it. All of sudden he became this other thing—totally the antithesis of what he was like. He was another man onstage. And when you went to see him after the show, he was that same jubilation, though not onstage anymore. The aura of that jubilation now surrounded him like a glow until he went to bed that night.

We had some wild times on the road in those days. I remember once when we played a theater in Princeton in 1975. We had utilized a mirror ball, like one of those they used in discos. We did this really spacey song, I think it might have been "Night," or maybe "Jungleland," and it was the spookiest thing. When Bruce hit a chord, all the lights went out except this one that was hitting the mirror ball. It shot everywhere and it was just wild. It scared even the band.

I remember another show we did at Arizona State University and we were at this theater designed by Frank Lloyd Wright. We were in there because no one else would book us at the time in that area, so we had to book ourselves, and that was the only hall we could get. I ended up promoting the show myself, which was okay because we made more money that way. I was real nervous, even before we went there, because they'd told me Frank Lloyd Wright had designed the theater and that it was this piece of art and all. We were used to playing in beer halls and gyms and clubs, so when we ended up in this piece of art, I thought Bruce would go nuts when he saw it.

We got to the theater and it was beautiful. There were these red stone blocks and these balconies up there and the place looked great. But it must have cost a fortune to build because it was so elaborate. Bruce didn't seem to pay much attention to the hall and he went out when the show began and played his usual show.

I looked out from the side of the stage and saw that up in the balconies the place was packed beyond capacity. I remember looking out there during "Twist and Shout" and the balconies had started to sway! They were moving up and down. I thought, "Jesus Christ, we're going to have a bunch of people crushed here because the balcony is not going to hold out any longer."

So I had Mike Batlan get down on his hands and knees and crawl out onstage when Bruce ended the song. He whispered up to Bruce and I had him tell Bruce to end it, because the balconies were going to collapse. And Bruce then looked up at the balcony and he could see it swaying. And he kept looking at it while he strummed his guitar. And suddenly, boom, he blasts into another song, oblivious to the balcony. I mean, this was Frank Lloyd Wright for Christ sakes, and we were liable.

Luckily it didn't collapse, but it sure looked like it might. I got him backstage after the show and just went wild. "You want to get people killed?" I asked him. He said, "Oh, there's elasticity built into those things." It

At the circus, circa 1974.

didn't phase him for a second, he had just gone right on playing his heart out.

Is Bruce Springsteen a man who lives to perform?

I'd have to say Bruce Springsteen is a guy who doesn't want to give this up. He's a guy who wants to keep stretching whatever his imagined limits are and keep pushing forward and forward and leave a nice, big huge legacy behind him. And I think that live performance is certainly part of that.

Can you see Bruce Springsteen onstage at 64 still rocking out?

He certainly won't be doing the same kind of thing onstage he does now but I think he'll find a way, the way some artists find a way in that some of them go to country music. I don't know if Bruce will make that change or if like James Dean, Bruce will just kind of cut out of the world. Bruce may not cut his life off—he doesn't seem like that kind of person at all—but he may say, "Look, I'm retiring." Like David Bowie or other bands, he might do it just to boost his popularity and then come back. Or he might do it like a Greta Garbo and that will be the end of it. You never know. But I think you're going to see a lot more of Bruce Springsteen before he makes any such determination.

The period between Tunnel of Love *and the new record is the longest period of time in Springsteen's career that he's gone without an album release. You saw what seemed like a long wait when you were putting* Born to Run *out, but that's nothing compared to this. What does Bruce think about during such a long layoff?*

He never worries about putting a record out. He thinks that no matter how slow he is, the world will wait for him. He thinks, "I'm Bruce Springsteen, and I command a certain amount of attention and no matter how long it takes me, when I'm done there will be an audience out there. If I do 55 shows, they will all sell out. I command that kind of attention and I know it."

He knows that some people will want to see him even without the E Street Band because some people will be curious. He knows he's a killer act. He knows that people come to see him sing his songs and his lyrics. Some people might like it better if Clarence Clemons was there playing sax, or if Bruce was with the E Street Band, or if he would play "Rosalita," but Bruce knows it's him they come to see. And given the choice, they are going to go see him.

If you would have continued on as Bruce's manager, how would things have been different?

We would have gone on to do a number of different things. We would have done a tent tour, which I had done an enormous amount of research into and I had presented it to the heads of CBS who thought it was a brilliant idea. I had mentioned it to Bruce in Phoenix and his face turned red with excitement. He really wanted to do it, I know he wanted to do it. I said, "Think of it Bruce, we won't have any problems with unions, we'll rig lights the way we want them. We'll have a whole midway. This has meaning with where you come from. It's a 6,000-seat tent so we don't have to go into 10,000 halls. In a lot of towns you can't fill a 10,000-seat hall so we have to go to small halls. This sort of makes it uniform." And what could be more newsworthy than Springsteen in a tent? Not since Sarah Bernhardt with the Shuberts, 1912, has there been something like that. So I investigated it and I had a circus boss tell me exactly what I needed to do, to get generators with mufflers so we'd have no noise, and we'd get Astro Turf and put a makeshift curb around in case it rained.

It was a very exciting idea. With an American original like this at this time, we were outdoing ourselves. I had this idea, and I think Jon put the clamp on the tent tour. Now I wasn't privy to any conversations, this is speculation on my part, but someone put the kibosh on it. The thinking on the other side of the fence might have been that this is one more example of Colonel Tom Parker, Circus Parker, Mike Appel making a circus act out of Bruce Springsteen. It was, of course, exactly the opposite.

He would have done a television special. At the time, the William Morris Agency called me up and said that Bob Dylan had gotten into a fight involving an NBC special. He was going to be getting a million dollars. So they called and asked me about Bruce doing it. So I asked if we could get a million and a half. And he said they will do anything you want. So I said I want something to go across the television screen that would say, "your television isn't fucked up." Basically, in short, "this is a show lit with entirely different values than most television shows." Then I'd do lighting in a club situation. I knew that the lighting would be different and we'd have total creative control so much so that if we didn't like it we could scrap it.

So that was the deal. It was an incredible deal. Dylan fell through so I ended up with Springsteen doing it. But it never came to pass because Springsteen and Landau didn't want to do it. So that was nixed.

You were very interested in getting Bruce into either television or film. How close did you come to getting him a movie deal?

I wanted to get him a part in the movie *King of the Gypsies*. I met with Dino DeLaurentis and we were going to

get Milos Forman to direct. We thought it would work out real great for Bruce. So we went up to meet Dino and he's this little Italian guy. Dino sees Bruce and says, "He looks the part but can he act?" We had no problem with the first part of the script but the second half was shit. So I asked for a screenwriter to work on it. And we met with Milos Forman. He flew in for the Hammersmith Odeon concert in London, and he came backstage. And everything was a go, but then the lawsuit came up and that ended it. People now see the movie, which was changed a whole bunch, and they said, "God, Bruce Springsteen in this!" But I had Milos Forman to do it. He did *Cuckoo's Nest*.

Once Larry Magid called me from Philadelphia and said, "Listen, Mike, I want to do Springsteen in JFK Stadium and I'm willing to pay half a million dollars for half a day's work and with percentages you'll walk away with a million dollars." I said, "Alright, that sounds reasonable." This was early in 1975. "But I said, it's a big huge place and we normally don't do these sort of things. How am I going to sell it to Bruce?" And he said, "Why don't we get 20 or 30 bands from Jersey who don't have any standing and let them go on first and make a day's event out of it and make it a carnival atmosphere. A battle of bands like he used to play. Let Bruce go on at midnight and play to two or three in the morning." I tried to pass that off and Bruce said, "I don't want to be part of an event." So that ended that.

I guess what it all boiled down to was that they didn't want to give Mike Appel any more power. The thing that pisses me off the most is the tent tour. That would have been on the covers of *Time* and *Newsweek* again.

You've told me before the story of trying to get Bruce to play the Superbowl. Can you relate that again?

Bruce had written this song called "Balboa vs. the Earth Slayer." I had this idea that Bruce could sing this anti-war song before the Superbowl. This was in 1972 before the first record. So somehow I actually got through to these people and told them about the idea and their response was "Who's Bruce Springsteen?" They didn't know him and they probably wouldn't know him today or go for the idea. But hey, at least I tried.

Tell me again about the experience taking Bruce on the road, opening up for Chicago. I think it's still hard for some people to believe that Bruce opened up for Chicago.

What you have to remember is that back then we couldn't choose. We had our records out but they hadn't sold anything. So we went on this tour and the

Oklahoma City, Okla., September 17, 1975.

first night was Madison Square Garden and it seemed like a giant place. It wasn't so bad though because the guys from Chicago were really great. And we figured they would probably just stand there and play so Bruce would look good.

And he did. Bruce really did great that night. He knocked them dead. So the next night the guys from Chicago wouldn't let us use their video. And things started to get worse from there.

It came to a head with this show in Philadelphia and it was bad. People were throwing Frisbees during Bruce's slow songs and it was not what he wanted. He came back to the dressing room after the show and he kicked over a chair and he had a fit. He said, "I don't want to play these big halls." And I said okay, we wouldn't play the big halls. I didn't know where else we were going to play because we didn't have much else but we ended up going back to small halls.

Was the Time *and* Newsweek *appearance the high point of your career managing Bruce Springsteen?*

That certainly was the high point, though my relationship was already somewhat damaged with Bruce. But it was such a high. Maybe it was the high point of our relationship.

When did the relationship start to unravel?

When Bruce started to rely on Jon Landau. He had a new guru. And this guru was more like a pal. Perhaps I was more of a surrogate father. I took on that role and that role didn't have long to live. Yet, pals, contemporaries, had more of a relationship with each other. And I couldn't possibly compete. Jon was a new guy and there's always that new-guy thing. Just being new has that appeal. I just think that maybe Jon Landau was able to appear to be less flamboyant than Mike Appel. Even when Jon speaks to you he speaks in much lower tones than Mike Appel. I can speak in a loud tone. Maybe that comes off as unprofessional and maybe it came off that way to Bruce.

How big an influence was Elvis Presley on Bruce's formative years?

TALK TO ME

I recently found the ticket stubs from when I took Bruce to see Elvis back in 1972 at Madison Square Garden. That was one hell of a show. He had this comedian open up who was so bad. It clearly was this total set-up done by the Colonel. He was so bad that people were screaming for Elvis.

Then when Elvis Presley came out, every female had their Sylvania Blue Dot camera there and it was world war three. He stood onstage for about 15 minutes and just waved to people. I've never been in a theater before with that many bulbs going off at once. The guy had not sung a note and he was just standing there.

After the concert Bruce turned to me and said, "The King." That was it. That was all that needed to be said. "The King." He held up beautifully all night long. He sounded great, he was thin, he was terrific.

Do you think seeing Elvis was a major influence on Bruce?

Well Bruce saw him in 1972 and Bruce didn't start doing those Elvis songs until later, 1974. It was years later before he seemed to feel okay about Elvis's songs.

Springsteen has always been famous for his use of cover songs. Do any stand out for you?

I loved "Every Time You Walk in the Room." And I loved the Mitch Ryder medley. I loved the original too. He did "Ring of Fire" once. Johnny Cash's "Ring of Fire." Before he did that he did the theme to "The Good, the Bad, the Ugly."

What music did you personally turn Bruce on to? At the time he was clearly heavily influenced by "Blonde on Blonde."

Bruce Springsteen was the sort of guy who had listened to lots of music. He was a student of history. He had heard lots of things. I remember one particular day when I told him I wanted him to listen to something. We were doing "Backstreets" and I said, "Let's try to do an identifiable solo." So I took him into the office and I played "Hello, Mary Lou" by Ricky Nelson. And James Burton plays the solo. And I pointed out how wonderful that solo was. That prompted the solo on "Backstreets."

How would you describe your present relationship, after all these years, with Jon Landau?

I think my relationship with Jon Landau is pretty good. We haven't had a harsh word since the end of the lawsuit. I think Jon certainly got what he wanted to get and I think that must be so satisfying to him that it would be unthinkable for him to have something bad to say about Mike Appel now at this late date. They've always gotten tickets for me.

How many times have you seen Bruce since the lawsuit?

Jeez, I don't know. I haven't kept count. I've seen him two or three times a year. A dozen times. And quite frankly my last conversation with him was only eight weeks ago and he said, "When you finish anything new I really am interested in hearing what you get into." I was rather surprised to think that he'd give a damn one way or the other. I know that he's always wanted to see me become successful because that would make him feel good, to see me have another hit and catch fire again. I'm sure both Jon and he are pulling for me.

Do you have any financial interest whatsoever in Bruce Springsteen's career at this point? Have you sold all your publishing rights?

I do not have any interest. He owns all the rights. I haven't owned any part of Bruce Springsteen since 1983 and 1984. That's a fact. People like to think that managers have been so shrewd and so clever that they will figure out a way to keep going. But that's not true in this case.

Was it a mistake to sell the publishing at that time?

Yes it was. Absolutely it was. It was stupid and I needed the money at the time. I live by my own rules. It's served me well in some ways and beat me over the head in others. It's been a learning process. I'm not always right. I wish I was. I'm a bit of a risk taker. Maybe fools rush in where angels fear to tread.

It's been reported that early on you mortgaged your house to keep the band above water financially. Is that true?

No. I didn't own a house. I rented. That's another fallacy. As much as I'd love to say that. I borrowed money from my father at the time, but that was about it.

One of the most infamous Mike Appel stories is about the time you sent out coal to radio stations who weren't playing the record. That story helped cement your reputation as being somewhat abrasive. What were you thinking about when you did it?

People always talk about the coal in stockings story. That came up because nobody was playing our record. And one day Bruce came up to me with this Christmas card of him sitting in Santa's lap and I thought it was great. So we sent it out to every radio station, hoping that it might help get them to play the record. This was when the record was selling like shit. And we included a note that said that everyone who doesn't play the record will get coal for Christmas.

By Christmas, no one was still playing the record. So we said, "Why not?" We got these charcoal briquettes and we stuck them in plastic bags and we put them in stockings and used silver paint to paint "coal" on the sides and send them out. We sent them to all the FM radio stations along with the original note again and the

Philadelphia, Pa., December 30, 1975. ►

picture. But what's funny about it is that after we sent it, a few stations called me up and said, "Sorry, we got your coal but why don't you mail us a record so we can see what this is about?" I didn't realize at the time that the reason we weren't getting played was because CBS hadn't serviced the record.

Did you ever have a relationship with Springsteen's parents? When you first signed him he really was young, and I wonder about their willingness to turn him over to you.

I certainly had spoken to Douglas and Adele, mostly to Adele since his father was kind of a silent character. But I'd speak to his mother on a regular basis. She'd always say, "Send me any news clippings on Bruce that you have." So we always sent them to her. I kept talking to her into 1976. She said to me "Are you boys going to be able to work things out?" I said I didn't know. I think she was just perplexed by the whole thing.

Was the lawsuit with Bruce Springsteen the hardest thing you've ever gone through in your life?

I think in the wake of the lawsuit, the period of trying to rebuild yourself, your reputation, that was hard. I went into motion pictures to find a place where I would have some skills but no enemies. But you just can't jump into that and I lost a lot of money doing that. I certainly would like a second crack at Hollywood and I'm sure I will have one.

Will there ever be a point in Mike Appel's life where you'll get some press and it won't be associated with Bruce Springsteen?

I hope so. At this point, it's hard for people to think about it in any other way since it was a precedent setting case and it got lots of attention. I've met other managers who have said to me, "I've had 20 huge acts like Bruce Springsteen and nobody knows who I am. And you had Bruce Springsteen and everyone knows you." I say, I wish I was them. It would make it a lot easier.

Again, many people think you were forced from the lawsuit not to speak about all this, that you somehow disappeared or were paid off not to talk. This is the first interview you've ever done with the press.

Mike Appel did disappear, but it wasn't because I was precluded from doing so. Nobody won or lost the lawsuit as such because it didn't go to trial. It didn't go to trial for a lot of reasons, the main reason being because they were losing so bad, they didn't dare. They lost five to nothing in the Court of Appeals. They had an injunction levied against them and that is an extremely rare tool. They lost five nothing. Now you want to go to trial? Are you kidding? I think "Fellows, whatever you thought was your case, okay, there's no case. So just lick your wounds, get CBS to pay off Mike Appel and

go about your lives, simple as that." Which is exactly what happened.

Your lawsuit with Springsteen is now frequently cited in other cases of contract law you said.

What was so crazy about the case was that if Mike Appel's contracts could be broken so easily, what about CBS's? CBS had contracts with producers and artists, so if Bruce could walk out on Mike Appel, then every production contract that CBS had with a producer could be broken. The record industry was not rooting for Bruce Springsteen—they were rooting for Mike Appel. Because if Bruce could walk out, contracts don't mean a damn thing. They stick and they have to stick or it's not a business anymore for anybody.

But in retrospect, did it really all have to go to this? Couldn't a compromise have been worked out? Did it have to get this messy?

Obviously not. It did in certain ways. It had to go down to where Mike Appel had to be gotten rid of, I think. Because it would have been very difficult for Landau and Springsteen to have to deal with me. It was on *Born to Run*. I was a particular personality and I had certain musical beds and they weren't Jon's. It was sometimes Bruce's and sometimes it wasn't. He could be swayed. I was not easily swayed. I think my love for his lyrics, that would have been a fight . . . I can't imagine.

I was stunned when I heard *Darkness on the Edge of Town*. I couldn't have been a part of that. I couldn't have made it. Those songs were, quite frankly, not good enough for me. It would have been a disastrous relationship. So actually Mike Appel got out right on time. Because what Bruce Springsteen did thereafter with Jon was their concoction and I can assure you that Mike Appel would not have gone along with that. It would not have flown. And he's had extraordinary success. And they might say it was good he didn't go with me because without me he had this success.

How would you want to be remembered if you could be the one to write history?

I'd want to be remembered for the exuberance, the joy, the road from nowhere to somewhere, that rock 'n' roll does have something to offer the masses. You can go from nowhere to somewhere. If I was part of a unit that offered and represented that for a moment in time, I'm overjoyed. If I was somehow selected to be in that coveted slot even for a brief time, I'm happy.

Have you ever heard the Springsteen song "Man at the Top"? The lyrics suggest the story of a kid that goes from nowhere to the top and then wonders what happens once he reaches it.

Don't know it. But I used to say, "Are we in it for the big bucks? Yep." We understood each other. I'm happy

Bruce ponders his first commercial endorsement.

that I was part of that and I've told him that too. He knows that.

Back in 1972 when Springsteen first played those two songs for you in your office that you describe as "horrible," did you ever see him becoming a star of the stature that he is now?

Yeah, I did. I always thought he was going to be a monstrous star.

Did Bruce see himself back then as someone who would ever be that famous?

I think it was a gradual process for Bruce. Bruce is someone who moves slowly. I'm one to leap. He hugs the earth. He's cautious. His background has created that kind of a person. Mine was more freewheeling. Maybe I had more success as a kid, and kids who had more take more chances. Kids who haven't had that much are more conservative. I think Springsteen is patient. Mike Appel likes to go for it. And that may be one portion, one fragment, of my undermining, and that gave them this image of me being some flamboyant crazy man, jumping around the world like a carnival barker trying to make some kind of circus act out of Bruce. That was absolutely not the case.

You know, maybe it did all come out right. Maybe it's right that Mike Appel got kicked out because maybe he's better off. I wanted something for him and it's not

what he got. Now he's bigger than life, and maybe that's better. I mean, maybe he thought he was better off with Landau and all his rock-critic friends. Maybe he thought that that circle would do better for him.

Nobody else loves his lyrics or considers them as important as I ever did. Or I wouldn't have done what I did. If I didn't, I wouldn't have gone out on a limb as many times as I did. If I wasn't absolutely seriously convinced that this guy was special and unique. I had blinders on—I couldn't see any other acts.

And yet, that all ended up with the two of you filing lawsuits against each other and testifying in depositions about betrayal. I know the lawsuit was an emotional ordeal for both you and Bruce. When you finally settled the suit, where were you at that particular time? Were you in your office here, or in a lawyer's office?

We were in a lawyer's office. We were at this big conference table. He signed his and initialled every page and then I came in and signed mine. We weren't even in the same room at the time.

I had run into him in the lobby. I was with Louis Lahav at the time. Bruce said, "What's the word?" I said, "Not much." He wasn't mad or anything; it was just this situation we were in. It was the end of a long, harrowing time in our lives. It was the end of it.

—*Charles R. Cross*

An alternate coverslick for the Darkness *album.*

COVER ME

. . . .

Behind the Design of Born in the USA

Making an album that's as successful as *Born in the USA* entails more than just writing and recording the songs. It also involves marketing and design. The packaging of the music and the classic design of the cover certainly contributed to the success of *Born in the USA.*

That design was the work of New York designer Andrea Klein. Her involvement with Springsteen stretches back to *Born to Run,* and she designed both the *Nebraska* and *Born in the USA* album covers. She also designed five of the seven singles sleeves of *Born in the USA,* most of the sheet music, the great songbooks to both *Nebraska* and *Born in the USA,* and the beautiful *Born in the USA* tour program. For several years she was the designer behind the look of Bruce Springsteen's printed work — an important job indeed. Much of the imagery the public associates with Bruce Springsteen's music comes from the work of Andrea Klein.

We sent *Backstreets* contributing editor Arlen Schumer, himself a New York graphic designer, to interview Klein on the making of an album cover. In this interview, she discusses the ideas and concepts behind *Darkness* and *Nebraska* and the making of the *Born in the USA* image.

· · · · ·

BACKSTREETS: *How did you begin at CBS Records?*
ANDREA KLEIN: I had taken a course in paste-ups and mechanicals and did very well in that class. The woman teaching the course was at one time the production manager at CBS Records, and when the class was finished, she sent three of us on an interview — she knew there was a job open — and I got the job!
What did you show the CBS people?
I must've shown them some work I had done in college — I graduated from Syracuse in 1971. I was a painter for about five or six years, and I had

a few paintings I had done that were used as jazz album covers. And then I showed them paste-ups and mechanicals, because that's what they wanted to see.
So paste-ups and mechanicals do pay off?
You don't get a job without them. Six months after I was in that department, I was promoted to junior designer.
Just from doing paste-ups?
I was doing some little bits of design work.
For John Berg?
And Paula Scher was very much a part of it. She was wonderful to work with. They used to throw work my way. I started out doing back covers of classical albums. They continued to give me more important work, and then I was promoted. They knew my intention was not to stay in paste-ups. Some people are there just to do that; that's all they want to do. Some of us who were doing paste-ups made it very clear that we did not want to remain in that area.
What did you think of Berg's previous work? Did you respect him?
Oh, completely. I think he's a genius.
The Born to Run *album cover was...*
Brilliant.
Well, Eric Meola's a great photographer...
But that's not why that album cover is great; I just don't believe that. An album cover is great because it's a great *graphic;* it's a package design. And an *art director* is the one who puts it together, who crops that picture, who picks the type, whose eye has made that look like what it does.
And yet the photographer seems to get the glory.
What I'm saying is that John Berg decided with Bruce what the photo was going to look like. He decided to make it black and white, decided to shoot him on a white, seamless backdrop, and chose to wrap the photo from front to back. It was John Berg's genius that created that cover.
One of the things I like about the Darkness *cover is the*

way the black and white inner sleeve pulls out from the color cover.

I designed the sleeve. It was on *my* typewriter. The type was originally typed out by me on an old manual typewriter.

Is the type a straight blow-up from crummy bond paper?

Exactly. I had been involved with the cover design and had met Bruce. He would come up to CBS — he had his fans by then, and he would come into my office with his sunglasses on. I was comping type, painting "Darkness on the Edge of Town" on clear acetate. He just sat there reading the paper — he obviously felt very comfortable. He just hung out.

There were many more typefaces to be done, and when it became obvious that this was going to take all day, Bruce said, "Look, I'll be at the studio. Come over when they're ready." And the next evening, with about fifty comps — they weren't all mine, everyone in the department was contributing — we went to the studio and spent quite a while there. John Berg had said, "Show 'em a million." We had them out against the wall on the floor so Bruce could see them all out in front of him. He'd go through them, "Okay, no...okay, yes..." It was fun. Bruce was very talkative and told some great stories. We picked the cover that night. And that's how *Darkness* happened.

I've heard Darkness *was the first album cover and promotion that Bruce took a real, personal involvement in, all the way to the final printing stages.*

He took a personal involvement mainly because he felt too commercialized from the *Born to Run* era. He wanted to make sure that the graphics that came out were not the least bit commercial and in no way was it going to be graphic and slick. He made sure he wasn't going to look too great. There was no retouching allowed, as always.

Who was making the decisions?

Bruce.

Bruce was acting as art director?

He makes all the decisions. You don't show him something you don't like.

So would you have retouched the cover shot?

Yes. I don't think *Darkness* is any great album cover, by *any* means. I don't think anybody does.

What about The River?

I had nothing to do with it. He was recording this out on the West Coast, and a friend of Bruce's...

Jimmy Wachtel "...for Dawn Patrol"?

◄ *Landover, Md., August 25, 1984.*

I think he was friendly with Jackson Browne, and that's how they hooked up. That's all I know.

To me, the cover of The River *is redundant. It's another disheveled close-up of Bruce.*

Yes, and very intentional on Bruce's part.

They should've made the back cover the front cover; it's a nice editorial image.

Oh, I don't agree at all. The whole package design is poor. The back has nothing to do with the front. I don't really like the type.

It was the most logical step after Darkness's *typewriter type, this hand-lettered* River *logo.*

It's the same thing. He was very deliberate about making sure nothing was "professional-looking." Bruce is into this stuff.

Tell me the whole story of your involvement with Nebraska.

I was at CBS and decided to leave, to spend more time with my nine-month-old son. One of the last days I was there, I got a call from Jon Landau Management. They wanted me to do the next cover. They wanted to present CBS with a finished mechanical that I would do. I was thrilled. So I met with Jon Landau that day, and soon after started meeting Bruce at the studio. He played me all the stuff. The album wasn't completed, so he would play some of the songs that didn't even end up on the album. He played me the music and we talked about it. He would explain to me how he feels about the album.

How did he word these feelings?

He played me the music — that's how he worded it, I mean. It was in the music; I understood it.

But did he try to verbalize it?

Yes, a little bit. He was very private about it. He didn't want anybody knowing about it. He knew it was very different from his other albums. We talked about a feeling that he had about the album and how he felt possibly about the image on the cover. Right away we both agreed it should be black and white. He didn't have any other particular ideas. He said stuff like he didn't necessarily have to be on the cover.

Did he have the title at that point?

No. So what I did then was decide to show him some portfolios of photographers' work, people that I knew who did great black-and-white photography.

What type of portfolios were you calling up? Were you thinking of the Robert Frank, Diane Arbus types?

Yes. I was showing him more of, I'd say, an "artsier" type of black-and-white photography, as opposed to commercial, slicker stuff. It just seemed right for this. There was a book Bruce had always loved which he showed me — *The Americans*, by Robert Frank! He also showed me some pictures of himself that he liked. And it wasn't because of how he looked. It was because of the *feeling* that was evoked in the pictures. And that's how he explains these things to me. He doesn't have to use a lot of words. I understand what he means. So anyway, I showed him some stuff, and he really liked David Kennedy's work. And I did also.

What was his work like?

David wasn't a very well-known photographer; he was well-known among us up at CBS. He was a twenty-five-year-old guy that really did some nice stuff. David had a commercial side to his work, and then there's his personal side, still-life photos, portraits, stuff he would exhibit if he had an exhibit. This [the *Nebraska* album cover photo] happened to be one of those pictures, which Bruce really loved.

Bruce saw it and said, "Hold it — that's the cover!"?

No, he just really liked that photo. He said, "Okay, let's go ahead, let's give it a shot."

And you were the middle man, the mediator?

So we did a marathon photo session up in Brewster, New York, at David Kennedy's house, an old family home, which was a lot of fun.

The inner sleeve photo seems like a James Dean Giant *kind of tribute.*

Bruce liked it; I would've *loved* it for a front cover. Bruce felt it was a little cold.

I always thought he had a great rapport with the camera.

He's actually very much at ease in front of a camera. But everything to him is *contrived*. When he looks at pictures of himself that were taken by a photographer in a photo studio, he feels very much that they're contrived. Which they are. So he always likes "on location" pictures — which are *just* as contrived!

So when did you get a title to work with?

The title wasn't picked until the very last minute. There was another possibility — the other title was going to be *January 3, 1982.*

The day he recorded it?

Because it was that journalistic kind of title. I guess Jon Landau and Bruce thought it wasn't a good name for an album; it was too hard to say. Jon Landau and Bruce went through lyrics in the songs, looking for a title. They talked about *Open All Night* as a possibility. They thought *Nebraska*

was more wide open. Then Bruce showed me an old Chuck Berry album cover that he liked. It had the same sort of cover layout.

And the back cover?

I was doing some big type, and Bruce certainly was anxious to see it, and finish it that night. So he came over with Landau and sat down for a while, as I comped it out. I played him a Roxy Music album, *Avalon*, which I love. He told me later that he got turned on to it that night. The mechanical was done, and that was it. They handed the tape over with the mechanical to CBS. No one at CBS knew anything about it.

How did CBS feel about the design being outside their control?

They loved the cover, but probably would have preferred a picture of Bruce. Bruce felt very strong about it. It was a very personal thing. He was thrilled when it went number...three? I was thrilled that I had the opportunity to do it. Bruce said *Nebraska* was his favorite album cover. I never took it for granted whether I was going to be asked again or not, so I was surprised and thrilled when they called me to do the *Born in the USA* album. I guess we developed some sort of communication bond.

Tell me about your involvement with Born in the USA.

I met with Jon Landau in the spring or summer of '83, and he played me the title song.

What was your reaction?

It was more like *Born to Run;* it had that great, great music, and the great lyrical aura of the whole album. It was that thrilling. We talked about the album, that it was a very important album for Bruce, because it was coming after *Nebraska*.

Important in what way? To reestablish him commercially?

Yes. Bruce actually had a fear — he expressed that he didn't think he had any fans out there. He said that it was four years since his last full band album came out. And he didn't go on the road with *Nebraska;* he didn't make any new fans. His fans had grown up, had gone to college and graduated. That's how both he and Jon felt. So they were very much ready to establish him again commercially. I met with Bruce, and he played me all the music, about sixteen cuts. Again, the album wasn't finished. So we sat down and talked about the cover, and right away we both agreed it should be *color*. Coming from *Nebraska* — boom! Rock 'n' roll! Color! And he was ready to *look good*, as opposed to

The River *cover sessions, October 1979.* ▶

the *Darkness* cover, where he deliberately did not look his best. But, as always, he feels an album cover of his music should be *emotionally* accessible. He talks about the *feeling* that he wants it to have. We'd go to a bookstore, he'd pick out books, and I'd take them home — it was that kind of process.

What were some of the ideas you were picking up on?
Pretty much American, a lot of color. Bruce had an idea, a book he really liked. It was a book of photographs, and maybe even some poetry, by Joseph Szabo, called *Almost Grown*. They were beautiful pictures of adolescents. Bruce really liked the pictures. All he would say was "I don't know . . . all I know is I like these pictures." Period. He didn't go any further with it. I said, "Okay, let's get hold of these pictures, and maybe I'll do a photo collage." Which is what I did, but there was quite a long period in between, going through pictures with Bruce.

Did you meet Joseph Szabo?
Yes. We kept finding pictures, editing pictures. To make a long story short, he outgrew the idea. All the while I had presented him with some ideas that I had, which is part of my job as an art director/designer. My main idea was to have Bruce come into the studio, a real, live, controlled, professional studio, a let's-get-some-beautiful-pictures-here-of-Bruce session. I wanted to do a graphic flag — Bruce against stripes. I thought stripes were beautiful, graphically.

Was he agreeable to that idea?
He definitely considered it, although he didn't right away jump to the idea. And then, at some point, he was ready. He said finally, "Okay, look, I don't have any other ideas, sure, let's try it, why not?" We talked then about photographers. I felt it was very important for Bruce to get comfortable with the photographer.

So Bruce felt comfortable with Annie Leibovitz?
He mentioned that he liked her; she knew that he liked her. I thought she'd be right, and I called her.

Had you worked with her before?
No. My main fear about working with Annie was that she would not be willing to work with tight art direction. She was a journalistic photographer for magazines like *Rolling Stone*; she didn't go out on jobs with an art director. Journalists don't work that way. I also had a friend who'd worked with her shooting Cyndi Lauper, and Annie very much liked to take control of it. Which sometimes is great if you need somebody like that.

But with so tight an idea. . .
You don't always need that good a photographer. But yet you do. So I explained to her that it was going to be heavy art direction, and she really appreciated my honesty. She really wanted to do it, she would've done it for free. She *loves* Bruce. We sat down and talked about a bunch of ideas. She felt once we had him in the studio, we should do whatever we could. We rented the studio next door to her, where we had a series of stage sets Bruce could just walk into. He was very impressed by the whole thing. He walked in, and the first thing he saw was this big painted flag. I hired a scenic painter to do a Rauschenberg-looking flag; it was done on canvas, about fifteen feet wide. I stapled it to the wall and made it real weird. Then we went down the street to this garage we rented and did the fire shot, one of Annie's ideas.

That's real fire?
You could see it on Bruce's face — he was a little nervous about it. He looked a little like, "What *are* we doing here?"

The fire shot seemed to come out of left field, having nothing to do with the established Born in the USA *image campaign. It's a nice enough Bruce shot, but seems very. . . contrived.*
Right. Then there was the Keith Haring painted flag. We hired him to paint the wall of the garage. That was another one of Annie's ideas.

Interesting. . .Bruce goes East Village.
Well, he didn't know from Keith Haring.

I'll bet Keith Haring didn't know from Bruce Springsteen!
He did. He really did. But as far as I was concerned, Annie wanted to use him, I didn't. But I didn't think Keith Haring and Bruce Springsteen would exactly be the right match. So then we went back across the street into the other studio, where we had one big taut flag. Bruce really loved the idea.

Was that famous opening scene from Patton *in your head at all?*
No. It did come up later. We went through all the photos, blew them up, and did comps of the album cover. But Bruce felt he looked a little schlumpy. He didn't want to look ambiguous — he wanted a clear face. So we decided to go back into the studio and get the picture he liked. At that point I decided I wanted bigger stripes, a more graphic look. We bought a flag that was twenty-five feet wide by

Tacoma, Wash., October 19, 1984. ▶

London, England, July 6, 1985.

fifteen feet high. It couldn't even fit in Annie's studio! So we went to Silvertop Studios in Queens, where commercials are shot, and rigged it up. We did a whole bunch of sessions.

When I first saw the cover, I expected to see Bruce's face on the other side.

Bruce hoped to have his face on the cover, because he didn't have it on the cover of *Nebraska*. When all was said and done, he just didn't like any pictures of himself. He liked this image the best; he picked it. It came from the idea of a back cover. Bruce had his hat in his pocket. That's how he is — he sticks his hat in his pocket. Great back cover! Even though some of us talked about it being the front cover, Bruce kept saying, "Yeah, but I can't put my *butt* on the cover."

When did he cross that hurdle?

I don't know. He went home one weekend and called me. "Well, I think we gotta keep fishing." In other words, start from scratch — and the album was nearly finished!! I got off the phone, and I was very depressed. I think I burst out crying. "Keep fishing"! I thought I was gonna lose my mind!

What were you, as art director of the project, happy with at that point?

There were so many photo sessions — we did seven sessions in a year and a half — that there were a few things I loved. There were some portrait photos I liked, frontal versions, and some great type designs. Anyway, that Monday I got a call from Bruce, that that was *it*. He got nervous. Just when it was time to really make a decision, he totally withdrew.

Saner heads prevailed?

Right. He spent the weekend with Chuck Plotkin.

"Thanks to Chuck Plotkin for his assistance. . ."?

Yes. Thanks to Chuck Plotkin for your influence! The way Bruce has taken his career that's *different* from other huge personalities is that he just maintains complete control of his own image. And one way he does that is by making sure, from the graphics side of it, he sees and approves every single solitary thing that goes out. It gets down to the slash mark on the cover; he didn't think it should be there. That's how involved he gets.

Considering that it was 1984, an election year, did you fore-

see the immense coopting of the album's flag imagery as patriotic propaganda?

I think Bruce, at one point, did picture it. He was a little bit afraid to use the flag. We all knew the flag was a great marketable image. That was clear to all of us. But it was more coincidental, as far as I'm concerned. I could be wrong. But the title of the song *is* "Born in the USA," and that's where it came from. I don't think being an election year had anything to do with it.

The double-page spread of the flag in the field, from the first tour book, was another keynote image.

It was taken by Robert Lewis, a young, very unknown photographer who's great. He went out to shoot Bruce during rehearsal, and in his spare time he took the flag out to the fields. I wanted to make it a *poster*. Bruce loved the picture; I guess he didn't like the way I designed the poster — I used skywriting. He thought that was funny but too cute. "Nice try, Andy."

The "Dancing in the Dark" 45 sleeve threw me a little, because it appeared before the album, and its type style gave me the impression Bruce was moving in some slick, modern

direction. Then the album came out with a completely different look.

Type has to do with the graphic. To me, Bodoni Bold [*USA*'s typeface] is a more classic American type; it's been used on stamps.

What's been the fallout from this album design?

I would say that some of the work I've gotten has been a result of the album. Recently, I got a call from Chris Blackwell at Island Records — he loved the Run-DMC album cover I had finished for Profile Records, not knowing I had done Bruce's cover. He found out later I had done it. So they've hired me to do a bunch of work.

Has Annie Liebovitz received more of the credit, in your estimation, for the great cover?

In a way she did. I saw an article about Bruce, and next to the album cover was "Annie Liebovitz's classic photo," and to me that was a real misrepresentation. In other circles, people looking for art directors have come to me, not caring that Annie took that picture. So it's not something I regret. I'm thrilled the album was such a success.

—*Arlen Schumer*

Spare Parts

Springsteen's Studio Sessions, 1966-92

Forced to Confess: New York, N.Y., March 1980. A **River** *cover outtake.*

SPARE PARTS
· · · · · · · · · · ·

Springsteen's Studio Sessions, 1966-92

---

hat follows is an attempt to document Springsteen's work in the studio from the beginning of his career to the present. No thorough or authorized documentation of Springsteen's recording sessions has been made public, so what's here has been pieced together from dozens of sources. We've done everything we can to ensure its accuracy and to correct errors perpetuated elsewhere.

Springsteen is one of the most prolific songwriters of the modern era. He's written over 1,000 songs; the recorded work on his nine Columbia albums is just the tip of the iceberg. Many of his songs have been recorded by other artists — "Because the Night" by Patti Smith, "The Fever" by Southside Johnny, and "Fire" by Robert Gordon — and there are hundreds of cover versions of Springsteen's songs, by artists as different as Johnny Cash and Air Supply. Looking back at the charts over the last decade, there has rarely been a time when one of Bruce Springsteen's songs wasn't in the Top 100, either in his own performance or a cover version. Until the release of *Born in the USA* it was said that Springsteen made more money from songwriting royalties than from sales of his records.

During the last decade, Springsteen has spent more time in the studio than almost any other artist. Several of his records have ended up taking years to record (the studio bill for *Darkness on the Edge of Town* was rumored to be over $250,000 in 1978 dollars). For all records since *Born to Run,* Springsteen and his producers have had to mull over recorded material that sometimes included three to four times the amount of music possible to release on a single record. And even when Springsteen put together a double record, *The River,* he didn't seem to find much economy of scale — that record alone had as many as 60 different songs

considered at various points for inclusion. For *Born in the USA,* which had 12 songs, Max Weinberg tells us the band recorded 80 tracks.

We have attempted to document both the songs released on Springsteen's albums and singles and the songs recorded but never released. There are two different kinds of unreleased songs, which we divide into two basic categories: outtakes and alternative tracks. Outtakes are completely recorded songs that were considered for release but did not make it onto a record. A good example of an outtake would be the song "Don't Look Back," which was written and considered for *Darkness* and then dropped off the record at the last minute, so late that early promotional material lists the song as being on the album. Alternative tracks include variant recordings, such as the rockabilly version of "You Can Look" that was recorded during *The River* sessions (it's essentially the same song as the released version but done with a different beat and nuance), as well as reference tracks or alternative mixes, which are songs that have already been recorded but that are remixed in the studio to create a different effect. For each record, there would be literally thousands of these different mixes. We've tried to indicate here only those that are dramatically different from the released version.

We also include under alternate tracks the many demos recorded both in the studio and with portable recording equipment. Demos are rough versions of a song, intended to demonstrate the song's lyrics, melody, and structure to other musicians. Some of these are hard to differentiate from studio outtakes.

When unclear about the recording history of a track, we've left it open rather than assign it to a session we're unsure of. We've left material out of these listings entirely, rather than list material we were uncertain about.

We are certain, however, that even these extensive listings represent only a small fraction of what has been recorded by Bruce Springsteen and the E Street Band. Particularly for the last two records, recording-session information is still rather sketchy, though with time we assume more of this data will come out. Sessions are listed roughly in chronological order. Where sessions were intended for a particular album, we list them under the name of that album. Whenever possible, we say where the sessions took place and the exact dates of the recordings. Under album sessions we list first the songs released from the session on albums, singles, and CDs; then we list outtakes and alternate tracks, with comments describing whatever we know about the songs or how they differ from released versions. Under each of these groupings, songs are listed alphabetically by title.

This listing is meant to provide insight and information about Springsteen's recording processes. Most of the material listed here is not available even through illegal bootleg channels. Please do not write us asking how you can obtain these songs.

— *Charles R. Cross*

THE CASTILES SESSION
May 18, 1966: Bricktown, N.J., Mr. Music Inc.

• Baby I
• That's What You Get

This session produced acetate pressings of a 45, three copies of which are still known to exist. Both songs were co-written by Springsteen and bandmate George Theiss during the car ride to the studio.

THE STEEL MILL SESSION
February 22, 1970: San Francisco, Calif.,
Fillmore Recording Studios

• Goin' Back to Georgia
• He's Guilty (Send That Boy to Jail)
• The Train Song

All three songs are Springsteen originals, chosen from among the more than 50 Springsteen compositions performed by Steel Mill during its two-year existence, 1970-1971. Springsteen plays lead guitar and sings. The sound of all three is bluesy and hard rocking, reminiscent of the British sound of the late sixties and early seventies. This widely circulated tape was recorded so that Bill Graham could evaluate the commercial potential of the band. After hearing the sessions, Graham offered the group a recording contract with an advance of $1,000, which, after a great deal of discussion, was turned down by the band.

THE HAMMOND DEMOS
May 3, 1972: New York, N.Y., CBS Studios

• The Angel
• Arabian Night
• Cowboys of the Sea
• Does This Bus Stop at 82nd Street?
• Growin' Up
• If I Was the Priest
• It's Hard to Be a Saint in the City
• Jazz Musician

A song containing some lyrics that would later appear in "Tenth Avenue Freeze-out." Original lyric sheet titles the song "The Jazz Musician (Man) Plays His Horn."
• Mary Queen of Arkansas
• Southern Son
• Street Queen

Springsteen joked in the studio that this song was his "Jerry Lee Lewis imitation."
• Two Hearts in True Waltz Time

This track was considered for Springsteen's first three albums.

This is Springsteen's solo audition tape, recorded for John Hammond in a rehearsal room next to his office in the CBS Building. Springsteen plays acoustic guitar throughout the recording, plus piano on "Jazz Musician" and "If I Was the Priest." On the original tape Hammond introduces the session by saying "Bruce Springsteen, Columbia Pop Audition, Job #79682." "Mary Queen of Arkansas" was the first song Bruce played and the session ended with "Cowboys of the Sea," whereupon Hammond thanked Bruce and asked him to wait while a technician copied the tape. The next day Hammond made Springsteen, and then-manager Mike Appel, an offer.

LONDON PUBLISHING DEMOS
June or July 1972: New York, N.Y., Media Sound

• Arabian Night
• Circus Song

This song went by many titles and underwent many changes before it finally appeared on the second album; other titles include "Circus Town" and "Wild Billy's Circus Story."
• Cowboys of the Sea
• Henry Boy
• If I Was the Priest
• Marie
• New York City Song

Also known under the title "Vibes Man." Would later evolve into "New York City Serenade."
• No Need

Also titled "She's My Westside Angel."
• She's Leaving
• Song for the Orphans

Included on an early song list for the *Born to Run* album.
• Southern Son
• Street Queen
• Tokyo

Also referred to by collectors as "Born to Win" and mistakenly listed on bootlegs as "And the Band Played." Also called "Shanghai."
• Visitation at Fort Horn

This song also underwent many title changes, and at various times was referred to as "Vision at Fort Horn" and "The Visitation." It also was mistakenly called "American Tune." It was in early consideration for the second and third albums and included on early acetates of the first album but removed in favor of "It's Hard to Be a Saint in the City."
• The Word

Also known as "I Never Heard the Word on You" and incorrectly as "The Song."

The above tape of Bruce's solo acoustic originals was put together to sell his songs to other artists. In 1972 it surfaced in London in the hands of Intersong Music. Though these songs have not been as widely circulated as the tape of the infamous Hammond demos, all of these tunes have appeared on bootleg recordings.

THE LAUREL CANYON DEMOS
June 1972-July 1974: Blauvelt, N.Y., 914 Sound Studios; New York, N.Y., CBS Studios, Media Sound, Angel Sound, Associated Studios and Wes Farrell Studios

Rehearsal, Bryn Mawr, Pa., February 25, 1974. ▶

- Ballad of the Self Loading Pistol

  An early ballad considered for the first two records. Early on may have been known as "The Shootout" or "Shoot Out in Chinatown." The lyrics refer to the "day I killed a man." Thematically the song is one of Springsteen's first efforts to write about the relationship between a father and son. The father in the song teaches the son to shoot a gun, which eventually leads to a killing. Pressed on an acetate by Laurel Canyon in 1972. Original lyric sheets title the song "The Story of the Self Loading Pistol."

- Cherokee Queen

  An early Steel Mill song also known under the title "Cradle Song." When Springsteen moved from a solo folk artist to fronting the E Street Band, this song was a major reference point for that transition. An earlier live performance of the song by the Bruce Springsteen Band was pressed on an acetate by Laurel Canyon in 1972.

- Janey Needs a Shooter

  Most likely first written in 1972 prior to the recording of the first album, and considered over the years for virtually every record Springsteen made up to and including *The River*. An early piano demo was pressed on acetate by Laurel Canyon in 1972. The song was also recorded with the full band for *Born to Run* and was one of the last outtakes left off that record. In 1977 Springsteen decided to reconsider the song and a rough version was recorded with the E Street Band during a rehearsal session. Warren Zevon eventually released his own take on this tune, using Springsteen's title but few of his lyrics.

- Missie

  A ballad recorded during a studio session for the first or second record. Only known tape is incomplete.

- Mother

  A title from one of the earliest Laurel Canyon lyric sheets from 1972. The mother in the song is called "mama" and she irons the character's communion suit. One of Springsteen's most direct Catholic songs. After writing this song, Springsteen listed the nine songs he considered his repertoire, perhaps his first conception of the listing for his debut album: "Arabian Nights," "Southern Son," "Growin' Up," "Jesse," "Mary Queen," "Marie," "The Jazz Musician," "Street Queen," and "Mother."

- Saga of the Architect's Angel

  An early ballad most likely written in 1972 but considered for several albums. An early acoustic demo was pressed on acetate by Laurel Canyon in 1972.

- There Are No Kings in Texas

  A soft ballad recorded as a publishing demo by Laurel Canyon. Seriously considered by Springsteen for the second record.

- Winter Song

  An early ballad featuring a wider range of piano playing than anything else in Springsteen's entire catalog. During the long instrumental break, Springsteen's playing sounds like George Winston. The lyrics personify the season describing it as an "ice metal whore." Pressed by Laurel Canyon on an acetate in 1972 but not known to collectors until 1990.

Between 1972 and 1975, Bruce Springsteen was a songwriting machine. Though Springsteen has always been a prodigious songwriter, no period in his career matches his output during these early days when he wrote hundreds, if not thousands, of songs. An old roommate of Springsteen's from this time period reports that every day at breakfast Springsteen would be working on a new song. Mike Appel says that he intentionally had Bruce come into New York every day, from his home on the Jersey Shore, even if there was no real business for him in the city: The idea was to make Bruce spend a couple of hours on a bus or train, which was where he wrote many of his songs.

Songwriting for Springsteen generally started first with lyrics. Bruce would write out lyrics in long hand all day long in one of the many notebooks he carried with him everywhere. Many of the songs he wrote only existed in lyric form and he never wrote music for them or recorded them. Those that were worked up into demos usually only

◀ **Greetings From Asbury Park, N.J.** *sessions, 1972.*

included Springsteen on guitar or piano. The material that Springsteen liked the most would be played for Hammond, Appel and occasionally the band. Springsteen and Appel had a very small budget for the first two records so very few songs were actually recorded in the studio: It was much more likely for a new song to be played in rehearsal or live in concert while Springsteen was deciding whether he wanted to include it on his album.

At some point Appel began to worry about copyright protection of the numerous songs Bruce had written, so an effort was undertaken to get official lyric sheets and at least demo recordings of the best of the material. In addition to the "London Publishing Demos" and the "Hammond Demos," at least two other demo sessions were undertaken to capture Springsteen's songs on tape (Bruce didn't write music at the time so there was really no other way to copyright his material). One Laurel Canyon assistant described running a tape for two full afternoons while Bruce cut song after song, playing guitar or piano into a crude reel-to-reel recorder.

After cutting these many demos, Springsteen also began the task of trying to put together the right songs to create his first album. Though there appears to be a dramatic shift in Springsteen's writing in 1972, away from the acoustic songs he first premiered for Hammond, and into songs that better suited the band he was assembling at the time, much of the acoustic and electric material overlaps. Five of the Hammond demos were reworked with the E Street Band and were included on Springsteen's first Columbia album. One of Springsteen's first lists of songs he was considering taking into the recording studio included both songs from the Hammond sessions and new material that had just been written. The list read (the titles are in Springsteen's shorthand): "Arabian Night," "Henry Boy," "I Heard the Word," "Growin' Up," "Two Hearts," "Lost in the Flood," "The Angel," "Bus Driver," "Saint in the City," "Visitation," "Mary Queen," and "Song to Orphans." If Springsteen would have put out an album with these twelve selections, it would have reflected more of an acoustic folk style than the record he eventually released.

While Springsteen was busy organizing his material, Mike Appel was trying to keep the business afloat. Appel realized that there might be money to be made in getting other artists to cover Springsteen's compositions, and to this end, the cataloging efforts were intensified. Some studio-quality demos were made of a few of the better songs and tapes were shopped around to various producers and performers. A handful of acetates was pressed of some of these early tunes, and in the last decade a few of these fragile acetates have surfaced on the collector's market and have helped shed light onto the many lost songs in the Bruce Springsteen catalog.

THE GREETINGS SESSIONS
June or July 1972: Blauvelt, N.Y., 914 Sound Studios
Released Tracks
- The Angel
- Blinded by the Light
- Does This Bus Stop at 82nd Street?
- For You
- Growin' Up
- It's Hard to Be a Saint in the City
- Lost in the Flood
- Mary Queen of Arkansas
- Spirit in the Night

According to Vini Lopez, these sessions lasted only about a week, with the basic tracks laid down in a single day, probably in June or July of 1972.

Springsteen first began to conceptually arrange his vast number of songs into an album in early 1972. One list of titles from this period simply calls it "the album." On it he listed these titles (again, the titles are in Springsteen's shorthand); side one, "Lost in the Flood," "Arabian Night," "Bus Driver," "The Angel," "Saint in the City"; side two, "Mary Queen," "For You," "The Jazz Musician," "Growin' Up," "Visitation." On this list Springsteen has put question marks after "Saint in the City" and "Mary Queen," suggesting that these were not his first choice for his album.

Another Springsteen attempt to put together an album on paper went like this: "Saint in the City," "Bus Driver," "The Angel," "Growin' Up," "For You," "Blinded by the Light," "Spirit in the Night," "Let the Words," "Visitation," and "Lost in the Flood." On this list Springsteen puts a question mark after "Lost in the Flood." After "Growin' Up" he has listed "violins," and after "Saint in the City," he has listed "bari sax." The fact that Springsteen would think of this release as "the album" indicates how much of himself he put into this record. Like many debut records in rock history, Bruce Springsteen had literally been waiting all his life to make this record.

1973 SESSIONS

May 1973: Richmond, Va., WGOE Studios

- The Fever
  Another Bruce original written as a publishing demo and eventually recorded by Southside Johnny. Though Springsteen's version was never officially released by Columbia, executives in the record company leaked many tape copies to radio stations in 1974 and 1975 to increase interest in Springsteen's career and garner airplay. Danny Federici plays piano on this track. Two other songs (possibly "Bishop Dance" and "Thundercrack") were also cut during this one-day session.

THE WILD, THE INNOCENT SESSIONS

July and August 1973: Blauvelt, N.Y., 914 Sound Studios

Released Tracks
- The E Street Shuffle
- Fourth of July, Asbury Park (Sandy)
  This song grew out of many earlier songs, including "Casper" and "Glory Road." On some set lists Bruce would title this song "Asbury Park," which is some indication as to how specific the tune was for him.
- Incident on 57th Street
- Kitty's Back
- New York City Serenade
  Grew out of "New York Song" and became a serenade when David Sancious joined the E Street Band.
- Rosalita (Come Out Tonight)
- Wild Billy's Circus Story
  Grew out of the earlier "Circus Story" and "Circus Town."

Alternative Tracks
- Fourth of July, Asbury Park (Sandy)
  Instrumental mix.
- Kitty's Back
  Different take, with slight lyrical and arrangement alterations.
- New York City Song
  An early version of "New York City Serenade" was recorded in the studio and at least two takes exist. Musically, and lyrically, this version differs dramatically from the released track and the chorus is "New York City kills her young."
- Rosalita (Come Out Tonight)
  Instrumental mix.
- Zero and Blind Terry
  Instrumental mix.

On an early sheet of paper from late in 1973, Springsteen selected his picks for what he wanted on his second record and the ten songs he chose were slightly different than the version that was eventually released. His choices were: "Thundercrack," "Rosalita," "Kitty's Back," "Fourth of July, Asbury Park," "Puerto Rican Jane" (alternate title for "Incident on 57th Street"), "New York City Serenade," "Santa Ana," "Circus Song," "Zero and Blind Terry," and "The Architect Angel."

Outtakes
- Phantoms
  An early alternate version of "Zero and Blind Terry" with completely different lyrics, though similar music. The characters here are "Jamie" and "Jesse," and the story is about friendship. The gang

theme that would later resurface in "Jungleland" is explored here. One line suggests "to be free is to be lonely." Also called "Over the Hills of St. Croix," when Springsteen performed this tune live in 1973.
- Santa Ana
  Also called "Contessa." Nice, mid-tempo love song, contains some lyrics that would later become "She's the One." Both "Santa Ana" and "Seaside Bar Song" were intended for inclusion on the second album, but the songs were vetoed by Columbia.
- Seaside Bar Song
  Also sent out as a publishing demo. Played live in 1973. On some set lists Springsteen called this song "Coupe Deluxe."
- Zero and Blind Terry
  This song was also considered for the third album.

These last three songs, along with "The Fever," "Bishop Danced" and "Thundercrack" were pressed as an acetate in the U.S. for Intersong, an English music publisher. The six songs recently were made into a bootleg compact disc titled "Forgotten Songs," pressed in Europe. An article which appeared in the October 4, 1975 issue of *Music Week* (the European equivalent of *Billboard*) interviews Adrian Rudge, the man in charge of Springsteen for Intersong. He says that he first received tapes from Springsteen in December of 1972 (likely "The Publishing Demos") and set up a deal in January to handle Springsteen's songs in the U.K. and Europe. At that time in 1975, Rudge told *Music Week* that he had 43 Springsteen songs available for other artists to cover.

OTHER SONGS 1972 TO 1975

The songs listed below are titles that show up on general lists of songs catalogued during this period. Some may have been recorded, and some may be variant titles of other songs. Some reflect lyric sheets that have been discovered or cataloged over the years. These songs are part of the large body of tunes Springsteen wrote around the time of his signing with Columbia, and in the prolific three years that followed. As opposed to the songs listed as album outtakes, most of these songs were never recorded in the studio or went beyond the demo stage. Many of these titles are from lists, like the one Adrian Rudge referred to, of material Springsteen had written.
- American Dream
  An early lyric sheet that includes some lines that would later become "Two Hearts in True Waltz Time." Filled with urban imagery like "garbage truck vigilantes."
- Angel Baby
  Included on early song lists for the third album. The song was listed on a 1972 inventory of songs Springsteen had written at that point.
- Angel's Blues
  A title from a lyric sheet from 1973.
- Angelina
  Listed on an early list of songs from 1972. A lyric snippet from this song contains the first two lines of "Thunder Road," but rather than Mary, the character with the swaying dress is "Angelina."
- Baby Doll
  A title from a 1972 inventory of songs.
- Balboa vs. the Earthslayer
  Anti-war song, circa 1972, that Mike Appel wanted Bruce to sing before the Super Bowl. The Super Bowl declined the offer. The song is almost science fiction in theme, with the Earthslayer "bursting" out of a graveyard.
- Ballad of Elmer the Pea
  A title from a 1972 list of songs.
- Before the Flood
  A title from a 1972 inventory of songs.
- Billy Boy
  A title from a 1972 inventory of songs.
- Bishop Dance
  Played live frequently in 1972 and 1973. A live version was performed on a "King Biscuit Flower Hour" broadcast. Probably recorded in 1973.

Rehearsal, Bryn Mawr, Pa., December 27, 1973. ▶

- Black Night in Babylon
  A Biblical drama complete with Moses, "Yul Bryner" (sic), and a pillar of fire. Most likely Springsteen's first song to mention "the promised land."
- Border Guard
  A title from a 1972 inventory of songs.
- Busted
  An early lyric sheet, probably from 1972, about someone "busted, locked in a jail house."
- California
  A lyric sheet that surfaced in 1990, most likely from this period.
- Calvin Jones and the Thirteenth Apostle
  Written around the time of the second album.
- Camilla Horn
  A story song about a movie star, described as "the new Garbo."
- Casper
  Probably written between the first and second albums; included some lyrics that would later be part of "Sandy."
- Danny Jones
  On a 1972 list of titles.
- Daytona Mission
  On a list of songs from 1973.
- Down at the Club
  A title from a 1974 list of songs.
- Down to Mexico
  One of the first tunes Springsteen wrote after signing up with Mike Appel. The song tells the story of James and Joey and their trip to Mexico, where James married Maria "in a little chapel."
- Dual
  Third album lyric sheet about a street fight.
- Elouise
  A partial lyric about a nun and a priest.
- Full of Love
  An early lyric sheet from 1974 most likely. Some of the lyrics are similar to those that later appeared in "Pink Cadillac."
- Funky Broadway
  A title from a 1974 lyric sheet.
- Glory Road
  Very early version of lyrics that later become "Thunder Road." Bruce also considered the titles "Orphans" and "Promised Land."
- Grandpa's Gone Down
  A title from a 1972 inventory of songs.
- Helen Blue
  A 1972 song that was written for the second album. Was possibly recorded with the band.
- Here She Comes
  Also called "Here She Comes Walking" on some lists, it was considered for the third album. A version of the song resurfaced in 1980 as the introduction to "I Wanna Marry You" on *The River* tour.
- Hidin' on the River
  The original lyrics to "Backstreets" were titled "Hidin' on the River," later to become "On the River," next "River," then "Fallin' on the Backstreets," and finally, simply "Backstreets." The original central character is called "Chrissie" in these lyrics.
- High Noon
  A title from a 1972 inventory of songs.
- How the West Was Won
  Title from a lyric sheet, possibly an alternate name for "Ballad of the Self Loading Pistol."
- It's Easy
  A title from a 1972 inventory of songs.
- It's Just You
  Listed on an early lyric sheet. Also called "It's You."
- Jambalaya
  Listed on a 1972 inventory of songs. Most likely refers to the Hank Williams' tune; however, the 40 other songs on this list were all original Springsteen songs.
- Jennifer
  Possibly recorded for the first album.

- Jesse
  Listed several times in early lists for the first and second album. The lyric sheet to this song was originally titled "Jimmy Boy" but was retitled "Jesse" by Springsteen.
- Killer's Paradise
  A third album lyric sheet also called "The Violent Ones."
- Lady and the Doctor
  Probably evolved from the Steel Mill song "I Am the Doctor."
- The Late Show
  A lyric sheet from the second record era. The song is about a judge's strange adventures in the jungle and with a jukebox that won't stop playing.
- Latin Song
  A title from a 1974 list of songs.
- Let the Words
  A title from a 1972 inventory of songs.
- Livin' in the Ghetto
  A song written during the third album sessions. An incomplete lyric about a street whore in Harlem, also titled "Harlem."
- Lonely Street
  A song that predates even the Hammond demos about a street where "nobody throws any stones."
- Lonesome Train
  From a 1974 list of songs.
- Lorraine
  A lyric sheet dating from the Hammond demos period. This is a simple love song about how the singer would like to catch his girl's affection in his glove.
- Love and Defiance
  A third album lyric about a guy whose girlfriend calls him a fool, so he buys a gun. Also considered at one point as a title for the album.
- Mary's Song
  A title from a 1974 lyric list.
- On a Day of the Cowboys
  A title from a 1972 song list. Not the song "Cowboys of the Sea," which was also on the same list.
- Orleans
  A 1972 song about jazz in New Orleans and the adventures of a "young apostle."
- Pretty Thing
  A title from a third album song inventory.
- Prisoner of Wars
  Written with most of the material for the first record in 1972. The song has references to Hitler and Israel.
- Prodigal Son
  A song dating from the time of the Hammond demos. Filled with violent and disturbing imagery, Springsteen would use many of the ideas in this song for later tunes. The song refers to a time when "love and hate" become indistinguishable.
- Randolph Street
  A song about an easier time when "hate was shallow," and love was easy. Written around the time of the Hammond demos.
- Saint Jimmy's Dream
  A *Born to Run* era lyric sheet also called "Someone," or "The Great Emperor of Casa Grande," or "The Great Race." Lyrics to this song were written during the sessions for the album but the song was most likely never recorded. The chorus went "Someone waits for me tonight" and the song included a line about Gino's Pizza.
- Scene #1 (She Comes Into My Room)
  A title from an early listing of *Born to Run* songs.
- Secret to the Blues
  Another revised version of a Bruce Springsteen Band song, then called "The Band's Just Boppin' the Blues." Played live in 1973, and possibly recorded for the first record.
- Sha La La
  A lyric sheet from 1973 with some lyrics that thematically resemble "Jungleland." Not to be confused with the Manfred Mann song.
- She's Got Nothing You Need
  A title from a 1972 inventory of songs.

Bruce in the studio with Steve Van Zandt, Ronnie Spector and Southside Johnny.

- She's Not My Woman
  A 1972 song about a woman who tempts the protagonist with her feminine charms.
- Shilo
  A 1972 song using a town's name as if it were a woman's name. The song contains references to San Francisco and Boston.
- Shoot out in Chinatown
  Listed on a title sheet as being considered for the third album.
- Small Town
  From a titles list circa 1973.
- Spanish Rose
  A title from a 1972 inventory of songs.
- Still There
  Lyrically similar to songs from the *Darkness* era though likely written in 1974. Hand-written lyric sheet surfaced in 1988.
- Street Fight
  A third album lyric written in 1974, but never completed.
- The Street
  A third album lyric about how city life ruins you.
- The Street Goes on Forever
  A title from a 1974 list of songs.
- Summertime (In My Mind)
  A 1972 lyric that surfaced in 1990. One line was about the "Wintertime cold in Alaska."
- Surrender at the Citadel
  A title from the third album era.
- Take Me Down
  A title from a 1972 song list. Also listed as "Take Me Down Easy."
- Ten Commandments
  A title from a 1972 song list.
- Texas Carnival
  A title from a 1972 song list.

- Theme from an Imaginary Waitress
  A title from a 1974 song list also called "Portrait of an Imaginary Waitress," subtitled "Fountainbleu." May have been the song that evolved into "Linda Let Me Be the One."
- Thundercrack
  Considered for both the second and third albums. Often performed live in 1973 and 1974. Springsteen also listed this tune on set lists as "Her Brains They Rattle."
- Thunderhill
  A third album lyric sheet about a singer who lives his life "in a senseless rage."
- Tonight
  Original title for the song "The Night." Lyrics from this evolved into both "Night" and "Factory." Not to be confused with a later song called "Tonight" from 1978.
- The Violent Ones
  An early *Born to Run* song that combined some of the ideas later used in "Jungleland" and "Born to Run." Also called "Killer's Paradise."
- Virgin Summer Nights
  An early alternate title to "She's the One." Also called "Wild One," and "Wendy's Theme."
- War and Roses
  Considered as a title track for the third album.
- War Nurse
  Written in 1972 right after "Randolph Street," probably on one of Bruce's bus rides into New York City. The story of a soldier's sweetheart who lived in a "rising sun." The next song Bruce would write was "Growin' Up."
- When You Dance
  Written with the material for the first record. The song makes reference to a "train stops once to hell." Contains some lines also used in "The Word."

- White House
  Written in 1972 and referring to a metaphorical house, not the President's home. Includes images of Mexico, a frequent theme of Springsteen's early work.
- Wisconsin
  A lyric sheet dating from 1972.
- Wild Billy's Lullaby
  Included on a title sheet for the third album. It can only be speculated that this song continued the same story-line as "Wild Billy's Circus Story."
- Wild Fire
  A third album lyric about dreams "burning like a distant fire."
- Wild Roses
  Written during the *Born to Run* sessions but never completed.
- You Mean So Much to Me
  Played live in 1973 and 1974, before Bruce gave it to Miami Steve for Southside's first album. Originally written for the Bruce Springsteen Band.

By 1974, Springsteen had a giant backlog of songs that could have been considered for any of the first three records. The influence of Appel and Hammond on Springsteen's writing in the early years was considerable as they encouraged Bruce to write a song a day. Appel tried to move Springsteen into an almost rock-opera mode of songwriting.

1974 SESSIONS
August–October 1974: Blauvelt, N.Y., 914 Sound Studios

Released Track
- Born to Run
  The first track recorded for Bruce's as-yet-untitled third album, with David Sancious on piano and Ernest "Boom" Carter on drums. Studio records show part of the recording of this song took place on August 6, 1974 from 10 p.m. to 11:30 p.m.

Alternative Track
- Born to Run
  At least four different mixes are known to exist that include strings, a female chorus, and one mix with a double-tracked lead vocal.
    "Born to Run" was the most complicated song that Bruce Springsteen had written at that point, and perhaps the most complicated song he ever wrote. The song originally was titled "That Angel" or "Wild Angels," and only as Springsteen fleshed out the lyrics did the line "born to run" come to him. The strongest image in the first few drafts, before the song was titled, was "the American night." Early versions of the song feature more Asbury Park images and more specific references to the Shore than the released version of the song. As the song developed, it included appearances from James Dean and Elvis Presley's "Heartbreak Hotel."
    The work for the third record began to show the influence of Jon Landau, who first came into the project as a sort of editor for the songs. With Landau's influence the record, and perhaps Springsteen's career, changed forever.
    When Springsteen first planned the third record, before he had even written the title tune, he wrote a list of songs titled "New Album" which included "Angel Baby," "Architect Angel," "Thundercrack," "Vision at Fort Horn," "Two Hearts," "Here She Comes," "Glory Road," "Janey Needs a Shooter," and "Jungleland." Needless to say, it would have been a dramatically different record from the *Born to Run* that was eventually released. Another list from what was most likely a few months later only included six titles but showed a change in the direction of the record. It listed "Latin," "Love So Fine," and "Park" as the three songs on side one. "Born to Run" started off side two, followed by "Hidin' on the River," and the album ended with "Jungleland." Yet another list further along in the process of writing, but probably before anything had been recorded, listed these tracks: side one, "Mary's Song, "Glory Road," "Down at the Club," "Lonely Night in the Park."; side two, "Born to Run," "Hidin' on the River," "The Night," "Jungleland."

After Springsteen wrote "Born to Run," the record changed in concept, format and style. Based on the idea that Bruce Springsteen might actually be able to write a hit record, CBS warmed up to the project and started the wheels in motion for the commercial push that began in early 1975. With less worry about the budget, Springsteen began to write in the studio and developed his habit of making every recording session stretch on until everyone involved reached the utter extremes of exhaustion. This style of recording meant cutting most songs live in the studio, then trying them as many different ways as possible. It was not uncommon for Springsteen to scrap an entire song but keep one line and add that to another new song. His style during this period was constantly to recycle and reassemble his material. While the resulting albums sound extremely finished and complete — both *Born to Run* and *Darkness* sound so mature and well thought out that it's easy to imagine they were recorded in one straight session — the technique was far from simple and involved literally years of studio work. This style of tedious rehearsal, writing, and revising in the studio would become a habit for Springsteen, and would be repeated during his recording sessions for his next six albums. Few artists in rock history have spent as much time in the studio as Bruce Springsteen.

October 1974: Blauvelt, N.Y., 914 Sound Studios

Outtakes
- A Love So Fine
  Recorded as an instrumental with new band members Max Weinberg on drums and Roy Bittan on piano. Considered for the third album.
- A Night Like This
  Studio records show a song with this title was recorded by Bruce on October 16, 1974 from 10 p.m. to 1 a.m.

THE BORN TO RUN SESSIONS
March–July 1975: New York, N.Y., Record Plant

Released Tracks
- Backstreets
- Jungleland
- Meeting Across the River
- Night
- She's the One
- Tenth Avenue Freeze-out
- Thunder Road

Alternative Tracks
- Backstreets
  Two rough takes exist with unfinished lyrics, one using the chorus "falling on the Backstreets." At least one alternative track was mixed with strings added. The original title of this song was "Hidin' on the River." Springsteen's first lyrics to this song note "Shirelles, 'Sha La La (Baby It's You)'" as inspiration for the start. Also noted near his original title are the words "early, late, virgin summer," referring most likely to the time element he hoped to capture.
- Jungleland
  One mix adds strings throughout the song. Another short rehearsal take of the ending adds a new piano part and vocals from Suki Lahav. This snatch of piano will be used on the *Born to Run* tour as an introduction to "Lost in the Flood."
- Meeting Across the River
  Multiple takes and mixes with varying amounts of horn.
- Night
  Rough take with double-tracked lead vocals.
- She's the One
  Early take included lyrics that later became "Backstreets."
- Thunder Road
  One complete take of Bruce playing the song in a slow acoustic arrangement. Another take, much like the one on the album, had "Chrissie's" dress waving. One other alternate starts the song off with more saxophone. Studio records show some recording for this song was done at the Hit Factory on April 19, 1975.

Outtakes
- Janey Needs a Shooter
  Though originally written and recorded before Bruce's first album, studio records from *Born to Run* confirm that this song was again recorded by the band and seriously considered for this album. The production notes show that Springsteen's chord notations included a suggestion that the song adopt a "Spanish style" change after the first chorus.
- Linda Let Me Be the One
  Probably the last song ruled out for inclusion on the album, it is a pleading, mid-tempo love song. The original lyric was called "Wendy Let Me Be the One." A production sheet during the mixing of the record indicates that this song was considered part of the album up until the actual pressing of the master. The lyrics bear some similar- ity to the early tune "Theme for the Imaginary Waitress (Fountainbleu)," so this song may have evolved out of those lyrics.
- Lonely Night in the Park
  Seriously considered for the album. This was an evolution of the song "Angel Baby," but the version considered for *Born to Run* had a new introduction and different lyrics. The song tells the story of "broken down doll Valentina" who worked as a topless dancer in Toyland and her romance with some surfers. Several different takes of this track were recorded and on one Springsteen wanted "high soprano voice like 'The Lion Sleeps Tonight,'" according to studio production records.
- Saga of the Architect's Angel
  A song from early in Springsteen's career that he seriously considered for the third record, and perhaps re-recorded during these sessions. It was one of the last songs left off the record.
- Walking in the Street
  One very rough take is known to exist. The style is similar to that of "Thunder Road," but the lyrics are not finished.

Many of the songs listed in the "Other Songs 1972/75" section may also have been recorded for *Born to Run*. The third album had been in planning for over two years, and the idea for what should be included changed wildly over time. One list from 1974 includes nine potential titles for the third album: "American Summer," "War and Roses," "Up From the Street," "Sometimes at Night," "From the Churches to the Jails," "The Legend of Zero and Blind Terry," "The Hungry and the Hunted," "Between Flesh and Fantasy," and "Jungleland." Another list around this time added even more choices: "American Blue," "Arcade," "N.Y.C. Dialogue," and "Appointment Across the River."

One concept for the album was for it to represent one full day in the character's life, starting with an alarm clock going off. That version of the LP had it starting and ending with "Thunder Road," opening with an acoustic version and closing with the full band take. That concept of the LP was eventually scrapped, but the idea that it represents an entire day remains subtly; the record begins with the sound of the morning in "Thunder Road," and ends late in the evening in "Jungleland."

THE DARKNESS SESSIONS
June–November 1977: New York, N.Y., Atlantic Studios
November 1977–April 1978: New York, N.Y., Record Plant

Released Tracks
- Adam Raised a Cain
- Badlands
  Take 23.
- Candy's Room
  Take 42.
- Darkness on the Edge of Town
  Take 28.
- Factory
  Take 28.
- The Promised Land
  Take 5.

- Prove It All Night
Take 49.
- Racing in the Street
Take 46.
- Something in the Night
Take 42.
- Streets of Fire
Take 28.

Takes noted above are the ones included on the album, with information from the studio production sheets for the record. Obviously, considering that the version of "Racing in the Street" used was the 46th take, a tremendous number of alternative takes exist. For the alternative tracks below, we've noted the most significant variations.

Alternate Tracks
- Badlands
One alternative mix with added guitar, one rough take with many unfinished lyrics. An early instrumental take had different guitar and saxophone parts.
- Candy's Room
Two different outtakes were combined to make the finished track. The music is from "The Fast Song," the words from "Candy's Boy," both recorded in late 1977 or early 1978.
- Darkness on the Edge of Town
An early rough take was recorded at Atlantic Studios in the summer of 1977. Another take includes an added rockabilly-style guitar part.
- Factory
One alternate take includes violin.
- The Promised Land
Same take as the released track, but the guitar solo is mixed out. This mix appeared on some of the first acetates of the LP.
- Racing in the Street
Two rehearsal takes: one with just Bruce's piano and vocals, and another full-band take that is close to the released track, but with many lyric changes.
- Something in the Night
A rough take recorded at Atlantic Studios in the summer of 1977.
- Streets of Fire
One rough take, similar to the released track, but with lyric differences in the final verse.

Outtakes
- The Ballad
Often misidentified as "Castaway" or "La, La, La," instead of the actual working title. A slow, unfinished, sleepy tune.
- Because the Night
Two very rough takes are known, at least one recorded at Atlantic Studios. Bruce never finished the song before he gave it to Patti Smith, but did finish it for performance on the 1978 tour.
- Bo Diddley Rocker
Working title for an obviously Diddley-inspired song often called "Goin' Back."
- Candy's Boy
A slow, organ-led song, the lyrics to which change slightly and become "Candy's Room."
- Don't Look Back
Replaced on the album by the title track at the last moment. The song is listed on early promotional material describing the impending release of the record. The take that was to be used was Take 3, recorded March 1, 1978. One rough take includes different guitar parts, and an instrumental reference mix is also known.
- Don't Say No
A rough rehearsal of a fast-paced tune, with unfinished lyrics.
- Drive All Night
Much longer than the version that later appeared on The River. Another short rehearsal has Bruce humming a proposed string section over the finished track.
- English Sons
Working title for a fast-paced song with driving vocals and guitars from Bruce. Often misidentified as "Endless Night."

- The Fast Song
Two rough takes of the music that will eventually be used in "Candy's Room." Recorded in late June 1977.
- Fire
A song Bruce wrote for Elvis Presley. (He went so far as to send a demo to Graceland.) Springsteen played the song on the Darkness tour.
- Frankie
Played live for a short time on the 1976 tour, this song was also recorded for the Born in the USA LP.
- Get That Feeling
Mid-tempo, Phil Spector-ish sounding tune.
- Hearts of Stone
This track recorded by the E Street Band is given to Southside Johnny. Vocals and solos are changed, but the basic track is left intact so that the released version is essentially Southside Johnny and the E Street Band.
- The Iceman
Some of these lyrics will later be included in "Badlands." Recorded in late 1977.
- I Wanna Be with You
One of the first tracks recorded for Darkness at Atlantic Studios.
- Let's Go Tonight
A slow song that will inspire both "Factory" and "Johnny Bye Bye."
- Outside Lookin' In
Another of the early songs recorded at Atlantic Studios.
- Preacher's Daughter
Recorded in late 1977, this song is similar in tempo to the '78-tour live performance of "She's the One," which also included a few lyrics apparently lifted from "Preacher's Daughter."
- The Promise
Originally titled "The Loser." Two versions exist: one rough rehearsal and one finished track. Seriously considered for the LP and perhaps for The River as well. Springsteen has said that this song is not about his legal battles around this time, as has been widely reported. Introducing this song in 1978, he said, "I wrote this soon after I wrote 'Born to Run'" which would put the time frame well before the lawsuit. The song was copywritten in 1979.
- Rendezvous
Another of the first tracks cut at Atlantic Studios. Played live 1976-1981 and later recorded by Greg Kihn.
- Say Sons
Working title for this rollicking song often incorrectly identified as "Down By the River." Ends with Bruce commenting, "This song should be one verse."
- Sherry Darling
Two rough rehearsal takes. Later re-recorded for The River.
- Spanish Eyes
Two rough takes of this unfinished slow tune.
- Talk to Me
Recorded by Bruce and the E Street Band. Bruce then gives the song to Southside Johnny who re-recorded it with the Jukes.
- Taxi Cab
A melancholy, unfinished song about driving through a city at night. Some lyrics appeared later in "Ramrod."
- The Way
Six different reference mixes of this song exist, plus one finished take. The song was seriously considered for the record, and is similar in tempo and feel to "Factory." A few lyrics from this dirge-like, brooding love song appeared later in "The River."

The Darkness recording sessions represent Springsteen's most prolific period. These were the first sessions where Bruce came into the studio and worked out his songs, as well as wrote new songs in the studio and this caused tremendous delays and increased expenses. Bits and pieces of many of the unreleased songs from these many sessions were worked into other songs that would appear later in his career.

New Orleans, La., September 7, 1975. ▶

Like most of his albums, this record only was completed after many false starts and numerous revisions. Several times during the sessions Springsteen thought he had a record done, only to reconsider and begin recording again. Several different titles and line-ups were considered along with numerous album cover designs. Alternative titles for the album included "Badlands" and "Racing in the Street." One list of songs on a cover slick for the "Badlands" variation had these songs on the record: "Badlands," "Streets of Fire," "Promised Land," "Independence Day," "Prove It All Night," "Candy's Boy," "Racing in the Street," and "Don't Look Back." Another line-up appearing on another alternative cover slick after the album started going under the title of *Darkness* looked like this: "Badlands," "Something in the Night," "Prove It All Night," "Factory," "Darkness," "Streets of Fire," "Racing in the Street," "Don't Look Back," "The Promised Land," "Adam Raised a Cain," and "Candy's Room."

1978 BAND REHEARSALS

October 1978: Location unknown

- The Ties that Bind
  This song is worked out many times during this loose rehearsal, held during a one-month break on the *Darkness* tour. After an arrangement was decided upon, this song was played live at the first show following the break, November 1, 1978, Princeton, N.J.
- Tonight
  This song was worked out for five or six takes, but never really went anywhere. The song does not appear again at any time in the future.
- I'm Gonna Treat You Right
  This song is also called "Wild Kisses." This is another song that was rehearsed but never played again.

1979 HOME DEMOS

1979: Holmdel, N.J.

- Chevrolet Deluxe
  Worked out for five or six takes. This is a sad epic not unlike "The River." The song uses a car as a metaphor for love, highlighted by a chorus of "I can't keep my payments up."
- Everybody's Looking for Somebody
- Held Up Without a Gun
  Acoustic, rockabilly-type version of the B-side.
- I Don't Know
- I Wanna Start a New Life
  Similar story to "Seeds," about packing up a life and moving away.
- Looking Out for Number One
  Strange lyrics about a "Mr. Outside."
- White Town
  There is a quirky reggae feel about this tune, which includes some lyrics that will appear in "Jackson Cage."
- You Can Look (But You Better Not Touch)
- You Gotta Fight
These demos show Bruce at home writing songs on acoustic guitar with a portable tape recorder. All the songs are in bits and pieces, and are not finished. "Chevrolet Deluxe" is being written over the course of multiple takes, and the one tape that has leaked of this tune, offers a fascinating example of Springsteen's writing style. Bruce starts with the chorus and then works out the verses over several takes, changing the lyrics, and the tone of the song, each time he runs through it.

THE RIVER SESSIONS

April 1979-August 1980: New York, N.Y., The Power Station

Released Tracks
- Be True
  B-side of the "Fade Away" single.

◄ *Philadelphia, Pa., December 1980.*

- Cadillac Ranch
- Crush on You
- Drive All Night
  Although it cannot be confirmed, the primary recording of this version probably took place during the *Darkness* sessions, but it was likely remixed and finished during *The River* sessions.
- Fade Away
- Held Up Without a Gun
  B-side of the "Hungry Heart" single.
- Hungry Heart
- I'm a Rocker
- Independence Day
- I Wanna Marry You
- Jackson Cage
- Out in the Street
- Point Blank
- The Price You Pay
- Ramrod
- The River
- Sherry Darling
- Stolen Car
- The Ties That Bind
- Two Hearts
- Wreck on the Highway
- You Can Look (But You Better Not Touch)

Alternative Takes
- Be True
  Seven rehearsal takes include double-track vocal and a later sax solo.
- Cadillac Ranch
  Rehearsal take with slight lyric changes and more guitar in the ending. One mix added screeching tire sounds to the background and fade-out. Another starts with a siren.
- Crush on You
  Two rehearsal takes with lyric changes and different sax parts.
- Fade Away
  Multiple rough mixes with alternate backing vocals are known.
- Held Up Without a Gun
  Longer, unedited version of the released track.
- Hungry Heart
  An instrumental rough mix.
- I Wanna Marry You
  Three different (numbers 8, 9 and 22) rough mixes alter organ and rhythm guitar.
- Out in the Street
  Had nine different rehearsal takes, all very similar to the released track. There are changes in drums, organ, and vocals.
- Point Blank
  Four rehearsal takes, all featuring radically different music with alternate lyrics and a screaming guitar solo. This is an excellent example of the kind of experimenting that Bruce does in the studio.
- Ramrod
  Three or four rough mixes, one with double-tracked vocals.
- Stolen Car
  Often called "Son You May Kiss the Bride." Begins with just piano in an alternative arrangement with many lyric changes. Recorded in 1979. When this song was registered with the Library of Congress, Springsteen denoted he was copyrighting the "revised version," suggesting that this outtake was the original take.
- Two Hearts
Alternative mix without back-up vocals from Miami Steve.
- You Can Look (But You Better Not Touch)
Rockabilly version of the song.

Outtakes
- Cindy
  Mid-tempo love song that was seriously considered for the album.
- From Small Things (Big Things One Day Come)
  A full-band rockabilly number given to Dave Edmunds. May date from the *Nebraska* sessions.

- I Wanna Be Where the Bands Are
  A searing, hook-laden pop song with a great guitar solo, back-up vocals and hand-clapping.
- Loose End
  One rehearsal take, "mix number one," was recorded in 1979. One finished take was seriously considered for the album. Mentioned by some members of the E Street Band as the strongest vocal track ever done by Springsteen in a recording session. Bruce's original lyric sheet titled this song "Loose End," not "Loose Ends" as it has been commonly known.
- The Man Who Got Away
  A title from notes Springsteen made in 1979 when he was considering releasing a single album.
- Mary Lou
  This rehearsal take is an early version of what became "Be True." Recorded in 1979.
- Restless Nights
  Another finished take of a driving rocker with nice organ work.
- Rickie (Wants a Man of Her Own)
  Seriously considered for the record, and rumored to have been written for Rickie Lee Jones, it is not unlike "Sherry Darling" in style.
- River Horse
  A title from a lyric sheet sold in an auction in 1991. Most likely from this era though perhaps a *Darkness* outtake. Incorrectly identified by the auction house as an early version of "The River." Chorus refers to how "yesterday is on the run."
- Roulette
  Three takes including one that will be released on the B-side of the "One Step Up" single in 1988. This track was recorded in 1979, the first track in *The River* sessions, but was quickly dismissed until its surprise revival in 1988. One other rough take exists with a double-track vocal. One of Springsteen's most intense guitar solos.
- Slow Fade
  An early title for "Fade Away" with different lyrics. This song title was confirmed when an early lyric sheet sold at a New York auction house in 1988.
- Take 'Em as They Come
  Three very polished rehearsal takes, one with an alternative verse, the other two with fades and finished endings.
- White Lies
  Often incorrectly identified as "Don't Do It to Me" or simply an alternative "Be True." The lyrics to this "Fiddler on the Roof"-sounding tune will evolve into "Be True." One of the three songs Max Weinberg said in 1991 would be his pick for a Springsteen unreleased box set.

The long *River* sessions can be divided into two sections: songs from 1979, when Springsteen was considering releasing a single album; and songs from 1980 when a two record set was decided upon, allowing Springsteen to rethink the concept of the album.

The original single album at one point was tentatively titled "The Ties That Bind" and some album covers were mocked-up using that title. In 1988, a lyric sheet was discovered that included some of Springsteen's notes for what he wanted on the single album. That line-up included, with Springsteen's titles: "The Ties That Bind," "Price You Pay," "Be True," "Ricky," and "Stolen Car." side Two: "I Want to Marry You," "Loose End," "Hungry Heart," "The Man Who Got Away," and "Ramrod."

As the sessions developed Springsteen was unhappy and decided he did not have the record he wanted. Springsteen continued to write new material and the band continued to record. Steve Van Zandt was essential to this album finally coming together, as his production assistance helped Bruce's idea of a double record finally jell. Even with a two-record set to work with, Springsteen still found it hard to fit all the material and "Held Up Without a Gun" was originally listed on the sleeve of the record, but left off both the album and the sleeve before it was officially issued.

◄ *Leaving the video shoot for "One Step Up" at the Wonder Bar, Asbury Park, N.J., February 15, 1988.*

THE NEBRASKA SESSIONS
January 3, 1982: Holmdel, N.J.

Released Tracks
- Atlantic City
- The Big Payback
  B-side of the "Open All Night" single in Europe.
- Highway Patrolman
- Johnny 99
- Mansion on the Hill
- My Father's House
- Nebraska
- Open All Night
- Reason to Believe
- State Trooper
- Used Cars
  It's unclear whether "The Big Payback" was recorded on January 3 along with the rest of *Nebraska* or if it is from a later date. It must have been written around this time, as the sound is very similar to *Nebraska*.

Alternative Tracks
- My Father's House
  An alternative track with 32 extra seconds of synthesizer coda appeared on the first CD mix of this album as pressed in Japan. The CD was recalled as soon as information about the alternative track was reported in the United States.

Though *Nebraska* was Bruce Springsteen's simplest album to record — he recorded it at home with a Teac Tascam tape deck — its history is the most mysterious. Only Springsteen and Mike Batlan were at the sessions, if you can call them that, and neither has been forthright about what was recorded that day in early January. Springsteen clearly set out to record demos for a new rock record, and eventually, at a later recording date as yet unspecified, these songs were cut in full-band arrangements. But the more those involved listened to the full-band version of these songs, the more they were convinced the original demos were more powerful. Springsteen then went back into the studio again and cut the songs solo. His goal was to produce better-sounding takes than his original demos which were considered at first to be so technically inferior they could not be mastered. The result from that session were solo studio takes that sounded stiff and unnatural and were too slick for the material. Late in the spring of 1982, Springsteen and Jon Landau decided to present CBS with the novel idea of releasing the actual original demo tape as the album. The response within CBS was less than enthusiastic but after some thought CBS allowed Bruce his creative freedom, knowing that his next record would be a rock 'n' roll album. *Nebraska* was rushed into production and caused great problems for CBS' manufacturing division. Many different masters were made of the record, trying to punch the sound out and make it fuller. The sound on the original tape lacked dynamics and at one point CBS considered putting it out as a cassette-only release. Chuck Plotkin eventually solved the mastering problem and the album was released with minimal production changes. The album was released worldwide in September of 1982. Other early titles that had been considered for the album included "Open All Night" and "January 3, 1982," reflecting the date of the original demo session.

THE BORN IN THE USA SESSIONS
Early 1982 to April 1984: New York, N.Y., The Power Station and the Hit Factory

Released Tracks
- Bobby Jean
- Born in the USA
  Also recorded during the *Nebraska* sessions acoustically.
- Cover Me
- Dancing in the Dark
  The last track written for the record, reportedly after Landau's request for a hit single.

- Darlington County
- Downbound Train
  Also recorded acoustically during the *Nebraska* sessions.
- Glory Days
- I'm Goin' Down
  Originally titled "Down, Down, Down," this was one of the last songs added to the record.
- I'm on Fire
- Janey, Don't You Lose Heart
  B-side of the "I'm Goin' Down" single. Nils Lofgren's replacement vocals are recorded shortly before the single is released in 1985. His first official recording with the E Street Band.
- Johnny Bye Bye
  B-side of the "I'm on Fire" single. Originally written and performed on the 1981 tour as "Bye Bye Johnny." This tribute to Elvis was played at a much slower tempo on the *River* tour. Co-credited to Chuck Berry, whose own song provided the title and first two lines. Grew out of the *Darkness* outtake "Let's Go Tonight."
- My Hometown
- No Surrender
  Early title was "Brothers Under the Bridges."
- Pink Cadillac
  B-side of the "Dancing in the Dark" single. Originally was written around the time of *Nebraska*. Bruce rejected a version recorded by Bette Midler but allowed Natalie Cole to release her cover of it later.
- Shut Out the Light
  B-side of the "Born in the USA" single.
- Working on the Highway

Alternative Tracks
- Bobby Jean.
  Unedited album version includes strange keyboard and the full count-in.
- Born in the USA
  Many takes of this song exist, dating as far back as the *Nebraska* sessions in 1982. Initially Springsteen did not think of the song as anthem-like and early demo versions are much more subdued. Acoustic takes exist in rough form and several band rehearsal versions were cut, including one where Springsteen shouts out orders to the band during the recording. Of the more developed band takes, one cut is almost seven minutes long, with a lengthy instrumental middle section. Another take is an edited version of the long one, cut by about a minute, and Springsteen's "Oh my God" lyric is mixed out.
- Cover Me
  Two different rehearsal takes, one without a lead guitar part, another with an extended guitar part that fades out.
- Dancing in the Dark
  Unedited take includes longer sax solo, and instead of fading out, a synthesizer coda finishes the song. Another rehearsal take includes Patti Scialfa on vocals.
- Darlington County
  Rehearsal takes include slight lyric changes and a different beginning and ending.
- Downbound Train
  Reference mix with more guitar and vocals in the middle section.
- Glory Days
  Alternative takes include an extra verse about Springsteen's father, which is edited from the finished track. Rehearsal takes have a full beginning and ending.
- I'm Goin' Down
  Rehearsal takes have full beginnings and endings.
- I'm on Fire
  Rehearsal takes are longer than the released track, but otherwise nearly identical to it.
- Janey Don't You Lose Heart
  Miami Steve on background vocals. The song ends with a 30-second synthesizer coda, much like that on the alternate "My Father's House."

- My Hometown
  A rockabilly version exists.
- Pink Cadillac
  Unedited take is longer than the official track. Seriously considered for the LP, probably the last song left off the record.
- Working on the Highway
  Rehearsal take with complete ending and slight lyric changes.

Outtakes
- Brothers Under the Bridges
  An early version of "No Surrender," with reworked lyrics.
- Child Bride
  Title from lyric sheet. Probably dates from early 1982 but may have been considered for this record.
- County Fair
  A country-inspired tune from early in the recording sessions. Perhaps also considered for an early version of *Nebraska*.
- Cynthia
  Sweet, playful love song with double-tracked vocals.
- Don't Back Down
  The title is known from several lyrics sheets and early recording notes for the album and a small snippet of rehearsal tape exists. Two versions of this tune are on one lyric sheet in Bruce's handwriting, one titled "'Don't Back Down' (rocking)," indicating that an acoustic track also was recorded.
- Down, Down, Down
  Early version of "I'm Goin' Down."
- Dream Song
  A song considered as a B-side but known only from Bruce's notes.
- (Drop on Down and) Cover Me
  Driving and radical version of what would become "Cover Me." Same basic lyrics, but with completely different music in the same tempo as "Roulette."
- Follow That Dream
  Loosely based on the Elvis Presley song, but with new lyrics and arrangement. One of the first songs considered for the album, this most likely dates back to 1983, and a series of demos Springsteen recorded in California.
- Frankie
  At least two rehearsal tapes exist, one with a sax solo, the other with harmonica. The song is slightly rewritten from the 1976 live version. Springsteen seriously considered putting this song on three different albums and thought enough of the 1984 take of the song that he included it on one of his final lists for the album.
- Little Girl Like You
  A rockabilly-styled uptempo tune. Springsteen considered this tune a B-side, while at least two band members voted for it to be included on the album.
- Man at the Top
  A slow ballad that sounds as close to autobiography as anything in Springsteen's oeuvre. Performed in concert only twice during the *Born in the USA* tour though frequently covered in concert by E Street Band member Nils Lofgren. Springsteen used a cassette version of the song to copyright the tune with the Library of Congress in 1984. This track was also considered for Springsteen's *Live* album but was dropped at the last minute to be replaced by "Badlands."
- Murder Incorporated
  Four different rehearsal takes with differing sax solos, guitar solos, and beginnings are in collector's hands. The professional mixing on these takes shows the song as fully developed and finished. Some of the band members have suggested at one point Springsteen felt he would build the album around this song. Springsteen thought enough of the tune to list it on a late cut of what he wanted on the record.
- My Love Won't Let You Down
  Relentless and driving rocker, with a strong guitar solo. Two rehearsal takes exist with different beginnings. Perhaps correctly titled "My Love," as it appears on early lyric sheets.

East Rutherford, N.J., August 1986. ▶

- None But the Brave
  Sax-led rehearsal take with ripping guitar solo.
- One Love
  A title from a recording session log book of Springsteen's.
- Protection
  Given to Donna Summer and eventually released by her. Bruce plays guitar on her version, but prior to giving the song away he considered it for his record. The song most likely dates from 1982. It was rehearsed for the *Tunnel of Love* tour with the Miami Horns, though it was never performed in concert.
- Robert Ford
  A country-styled mid-tempo number that bears a thematic resemblance to the material released on *Nebraska*.
- Seven Teardrops
  A title mentioned in interviews and based on a story of a man with seven teardrops tattooed on his cheek.
- Sugarland
  A song about the plight of a farmer who burns his fields out of frustration. An early demo take exists on which Bruce may be playing all the instruments with a drum machine providing the beat. The song was also most likely recorded with a full band arrangement.
- This Hard Land
  This up-tempo, *Nebraska*-styled song was seriously considered for the album and dropped in the final cut. In late 1991 Max Weinberg listed this tune, along with "White Lies" and "None But the Brave," as one of his top picks for a retrospective of unreleased Springsteen songs.
- T.V. Movie
  A title mentioned by E Street Band members as a tune they recorded in 1983.
- Wages of Sin
  Another country-influenced mid-tempo song written early during the recording sessions.
- Your Love is All Around Me
  An uptempo love song from early in the recording sessions.

Much like the period of 1972 to 1975 early in Bruce's career, the period from 1982 to 1984 is blurry as to when songs were written. Since tapes of the full band recordings of the *Nebraska* songs have yet to find their way into collector's circles, we are left with little information as to what songs from this time were written for the follow-up to *The River* and which songs were for the record that became *Born in the USA*. The ten songs that appear on *Nebraska* probably represent only a fraction of the songs that were written between 1981 and 1982, and clearly the songs that did not fit thematically on that project were held over and considered for the rock 'n' roll record that was to follow. "Spare Parts," which was eventually recorded for *Tunnel of Love*, is rumored to have been one of the other songs written during this prolific period.

Of the outtakes from the *Born in the USA* sessions, many are rough demo takes most likely recorded in California in early 1983 by Bruce himself, playing all the instruments over a drum machine. This set of material would include songs like "Sugarland," "Follow That Dream" and "Robert Ford." Another set of demos including songs like "Born in the USA" and "Downbound Train," date back to the time of *Nebraska* and were originally worked up as acoustic numbers.

Armed with his many demo recordings, Springsteen began rehearsing and recording with the E Street Band in early 1982 and continued on and off through to April 1984, with the bulk of the work taking place in early 1984. Most of the songs that were included on the eventual release were songs first recorded in late 1982. It has been theorized that halfway through the sessions Springsteen considered releasing an album titled "Murder Incorporated," but others contest this point. At least three times before April of 1984, sources within CBS announced a new Springsteen album was imminent, though whether those pronouncements were wishful thinking on the part of the label, or a signal that Springsteen had momentarily felt he had a completed project, is not known.

In the course of producing the album, Springsteen wrote, recorded or considered nearly 100 different songs. Tunes would be considered one month then fall out of favor with Bruce, only to later resurface and be re-recorded. To help weed out some of the material, Springsteen actually sat the band members down and had them vote for their ten favorite tracks. Springsteen's own vote for the album, probably from the middle of 1983, shows a remarkably different record than the one that was released. His list contains the following songs, most likely in the order he planned them to appear on the record: "Born in the USA," "Murder, Incorporated," "Downbound Train," "Glory Days," "This Hard Land," "My Love," "Bye Bye Johnny," "Frankie," "Down, Down, Down," "Working on the Highway," and "I'm on Fire." On the same note Springsteen also wrote a list of B-sides including "Don't Back Down," "Sugarland," "One Love," "Little Girl Like You," "Dream Song," and "Don't Back Down (rocking)." Of the eleven songs Springsteen lists as his choices for the album at that moment, less than half would appear on the final record, and four of those top picks remain unreleased even on B-sides.

Early in 1984, Springsteen finally felt the project had jelled into an album though it lacked a hit single. On urging from Jon Landau, Springsteen crafted "Dancing in the Dark" and the project was finished and sent to CBS. "No Surrender" was one of the last songs added to the album and an early prototype for a CD package lists "Pink Cadillac" as one of the cuts on the record, omitting "No Surrender" and "I'm Goin' Down."

THE TUNNEL OF LOVE SESSIONS

January-June 1987: Rumson, N.J.; Los Angeles, Calif., A&M Studios and Kren Studios; New York, N.Y., the Hit Factory

Released Tracks
- Ain't Got You
- All That Heaven Will Allow
- Brilliant Disguise
- Cautious Man
- Lucky Man
  B-side of the "Brilliant Disguise" single.
- One Step Up
- Spare Parts
- Tougher Than the Rest
- Tunnel of Love
- Two Faces
- Two for the Road
  B-side of the "Tunnel of Love" single.
- Valentine's Day
- Walk Like a Man
- When You're Alone

The sessions for *Tunnel of Love* still are unclear, primarily because Springsteen has done so few interviews in the past couple of years. Bruce has said that most of the record was recorded in his house. Pictures taken there show a basic home studio. He's also said that the two B-sides were all the extra material he was happy with; the fact that an older outtake, "Roulette," was used as the B-side to the third single from the album reinforces this.

Springsteen started recording this record in 1986, first in Los Angeles with noted country session players, and then in New York, but what came out of those sessions is uncertain; security was extraordinarily tight. This is further clouded by the fact that, unhappy with those sessions, Springsteen moved the whole process of recording back into his house. Exactly how much material he recorded or how long he worked on it is unclear. Band members were brought in to replace instruments already recorded by Springsteen solo. Max Weinberg recorded new drum parts to replace drum machine tracks and embellished the drum machine tracks on other songs.

1988-1990 SESSIONS

Los Angeles, Calif., A&M Studios, Kren Studios, the Record Plant and One on One Studios; New York, N.Y., the Hit Factory

Released Tracks

- Chicken Hips and Lizard Lips
  Released on the *For Our Children* benefit album from Walt Disney Records in early 1991. Most similar in style to "The Big Payback" from the *Nebraska* sessions, Springsteen said he found this tune on one of his son Evan's children's cassette. The song was written by John Cassidy. Springsteen plays guitar and sings on this song. According to one source, Springsteen also recorded "Pony Boy" during this session, as a duet with Patti Scialfa, but choose to release "Chicken Hips and Lizard Lips." The album benefited the Pediatric AIDS Foundation.

- I Ain't Got No Home
  Recorded in early 1988, mostly likely in New York City at the Hit Factory. This song was written by Leadbelly and Springsteen's version was released on the benefit album *Folkways: A Vision Shared*. A different take, most likely from a tour rehearsal or a soundcheck, also exists and is featured on the promo LP *Folkways: A Vision Shared Innerchords*.

- Vigilante Man
  Released on the *Folkways: A Vision Shared* collection and most likely recorded in early 1988 at the same time as "I Ain't Got No Home." An alternative version appears on the *Folkways* promo album.

- Viva Las Vegas
  Released on the *NME* benefit album *The Last Temptation of Elvis* in the United Kingdom in early 1990, this represented the first recording by Bruce Springsteen without the E Street Band. Recorded on September 13 and 14, 1989 at One on One Studios in Los Angeles, and mixed five days later at A&M Studios, the song was produced by Springsteen, Jon Landau and Chuck Plotkin. Toby Scott was the engineer with assistance from Bill Kennedy. The session musicians used on this track include Ian McLagan (piano, organ), Bob Glaub (bass), and Jeff Porcaro (drums). Springsteen plays all the guitars and does all vocals. Roy Carr was the executive producer of the record and he said he first suggested concert versions of "Follow That Dream" or "Can't Help Falling in Love," but that Springsteen came up with the idea of covering "Viva Las Vegas," the title tune of one of Elvis Presley's latter era movies. *The Last Temptation of Elvis* album benefited the Nordoff Robbins Music Therapy charity.

HUMAN TOUCH SESSIONS

Spring 1990-Winter 1991: Los Angeles, Calif., A&M Studios and One on One Studios.

Released Tracks

- All or Nothin' at All
- Cross My Heart
- 57 Channels
- Gloria's Eyes
- Human Touch
- I Wish I Were Blind
- Long Goodbye
- Man's Job
- Pony Boy
- Real Man
- Real World
- Roll of the Dice
- Soul Driver
- With Every Wish

Bruce's longest-ever gap between records was finally broken in the Spring of 1992 with the concurrent release of *Human Touch* and *Lucky Town*. The *Human Touch* sessions began in 1990, with the majority of recording taking place the following year. The band for the record was Randy Jackson on bass, Jeff Porcaro on drums, Springsteen himself on guitar and E Streeter Roy Bittan on keyboards. The sessions also marked the first time since the recording of "Born to Run" in 1974 that Bruce and former E Street Band member David Sancious had worked together in the studio; a reunion spawned by Sancious's participation, as a member of Sting's band, in the 1988 Amnesty International tour. The basic line-up was further augmented by guest appearances from Mark Isham on trumpet and additional vocals by Sam Moore (of Sam and Dave), Bobby Hatfield (of the Righteous Brothers), Bobby King and Patti Scialfa. Production credits were divided four ways between Springsteen, Bittan (who also co-wrote "Roll of the Dice" and "Real World"), Jon Landau and Chuck Plotkin.

Many of the songs on *Human Touch* were written prior to 1991. "Roll of the Dice," was first mentioned in connection to an early 1990 session with drummer Steve Jordan. Also, "Soul Driver," "57 Channels" and "Real World" were first performed at the November 1990 Christic Institute benefit shows in Los Angeles, in sparse acoustic arrangements. Singer Sam Moore's participation in the sessions was reported in 1990, and drummer Jeff Porcaro gave some details on the recording sessions to a European journalist in September of the same year. It has been suggested that Springsteen was close to releasing an album in the second half of 1990, but pulled back around the time his first child Evan was born, deciding instead to continue working on the material. By the time the album was finally released, Springsteen had already fathered another child, Jessica.

LUCKY TOWN SESSIONS

Fall and Winter 1991: Los Angeles, Calif., Bruce Springsteen's Home.

Released Tracks

- Better Days
- Big Muddy
- Book of Dreams
- If I Should Fall Behind
- Leap of Faith
- Living Proof
- Local Hero
- Lucky Town
- My Beautiful Reward
- Souls of the Departed

The surprising release of two different Springsteen records on the same day took many fans by surprise. Unlike the double album *The River*, or the two volume Guns N' Roses *Use Your Illusion*, Springsteen chose to issue recordings from two different sessions simultaneously. *Lucky Town* was reportedly recorded over just eight weeks of sessions at Springsteen's home recording studio in the Hollywood Hills. Bruce apparently commenced the sessions expressly to record one more song for *Human Touch*, and ended up with enough material for a second release. Though Randy Jackson and Roy Bittan play on both records, for *Lucky Town*, Springsteen was joined by drummer Gary Mallaber and singers Lisa Lowell and Soozie Tyrell.

PROVE IT ALL NIGHT

Springsteen's Performances, 1963-92

Tying Faith Between Our Teeth: Tacoma, Wash., May 5, 1988.

PROVE IT ALL NIGHT

. . . .

Springsteen's Performances, 1963-92

Bruce Springsteen's live performances are his legacy. Though he sold 17 million copies of *Born in the USA* and has enjoyed record sales from all albums combined upwards of 30 million copies, his live shows have had the most enduring impact on his fans. At times the studio has been a difficult place for Springsteen, but onstage he acts at times as if he was born in the spotlight. No other rock performer in history has established a reputation for such searing stage shows, and no one has continued in that tradition for so long. Bruce Springsteen proves it all night, every night he gets on stage.

From the day he bought his first guitar, Bruce Springsteen began to establish his reputation as a player. Early in his career, back when he was performing in small Jersey Shore clubs like the Upstage, he was known more as a guitar player than a singer. At the time his reputation was as a Clapton-inspired lead guitarist, though the sound of those early groups seemed more influenced by the Allman Brothers. In early pictures from those days, Springsteen looked better onstage than he ever looked off — it was almost as if there were two different Bruce Springsteens and that by strapping a guitar on, Bruce became some sort of super version of his other self. Offstage he was always described as shy and thoughtful, while onstage he was as sure of himself as any young man could be.

Though it is not uncommon for artists to survive on their concert fees, what may be surprising about Bruce Springsteen is just how many years concert revenues were his major, and sometimes only source of income. Well into the recording of *Born to Run*, Springsteen and the E Street Band were forced to take time off from recording to play shows to make enough money to pay the rent. It was not uncommon, even as late as 1974, for band members to come back from a show with less than $100 in their pockets.

Even though money is no longer a problem for him, it still sometimes seems as if Bruce Springsteen *needs* to play live. During the times when the band isn't touring behind a record, Springsteen frequently makes surprise guest appearances in clubs. He seems perennially ready to strap on a guitar and shout out "Lucille," even if he's backed up by the rawest guitar band in the land. During the summer of 1982, right after recording *Nebraska* and at the point where he wasn't playing regularly with the E Street Band, Springsteen played in Shore clubs more than 40 times, almost as many dates as most bands schedule when they go out on paying tours. None of those appearances were scheduled, and Springsteen wasn't paid a dime for any of them. He played to crowds as small as 20 people, and the tradition continues to this day on the Jersey Shore.

What follows is the most complete list ever assembled of Springsteen's live performances, including information about what songs were performed. It would be impossible to print every known set list without turning this book into an encyclopedia, so we've given the basic set list for every tour, and noted significant changes. We've also given set lists for unusual or important shows.

You'll find noticeable differences between this list and lists that have appeared in other books. We've attempted to double-check all information to make this list as accurate as possible, relying on *Backstreets'* network of writers, collectors, and subscribers around the world to confirm exactly what was played at a particular show. Even this list, however, is nowhere near complete or totally accurate; we'd appreciate information or updated information other fans can provide. Write us.

. . . . . .

1963 Freehold, N.J., Elks Club
This is one of the venues played by Bruce in his first band the Rogues. At age thirteen, Springsteen is only a member of this band, but he

does play other clubs, high school dances and hospital benefits with the group for about a year.

1965 Woodhaven, N.J., Woodhaven Swim Club
The Castiles, managed by Tex Vinyard, play their first show ever. The group will play together until 1968. Other common venues for the band are The Left Foot, a teen club in Freehold; The Surf 'n' See Club in Sea Bright, N.J.; and Le Teendezvous in New Shrewsbury, N.J. Bruce sings lead on "Eleanor Rigby," "My Generation," Hendrix's "Purple Haze" and "Fire." A wedding reception set list from '65 or '66 includes standards like "Summertime," "Sentimental Journey," "Never on Sunday," "In the Mood," and "Moon River." Contemporary songs on the list include "I Got You Babe," "Money," "Satisfaction," and "You've Lost That Loving Feeling."

4/22/66 Matawan, N.J., Matawan-Keyport Roller Dome
The Castiles participate, along with over 20 other area bands, in a "battle of the bands." Admission to the event is two dollars.

5/18/66 Bricktown, N.J., Mr. Music, Brick Mall Shopping Center
Bruce and the Castiles record "That's What You Get" and "Baby I," co-written by Springsteen and George Theiss during the car ride to the studio. At least three acetates of this recording are still known to exist.

7/29/66 Hazlet, N.J., Loew's 35 Drive-In
A newspaper article previewing the concert describes the event as "Dance night, tomorrow night at Loew's 35 Drive-In Theatre will help the theatre celebrate its tenth-anniversary. . . . Starting at 7 p.m., The Castiles, a local rock 'n' roll band, will provide music with a beat very different from other rock bands. Their uniqueness has made them great favorites with the teen set."

11/24/66 Freehold, N.J., Freehold Regional Dance

3/10/67 Freehold, N.J., Hullabaloo Scene Teem Dance Club

6/9/67 Freehold, N.J., Freehold Regional High School
The Castiles play for the "Senior Farewell Dance."

11/3/67 Middletown, N.J., Hullabaloo Club
Bruce meets Steve Van Zandt here. Van Zandt's band, the Shadows, plays the next night. The Hullabaloo Club bills itself as "a groovy kind of fun. Strictly for teenagers. With dancing, live entertainment and refreshments."

12/67 New York, N.Y., Cafe Wha?
The Castiles play a series of impressive sets here during December and part of January, but the group splits up soon after.

6/16/68 Long Branch, N.J.
The Castiles participate in a YMCA-sponsored "battle of the bands."

2/14/69 Long Branch, N.J., Italian American Men's Association
Bruce forms a short-lived new band called Earth. This show is their only known appearance under that name. The poster bills the show as "St. Valentines Day Massacre Featuring Earth."

5/23/69 Ocean, N.J., Pandemonium
Bruce joins a new band formed by Danny Federici and Vini Lopez called Child, and this night they open for James Cotton. Bass player Vini Roslin joins the band a short time later. The band often plays here and continues to do so as Steel Mill until the Pandemonium burns down in 1970. One of the highlights of any Child show was their cover of Buffalo Springfield's "For What It's Worth."

6/1/69 Richmond, Va., Monroe Park
Set list is said to have included "Voodoo Chile," "Jennifer," a Springsteen original, and "Crown Liquor" written by Billy Chinnock. This was a rare afternoon show and was free.

6/13/69 Long Branch, N.J., The Auction

6/14/69 Long Branch, N.J., The Auction

7/15/69 Ocean, N.J., Pandemonium

7/20/69 Ocean, N.J., Pandemonium
The band reportedly becomes upset when the audience stops watching the show and instead watches television coverage of Neil Armstrong's first steps on the moon.

8/29/69 Sea Bright, N.J., Oceanside Surf Club

9/19-20/69 Richmond, Va., The Center

11/1/69 Richmond, Va., Virginia Commonwealth University

11/20/69 Richmond, Va., The Center
The band hears of another group from Long Island also called

"Child," and changes its name to Steel Mill. For this show they are billed as "Steel Mill — Formerly Child of N.J." Tickets are $2.00 and the performance includes a light show.

12/12/69 West Long Branch, N.J., Monmouth College
For this show the band is promoted as "Steel Mill — Child under an assumed name." The band now includes Springsteen, Federici, Lopez and Roslin; Roslin will eventually be replaced by Steve Van Zandt. They are managed by Carl "Tinker" West, who quickly books them on a tour of California.

1/13/70 San Francisco, Calif., The Matrix.
In a review in the *San Francisco Examiner* Philip Elwood calls Steel Mill "the first big thing that's happened to Asbury Park since the good ship *Morro Castle* burned to the waterline off that Jersey beach in '34." Set includes "The War Is Over," "Lady Walking Down by the River," "Jeannie, I Want to Thank You," "He's Guilty," and "The Train Song."

2/12/70 San Francisco, Calif., The Matrix

2/14/70 San Francisco, Calif., The Matrix

2/22/70 San Francisco, Calif., The Fillmore Record Studios
At the request of Bill Graham, Steel Mill enters the studio and records a three-song demo of "Goin' Back to Georgia," "The Train Song," and "He's Guilty." Graham liked the songs and makes an offer to sign them to Fillmore Records, which Tinker declines. The band returns to New Jersey, where they eventually add Robbin Thompson from Richmond as a second vocalist.

2/27-28/70 Richmond, Va., The Center
A partial set list exists: The Judge Song/Jeannie, I Want to Thank You/You Say You Love Me/California Blues/I am the Doctor/Goin' Back to Georgia/America Under Fire/The War Is Over/On the Road/ Sweet Melinda/Crown Liquor/Lady Walkin' Down by the River.

4/18/70 Ocean, N.J., Ocean County College
The band is promoted as "Steel Mill, Just Back from San Francisco."

4/24/70 West Long Branch, N.J., Monmouth College

5/4/70 West Long Branch, N.J., Monmouth College
Set includes "I am the Doctor" and "He's Guilty."

5/10/70 West Long Branch, N.J., Monmouth College

5/16/70 Richmond, Va., Virginia Commonwealth University
Set includes "For What It's Worth," and "Sweet Melinda."

5/23/70 Richmond, Va., Virginia Commonwealth University

6/13/70 Bricktown, N.J., Ice Palace

6/21/70 Atlantic Highlands, N.J., Clearwater Swim Club

7/17-18/70 Asbury Park, N.J., The Sunshine Inn

7/27/70 Asbury Park, N.J., The Upstage Club

8/8/70 Long Branch, N.J., The Beachcomber
Steel Mill performs at the first annual "Nothing's Festival."

8/14/70 Richmond, Va., Marshall Street Parking Deck

9/11/70 Atlantic Highlands, N.J., Clearwater Swim Club
This show ends in a near riot when police pull the plug. Twenty-one people are arrested for drug use and other infractions and the police force becomes the target of a petition drive calling for a probe of their tactics. The issue blossoms into a giant controversy, drawing lines between the liberal youth and conservative elders of the township. The issue dominates the local press for days. During the melee, Danny Federici allegedly assaults a police officer; however, he escapes arrest that night by disappearing into the crowd during a sing-along, hence his nickname "Phantom Dan."

9/19/70 Point Pleasant Beach, N.J., Beacon Beach
Steel Mill performs with others in a benefit concert to raise money for the legal fund of the 21 people arrested at the Clearwater Swim Club show. The benefit raises $200.

11/2/70 Richmond, Va., University of Richmond
Interesting early set of both covers and originals: Do It With a Feeling/Cherokee Queen/Look to the River/Not Fade Away/When You Dance/Goin' Back to Georgia/Got My Mojo Working/It's All Over Now, Baby Blue.

11/20/70 Richmond, Va., The Center

11/27/70 Asbury Park, N.J., The Sunshine Inn
Billed as "Monmouth County's Biggest Concert Ever." Steel Mill is third on the bill behind Black Sabbath and Cactus.

The only known color photograph of the Castiles performing. Bruce is at the microphone wearing sunglasses.

1/12/71 Long Branch, N.J.
1/18/71 Sayreville, N.J., D'Scene
Twelve-song set lasting over two hours.
1/22-23/71 Asbury Park, N.J., The Upstage Club
Billed as Steel Mill's final shows.
4/16-17/71 Asbury Park, N.J., The Upstage Club
Billed as the "Bruce Springsteen Jam Concert."
5/14/71 Asbury Park, N.J., The Sunshine Inn
First show as Dr. Zoom and the Sonic Boom, made up of Springsteen, Federici, Lopez, Van Zandt, David Sancious, and Garry Tallent, in a rotating line-up with numerous other Shore musicians, including Southside Johnny, Bobby Williams, Kevin Connair, Danny Gallagher, John Luraschi, Kevin Kavanaugh, Al Tellone, Johnny Waasdorp, and a group of female backup singers known as the Zoomettes.
5/15/71 Union, N.J., Newark State University
7/10/71 Lincroft, N.J., Brookdale Community College
The unwieldy size of Dr. Zoom leads Bruce to trim down the band to what becomes "The Bruce Springsteen Band." The band is made up of the principal members of Dr. Zoom, joined at certain shows by the horn section of Harvey Cherlin and Bobby Feigenbaum and the back-up vocals of Francine Daniels, Barbara Dinkins, and Delores Holmes. The band headlines the second annual "Nothing's Festival."
7/11/71 Asbury Park, N.J., The Sunshine Inn
The band opens for Humble Pie and receives a positive review from Joan Pikula in the *Asbury Park Evening Press.*
7/29/71 Sayreville, N.J., D'Scene
8/7/71 Asbury Park, N.J., The Sunshine Inn
9/71 Asbury Park, N.J., The Student Prince
The band plays here every Friday, Saturday, and Sunday night in September, with Springsteen billed as "That Sensational Soul Man." Sunday show features a happy hour and free dinner buffet. Southside

Johnny often sits in with the band here, adding his bluesy harmonica and vocals.
9/1/71 Long Branch, N.J., City Park
Billed as the Bruce Springsteen Blues Band. A partial set list exists, consisting mostly of covers: Little Queenie/Bright Lights, Big City/Ballad of Jesse James/Jumpin' Jack Flash/Festival/You Better Be Nice to Me/Route 66/The Night They Drove Old Dixie Down/ Dance, Dance, Dance/Jambalaya.
10/23/71 Richmond, Va., University of Richmond, Keller Hall
10/31/71 Long Branch, N.J., National Guard Armory
12/17/71 New Brunswick, N.J., Rutgers University
Also on the bill are Southern Conspiracy and Power House.
2/4/72 Richmond, Va., Back Door Club
2/14/72 Asbury Park, N.J., The Sunshine Inn
The band reportedly opens for Crazy Horse, though it is questionable whether this actually occurred.
2/16/72 West Long Branch, N.J., Monmouth College
Billed as the "Save a Tree Concert."
2/26/72 Richmond, Va., Back Door Club
Set includes "Down to Mexico," "Something You Got," "All I Wanna Do Is Dance," and "I Remember."
4/15/72 New Brunswick, N.J., The Ledge, Rutgers University
Last known show as the Bruce Springsteen Band, though an undated poster from 1972 has the band playing a George McGovern benefit.
5/2/72 New York, N.Y., CBS Building
Bruce has his now-famous 15-minute audition with John Hammond, set up by Mike Appel, who has now become Springsteen's manager. Bruce ends up playing at least two hours and earns a recording session the next day. Appel later describes Bruce as "literally jumping in the air running down the street after the audition."
5/2/72 New York, N.Y., The Gaslight Club
Show is hastily arranged by John Hammond.

8/30/72 New York, N.Y., Max's Kansas City
Part of the show is recorded for the "King Biscuit Flower Hour," and "Bishop Dance" is later aired on the very first King Biscuit radio special. The song is later rebroadcast during the pre-concert special before the Stockholm '88 radio simulcast.

11/12/72 York, Pa.
According to Laurel Canyon records, the first show with the new E Street Band, whose lineup includes Springsteen, Danny Federici on organ, Clarence Clemons on saxophone, Garry Tallent on bass, and Vini Lopez on drums.

12/7/72 Ossining, N.Y., Sing Sing Prison
Bruce and the band get a full dress rehearsal in an unusual prison gig.

12/29/72 Dayton, Ohio, Hara Arena
Bruce and the band open two dates in Ohio for Sha Na Na.

12/30/72 Columbus, Ohio, Ohio Theater

1/4-7/73 Bryn Mawr, Pa., The Main Point
Springsteen makes his first Main Point appearance opening for Travis Shook. Over the years this becomes one of his favorite venues.

1/5/73 *Greetings From Asbury Park, N.J.* is released in the U.S.

1/8-13/73 Boston, Mass., Paul's Mall
The E Street Band play a week of two-show-per-night dates at this small rock club.

1/10/73 Boston, Mass., WBCN Studios
Bruce does his first major radio interview and an acoustic set, a practice he will continue in many cities during the next two years. Satin Doll/Bishop Dance/Circus Song/Song for the Orphans/Does This Bus Stop at 82nd Street/Blinded By the Light.

1/15/73 Villanova, Pa., Villanova University

1/17-21/73 Roslyn, N.Y., My Father's Place

1/24-28/73 Chicago, Ill., The Quiet Knight

1/31-2/5/73 New York, N.Y., Max's Kansas City
Cashbox Magazine: "Suppose the music of Dylan, Van Morrison, Leon Russell and the Band were erased from all memory, and that, lo and behold, a newcomer makes the scene and with the deftness of all the forenamed fills that void. Thus it happens that, free of any Woodstock, L.A. or British environmental influences, in drops Bruce Springsteen from Asbury Park, N.J., upon John Hammond at Columbia. . . . This newcomer undoubtedly deserves the stature of a performer who will be rising to fame quickly and will remain there for a long time. Bruce Springsteen is THE performer of the '70s."

2/10/73 Asbury Park, N.J., The Sunshine Inn
Billed as "New Jersey's Own Superstar."

2/11/73 South Orange, N.J., Seton Hall University

2/14/73 Richmond, Va, Virginia Commonwealth University

2/16/73 West Long Branch, N.J., Monmouth College
Following the show, Springsteen is scheduled to play three weeks of dates on the West Coast as an opening act for Paul Butterfield, but the Northwest portion of the tour is cancelled, and the band play only a few California dates.

2/26/73 Los Angeles, Calif., The Troubadour
Bruce and the band appear at the Troubadour's "hoot night," a regular open mike for singer-songwriters. Peter Jay Philbin (later Bruce's A&R rep at Columbia) in the *Los Angeles Free Press:* "But it was Bruce Springsteen who made the crowd collision, the stepped-on toes, the smoke-pained eyeballs, the walk away from the war TV set all worthwhile. Let me put it to you this way: Never have I been more impressed with a debuting singer than I was with Bruce Springsteen on Monday night." Six-song set includes "Mary Queen of Arkansas."

2/28/73 Stockton, Calif.
Opening for Paul Butterfield. Other opening dates in Bakersfield, San Jose and Los Angeles are cancelled.

3/2/73 Berkeley, Calif., Community Theater
The E Street Band picks opening dates for Blood, Sweat and Tears here and in Santa Monica.

3/3/73 Santa Monica, Calif., Santa Monica Civic Auditorium

3/12-17/73 Boston, Mass., Oliver's

3/18/73 Kingston, R.I., University of Rhode Island

◄ *Lenox, Mass., September 23, 1975.*

3/23/73 Providence, R.I.

3/24/73 Niagara, N.Y., Niagara University

3/29/73 Kutztown, Pa.

4/1/73 New Brunswick, N.J., The Ledge, Rutgers University
Headlining show opened by Heavy Trucking and Southern Conspiracy.

4/7/73 Norfolk, Va.
Some southern dates scheduled for the following week, including a show in Atlanta, are cancelled.

4/13/73 Villanova, Pa., Villanova University

4/14/73 Richmond, Va.

4/18/73 Lincroft, N.J.

4/23/73 Hartford, Conn., Shaboo

4/24-25/73 Bryn Mawr, Pa., The Main Point
Part of this show is later broadcast on WMMR radio, Philadelphia. Set includes "New York Song," which will evolve into "New York City Serenade" when David Sancious joins the band. Partial set list: New York Song/Circus Song/Spirit in the Night/Does This Bus Stop at 82nd Street/Santa Ana/Tokyo/Thundercrack.

4/27/73 Athens, Ohio, Convocation Center, Ohio University
Festival appearance with Blood Sweat and Tears, the Eagles and Billy Preston.

4/28/73 College Park, Md., Field House, University of Maryland
Bruce and the band are on a triple bill opening for Chuck Berry and Jerry Lee Lewis. They also serve as Berry's backup band. Springsteen recounted the story in the film about Berry called *Hail, Hail, Rock 'n' Roll*, saying that Berry came on and began playing without filling the band in on what number he was starting with. Springsteen described it as "total panic" as the band tried to figure out both what song and what key Berry was playing. At one point during the show Springsteen says Berry came over and told them "Play for that money, boys," but Springsteen says the band wasn't getting paid for backing him. Tickets to the show were $5.50 and Springsteen's name was misspelled in the newspaper ads as was a frequent occurrence at this time.

5/1/73 University Park, Pa., Penn State University
This date is often attributed to the CBS Records convention in Los Angeles, but Laurel Canyon records indicate the band was paid for a show at the university on this date, and that the CBS convention occurred in July.

5/5/73 Providence, R.I.

5/6/73 Amherst, Mass., Alumni Stadium, University of Mass.
Opening for Cold Blood and It's a Beautiful Day.

5/11/73 Columbus, Ohio, Ohio State University

5/12/73 Niagara, N.Y., Niagara University

5/24-26/73 Washington, D.C., Childe Harold

5/30/73 Fayetteville, N.C., Cumberland County Civic Center
First show opening for Chicago. Bruce will become so disillusioned during this tour that he refuses to play arenas again until 1976. In order to join the Chicago tour, Springsteen turns down two dates in Florida opening for Stevie Wonder.

5/31/73 Richmond, Va., Alfa Studios
Acoustic set is recorded and later broadcast on WGOE radio, Richmond. Satin Doll/Does This Bus Stop at 82nd Street/Circus Song/Growin' Up/New York Song/You Mean So Much to Me.

5/31/73 Richmond, Va., Coliseum
Short opening set includes "Santa Ana," "Secret to the Blues," "Tokyo," "Thundercrack."

6/1/73 Hampton, Va., Coliseum

6/2/73 Bethesda, Md., WHFS radio studios
Five-song acoustic set: Satin Doll/Circus Song/New York Song/Growin' Up/Mary Queen of Arkansas.

6/2/73 Baltimore, Md., Civic Center

6/5/73 New Haven, Conn., Veterans Memorial Coliseum

6/6/73 Philadelphia, Pa., The Spectrum

6/8-9/73 Boston, Mass., Boston Gardens

6/10/73 Springfield, Mass., Civic Center

6/13/73 Binghamton, N.Y., Broome County Memorial Arena
Seven-song set, opening for Chicago. Spirit in the Night/Does This Bus Stop at 82nd Street/Phantoms/Secret to the Blues/Take Me Out

to the Ballgame/Seaside Bar Song/Thundercrack. "Phantoms" will later evolve into "Zero and Blind Terry."

6/14-15/73 New York, N.Y., Madison Square Garden
Chicago tour ends.

6/22-24/73 Seaside Heights, N.J., Fat City
David Sancious's first shows with the band. Following this show, the band spends a week in the studio beginning work on the second album.

7/5-9/73 Bryn Mawr, Pa., The Main Point
William K. Mandel in the *Philadelphia Evening Bulletin*: "Springsteen's genius — yes, I do think he's a genius — lies in his ability to take everyday situations and write songs that are as different as though he were describing scenes on Mars. Then again, he can take weird situations — a surreal circus, for instance — and write a song that in tune, words and actual performance evokes a very special feeling, elicits a sympathetic vibration in the listener that sighs in unison, 'yes, that is really weird and we can share it'."

7/18-23/73 New York, N.Y., Max's Kansas City
Seven-song set now features Sancious on piano. The band co-headlines with Bob Marley and the Wailers. New York City Serenade/Sandy/Spirit in the Night/Does This Bus Stop at 82nd Street/Something You Got/Zero and Blind Terry/Thundercrack.

7/27/73 Los Angeles, Calif., Ahmanson Theater
Bruce performs at the four-day CBS convention in Los Angeles. "Thundercrack"and "Circus Song" are shot for a promotional video. The live "Circus Song" later appears on a CBS Playback single.

7/31-8/2/73 Roslyn, N.Y., My Father's Place
Terrific show on the 31st, 60 minutes of which are broadcast on WLIR radio, Long Island, N.Y. Set includes "You Mean So Much to Me," written around 1971 and played then by the Bruce Springsteen Band. Sandy/New York City Serenade/Spirit in the Night/Does this Bus Stop at 82nd Street/Saint in the City/You Mean So Much to Me/Thundercrack. A Texas tour in mid-August, including multiple night stands in Houston and Dallas, is cancelled to allow for more studio time.

8/5/73 Asbury Park, N.J., Convention Center

8/20-26/73 Boston, Mass., Oliver's
Neal Vitale in the *Boston Globe*: "The set began with a slow, acoustic number, with Bruce accompanied by his own guitar and an accordian, harking back both to the first album and to his languid reticence of earlier in the evening. But slowly, as the rest of the band joined in (adding so tasty bits of sax, organ, piano, bass, drums, mellotron and vocal harmonies), things turned more funky, as they slid into an updated rhythm 'n' blues style, modernized by a shot of rock 'n' roll. . . . It became obvious, as Wednesday night faded into Thursday morning, that this had been the sort of gig to be long remembered; the feeling was that of having seen a totally brilliant, unique, soon-to-be-a-giant artist in his early days before he becomes a star."

8/31-9/2/73 Seaside Heights, N.J., Fat City

9/7/73 Franklin, Mass., Pieri Gym, Dean Junior College

9/8/73 Pittsburgh, Pa., Carnegie-Mellon University
Following this date, shows in Syracuse and Miami are cancelled.

9/28/73 Hampden Sydney, Va., Hampden-Sydney College

9/29/73 Waynesburgh, Va., Waynesburgh College

9/30/73 Stony Brook, N.Y., State University of New York

10/6/73 Villanova, Pa., Villanova University

10/15-18/73 Boston, Mass., Oliver's

10/20/73 West Rindge, N.H., Franklin Pierce College

10/26/73 Geneva, N.Y., Hobart College

10/29-31/73 Bryn Mawr, Pa., The Main Point
Roadie Al Tellone guests on baritone sax. The band plays three songs from the second album which has just been sent to radio stations. Sandy/New York City Serenade/Spirit in the Night/Does This Bus Stop at 82nd Street/E Street Shuffle/Growin' Up/Walking the Dog/For You/Lost in the Flood/Saint in the City/Zero and Blind Terry/Blinded by the Light/Thundercrack.

11/3/73 Houlton, Maine, Rickler College

◄ *The* Darkness *tour, 1978.*

11/5/73 *The Wild, the Innocent and the E Street Shuffle* is released in the U.S.

11/6-10/73 New York, N.Y., Max's Kansas City

11/11/73 Trenton, N.J., Kendall Hall, Trenton State College
According to an article in the Trenton State College newspaper *The Signal*, acoustic guitarist David Bromberg was originally scheduled to headline this show, but refused the offer when he heard that Springsteen was going to open his show. A very unusual set includes "Walking the Dog," "634-5789" and "Twist and Shout."

11/14-16/73 Roslyn, N.Y., My Father's Place

11/17/73 Maneryonk, Pa., Roxy Theater

11/25/73 Amherst, Ma., University of Massachusetts
Opening for John Mayall. A show on the 30th Virginia Commonwealth University in Richmond is cancelled because of contractual problems.

12/1/73 Hamden, Conn., Quinnipiac College

12/6-8/73 Washington, D.C., Childe Harold
Forty-five minute live broadcast by WGTB radio, Washington, D.C., on 12/6/73, including the first known performances of "Let the Four Winds Blow" and "Kitty's Back." Set also includes "For You," "Walking the Dog," "E Street Shuffle" and "Does This Bus Stop at 82nd Street."

12/14/73 Shelton, Conn., Pinecrest

12/15/73 Garden City, N.Y., Nassau Community College

12/20/73 Providence, R.I., Roger Williams College

12/21-22/73 Cherry Hill, N.J., Earlton Lounge

12/23/73 Cassville, N.J., Rova Farms
Outdoor festival appearance.

12/27-30/73 Bryn Mawr, Pa., The Main Point

1/4-6/74 Boston, Mass., Joe's Place
At least one show is both filmed and professionally recorded for use in a Multiple Sclerosis charity television special which never airs. A terrific 14-song set includes the premiere of "Rosalita." New York City Serenade/Spirit in the Night/Does This Bus Stop at 82nd Street/Walking the Dog/Saint in the City/Kitty's Back/Thundercrack/You Mean So Much to Me/Growin' Up/Let the Four Winds Blow/Zero and Blind Terry/Blinded by the Light/For You/Rosalita/Twist and Shout.

1/12/74 Parsippany, N.J., Joint in the Woods
Similar show to the above, but includes the only known performance of "Ring of Fire."

1/19/74 Kent, Ohio, Kent State University
This show is believed to have included the first performance of "Incident on 57th Street." The band is flown from New York to Cleveland specifically for this gig.

1/25/74 Richmond, Va., The Mosque
"Rosalita" ends the set and will be played at nearly every show from now until 1984. Spirit in the Night/New York City Serenade/Blinded by the Light/Let the Four Winds Blow/Kitty's Back/For You/Rosalita/Twist and Shout. A poster advertises the show by saying "Brucie's back in town."

1/26/74 Norfolk, Va., Chrysler Hall
The Charlie Daniels Band opens the show. Set includes "Thundercrack."

1/29/74 Nashville, Tenn., The Music Emporium

2/1/74 Cleveland, Ohio, Allen Theater

2/2/74 Springfield, Mass., Field House, Springfield College
Springsteen headlines the "Winter Weekend Concert."

2/7-9/74 Atlanta, Ga., Poor Richard's

2/12/74 Lexington, Ky., Student Center, University of Kentucky
This appears to be the last date played by Vini Lopez with the E Street Band, as shows booked in Toledo and Columbus are cancelled.

2/23/74 Cookstown, N.J., The New Satellite Lounge
Two shows in one night. Ernest "Boom" Carter plays his first show with the E Street Band.

2/25-27/74 Bryn Mawr, Pa., The Main Point

3/3/74 Washington, D.C., Gaston Hall, Georgetown University
110-minute show on 3/3/74 is broadcast live on WGTB radio, Washington, D.C. Wild Billy's Circus Story/New York City Serenade/Spir-

it in the Night/Walking the Dog/Sandy/E Street Shuffle/Saint in the City/Kitty's Back/For You/Rosalita.

3/7/74 Houston, Tex., Liberty Hall

After two attempts, Bruce and the E Street Band finally make it to Texas, where they are warmly received, thanks in part to a great deal of local radio airplay. Houston becomes one of the first cities outside of the eastern seaboard to get strongly behind Springsteen.

3/8/74 Houston, Tex., KILT Studios

Acoustic set broadcast includes "Something You Got" and "Satin Doll."

3/8-9/74 Houston, Tex., Liberty Hall

Performance on 3/9/74 is broadcast live on KILT radio, Houston. Same set as 3/3/74, but "Blinded by the Light" is played and "Sandy" is not.

3/10/74 Houston, Tex., Liberty Hall

Show on 3/10/74 opens with "Mary Queen of Arkansas" followed by "The Fever," played at the request of fans who have heard the song on the radio, thanks to a tape sent out by Laurel Canyon. Clarence also takes center stage for the barroom classic "Gimme That Wine." Mary Queen of Arkansas/The Fever/Spirit in the Night/Gimme That Wine/E Street Shuffle/Something You Got/Saint in the City/Does This Bus Stop at 82nd Street/Kitty's Back/Ride on Sweet William/Thundercrack/For You/Rosalita.

3/15-16/74 Austin, Tex. Armadillo World Headquarters

Two shows per night. At least one set is filmed professionally, but never issued or used in any form.

3/18-21/74 Dallas, Tex., Gertie's

Because of demand, these shows are moved from the smaller Mother Blues club. *The Dallas Times Herald* describes Springsteen as a "songwriter-guitarist" who "produces a resilient song with a steady beat punched out by an excellent bass player. Jazz-influenced numbers and some near-Frank Sinatra ballads fill out his set."

3/24/74 Phoenix, Ariz., Celebrity Theater

Bruce headlines this show opened by Leo Kottke. The set opens with "Wild Billy's Circus Story" and includes Bruce's solo piano performance of "For You." Phoenix becomes the band's second major western market (along with Texas), and would play host to some of their biggest shows over the next 18 months. He sells out this theater (one of the biggest the band had played to date), largely on the strength of a great deal of local airplay on KDKB. Springsteen was originally scheduled to play Phoenix three months earlier on tour with Roger McGuinn, but the show was cancelled. Phoenix was also part of the cancelled Paul Butterfield tour itinerary a year earlier.

The day before the show, Springsteen plays deejay on KDKB and describes the experience in the *New Times*: "Got to play all my favorite records. Because you go to these stations, you come in, you sit down and the guy goes, 'Okay, what do you want to talk about?' And I don't want to talk about anything. I don't want to talk about Nixon, I don't want to talk about sidewalks. I don't have nothing to talk about. So sometimes, they just let me whack away at their records. People will get a better idea of where you're at from the records you play — you know, you play 'Surfer Girl' and then you play 'Sandy' and there's an understanding right away, (more) than if I sat there for a half hour and bullshitted 'Well, "Sandy" is about living at the beach,' you know? And if you play 'Born to Be Wild' you flash on the connection. There's no way you can talk about it. Music itself is the easiest explanation." About the reception in Phoenix, Springsteen tells the paper, "We have never ever in my life gotten receptions like this latest tour. It just doesn't happen. Ask my manager. Who the hell thought that anybody was going to come see us in Phoenix, Arizona?"

4/5/74 Chester, Pa., Macmorland Center, Widener College

4/6/74 Pemberton, N.J., Burlington County College

4/7/74 South Orange, N.J., Seton Hall University

4/9/74 Boston, Mass., WBCN Studios

Forty-five-minute acoustic set including the only known acoustic version of "Rosalita." Satin Doll/Does This Bus Stop at 82nd Street/Growin' Up/Wild Billy's Circus Story/Sandy/Rosalita.

4/9-12/74 Cambridge, Mass., Charlie's Bar

Originally scheduled for Joe's Place, but moved when that club burns down. One of the show's at Charlie's is held as a benefit for Joe's Place owner Joe Spadafora.

4/13/74 Parsippany, N.J., Joint in the Woods

4/18/74 West Long Branch, N.J., Monmouth College

4/19/74 New Brunswick, N.J., New Jersey State Theater

4/20/74 Collegeville, Pa., Ursinus College

4/26/74 Providence, R.I., Alumni Hall, Brown University

4/27/74 Storrs, Conn., University of Connecticut

Laurel Canyon records also indicate a show at the University of Hartford on this day.

4/28/74 Swarthmore, Pa., Swarthmore College

Outdoor show in a natural amphitheater.

4/29/74 Northampton, Pa., Roxy Theater

5/4/74 Upper Montclair, N.J., Montclair State College

5/6/74 Newtown, Pa., Bucks County Community College

5/9/74 Cambridge, Mass., Harvard Square Theater

Bruce opens for Bonnie Raitt. This show is attended by Jon Landau and results in a rave review in *The Real Paper* which includes the quote "I saw rock 'n' roll future and its name is Bruce Springsteen." In response to the attention the quote receives in other media, and growing fan support within certain segments of the company, Columbia begins using the quote in advertising and promotional materials, marking a dramatic shift in the label's overall feelings towards Springsteen. Bruce adds "I Sold My Heart to the Junkman" to the regular set. Other sources claim both "Born to Run" and "She's the One" premiered here, but this cannot be confirmed. Partial set list: New York City Serenade/Spirit in the Night/I Sold My Heart to the Junkman/Does This Bus Stop at 82nd Street/Saint in the City/The E Street Shuffle/Kitty's Back/Rosalita. A show the following night in Providence is cancelled.

5/11/74 Teaneck, N.J., Fairleigh Dickinson University

Bruce turns down an opportunity to open for the Eagles at the Academy of Music in New York City to play this small show. Dates following in Glassboro, N.J., and Greenville, Tenn., are cancelled.

5/24/74 Trenton, N.J., War Memorial

5/25/74 Radnor, Pa., Archbishop Carroll High School

5/28-29/74 Bryn Mawr, Pa., The Main Point

5/31/74 Columbus, Ohio, The Agora

6/1/74 Kent, Ohio, Kent State University

Bruce opens for Black Oak Arkansas.

6/2/74 Toledo, Ohio, The Agora

6/3/74 Cleveland, Ohio, The Agora

Sixty minutes of the show are broadcast live on WMMS radio, Cleveland. Songs broadcast are Spirit in the Night/E Street Shuffle/Sandy/Tokyo/Rosalita/Let the Four Winds Blow/You Never Can Tell/I'm Ready. A number of dates in the South (some opening for the Guess Who), including Oklahoma City, Arlington, Tex., and Houston, are cancelled, as is a date opening for Frank Zappa in St. Louis on July 5th. Scheduled dates in Kansas City on the 19th, and a week of dates in Memphis beginning on the 26th may have been fulfilled, though this cannot be confirmed. It is very likely that during the gap between this show and the concerts at the Bottom Line, that the band traveled to 914 Sound Studios in Blauvelt, N.Y. and recorded the first track for Bruce's third album, "Born to Run."

7/12-14/74 New York, N.Y., The Bottom Line

"Jungleland" premieres on 7/13/74 in a version much different from the final released version. The song is much longer and more jazz-styled, and omits the now-famous saxophone solo. Then She Kissed Me/Spirit in the Night/Does This Bus Stop at 82nd Street/E Street Shuffle/Saint in the City/No Money Down/Jungleland/Born to Run/Sandy/Kitty's Back/New York City Serenade/Rosalita. To play the Bottom Line gigs, Bruce turns down opportunities to open for Chuck Berry and Z.Z. Top, and cancels an appearance at the Ozark Music Festival in Sedalia, Mo. The reaction to Jon Landau's quote begins to turn attention is Bruce's favor, and the band travels to the West Coast at the end of the month to play a few select dates, including a CBS showcase at the Troubadour.

7/25/74 Santa Monica, Calif., Santa Monica Civic Auditorium

Michael Davis in *Phonograph Record*: " . . . the crowd had already been

Dallas, Tex., September 16, 1974.

worn out by Bruce Springsteen . . . from the third song on, each number was followed by a standing ovation. The Civic didn't sound half empty during Springsteen's set, that's for sure. If Columbia doesn't put out a live album by this man soon, they're crazy." Bruce opens a gig for Dr. John, though for one of the first times, Bruce is given "100 percent special guest star" billing, meaning his name is mentioned as prominently as Dr. John's in all advertisements for the show.

7/26/74 San Diego, Calif.

7/27/74 Phoenix, Ariz. Celebrity Theater
Again thanks to radio airplay and enormous word-of-mouth reviews of Bruce's last show in the area, this Phoenix gig is Bruce's biggest paying night to date, drawing well over 3,000 people.

7/28/74 Tucson, Ariz., Tucson Raceway
Outdoor gig at this motor speedway.

7/30/74 Los Angeles, Calif., The Troubadour
An very important gig in Springsteen's career. By all accounts the outstanding performance here helps establish him in Southern California, and converts many formerly apathetic critics and Columbia employees to his camp. The set opens with "Incident on 57th Street" and closes with "Sandy," a few minutes before 4 a.m. A date at the famed Hollywood Bowl during this trip west is discussed, but never goes beyond the planning stages.

8/3/74 New York, N.Y. Central Park Music Festival
Another important gig in the quickly blossoming career of Springsteen, and his first non-club show in New York City, apart from the Chicago shows. Though Bruce is originally scheduled to close the show (replacing Boz Scaggs), he instead opens for the Canadian female crooner Anne Murray in front of 5,000 fans. Springsteen's then manager Mike Appel: "After tickets went on sale, and had not sold very fast, Murray's manager went to the promoter and said, 'Hey. Anne's the bigger star, has sold a lot more records, and tickets aren't yet selling so she should be on top.' The manager made a real big deal of it. So the promoter let Murray's manager have his way, saying how-

ever, nobody is going to want to come on after Bruce. So the show went off. Bruce did an abbreviated set, but it was 75 minutes. Then when he was over, literally 90 percent of the crowd left, there were maybe 150 people left. Murray came on and even the crowd that was left started screaming 'Bruce,' which she thought was 'boos'."

8/9/74 Lenox, Mass., Tanglewood Music Festival

8/13/74 Newark, Del., The Stone Balloon
Rescheduled date from cancelled July gig.

8/14/74 Red Bank, N.J., Carlton Theater
Two shows in one night. David Sancious and Ernest Carter quit the E Street Band following this show, forcing the cancellation of a number of dates in early September.

9/8/74 Asbury Park, N.J., Stone Pony
Bruce and others guest with Southside Johnny.

9/19/74 Bryn Mawr, Pa., The Main Point
First shows for Max Weinberg and Roy Bittan with the E Street Band. Also joining the band on violin is Suki Lahav. Two shows in one night, the first beginning at 9:30, the second commencing 20 minutes after midnight, serve as full dress rehearsals for the new band.

9/20/74 Philadelphia, Pa., Tower Theater
3,000 seats sell-out with just two days advance notice. Much like Phoenix, Springsteen's popularity in Philly seems to grow exponentially with each performance.

9/21/74 Oneonta, N.Y., Ballroom, SUNY

9/22/74 Union, N.J., Kean College

10/4/74 New York, N.Y., Avery Fisher Hall
In retrospect, an enormously important date for Springsteen, as his first headlining show, outside of the clubs, in New York City. Again, thanks to the publicity surrounding Landau's quote, this show receives unprecedented media coverage locally, nationally, and internationally. The reviews are uniformly excellent, including a rave in *Record World* where David McGee (who in the late '80s would slam Springsteen's treatment of roadies Mike Batlan and Doug Sutphin in

New Musical Express) calls Bruce, "a truly original artist; an artist who is eminently appropriate for his time; an artist who is destined to leave an indelible mark on the music." Greg Waller in the *Village Voice* writes, "More than any other rock vocalist I have ever heard in live performance, Bruce Springsteen can articulate a lyric, to locate his delivery at the lyrically appropriate point between whisper and shout. . . . I can only swallow my superlatives and confess to being blinded by the light." Even Ellen Willis in the staid *New Yorker* saw fit to comment, "his recent performance at Avery Fisher hall was the best yet. . . . I'm not yet ready to endorse Jon Landau's rash proclamation that Springsteen is the future of rock and roll, but in the present he sure provides a good night out."

"She's the One" is the third song to be performed live from the as-yet-untitled third album. At this point the song still contains some lyrics that will later be worked into "Backstreets." Incident on 57th Street/Spirit in the Night/Does This Bus Stop at 82nd Street/Cupid/Saint in the City/Lost in the Flood/She's the One/Jungleland/A Love So Fine/Kitty's Back/New York City Serenade/Rosalita/Sandy/Quarter to Three.

10/5/74 Reading, Pa., Albright College
10/6/74 Worcester, Mass., Clark University
10/11/74 Gaithersburg, Md., Shady Grove Music Fair
Tom Zito in the *Washington Post*: "It is quickly apparent why Bruce Springsteen . . . is soon going to be a name to reckon with. Springsteen's not just a desperately vivid lyricist, or an ace guitarist. He turns into a Marlon Brando rock performer on the stage in his black leather jacket, raggedly red shirt and jeans, clutching his fists, flailing his arms and stomping around the stage like a method actor psyching his lines out of himself." Martin Mull opens the show.
10/12/74 Princeton, N.J., Alexander Hall, Princeton University
Similar set to 10/4/74, with "A Love So Fine" as the encore.
10/18/74 Passaic, N.J., Capitol Theater
Craig Zeller in the *Aquarian*: "Bruce Springsteen hit the stage and proceeded to shake it up like it's never been shook before. He absolutely exploded into the audience. From the opening song, the anguished "Incident on 57th Street" done simply with a beautiful piano-violin accompaniment, Springsteen had me transfixed." Dan Fogelberg and John Sebastian open the show. Again, similar to the basic set of 10/4/74, but with the addition of Ben E. King's "Spanish Harlem."
10/19/74 Schenectady, N.Y., Union College
Show includes "Spanish Harlem" and "Lost in the Flood."
10/20/74 Carlisle, Pa., Dickinson College
10/25/74 Hanover, N.H., Spaulding Auditorium, Dartmouth College
10/26/74 Springfield, Mass., Springfield College
A date in Millersville, Pennsylvania, the following day is cancelled as Bruce comes down with laryngitis.
10/29/74 Boston, Mass., Music Hall
Set includes "Cupid." Peter Gelzinis in the *Herald American*: "The show was built around the personality of a gang leader. Bruce Springsteen is a fine actor who turned the stage into a street corner. The sounds of Clarence Clemons's super sax could pass for a cruising police car, Dan Federici's grumbling organ could signal a rumble on the way, Roy Bittan's piano along with Suki Lahav's brilliant violin work created the tenderness that street people often hide under a swagger they learn when imitating the tough guys is all that matters in life. . . . Holding his guitar like a machine gun and jumping around stage and looking like a cross between Brando in *The Wild One*, Elvis and Jerry Lee Lewis all in one — his gravely, city-worn voice screamed out his story."
11/1-2/74 Philadelphia, Pa., Tower Theater
Bruce's audience grows in his home away from home, Philadelphia, as two shows here draw over 4,000 people.
11/6-7/74 Austin, Tex., Armadillo World Headquarters
Posters say "The Lone Star Comes Back to Texas."
11/8/74 Corpus Christi, Tex., Ritz Music Hall
11/9/74 Houston, Tex., Music Hall

◄ *Philadelphia, Pa., May 26, 1978.*

A final night on the Texas tour in Dallas is cancelled. Upon returning to the East Coast, recording begins again at 914 Studio in Blauvelt.
11/15/74 Easton, Pa., Lafayette College
11/16/74 Washington, D.C., Gaston Hall, Georgetown University
11/17/74 Charlottesville, Va., University of Virginia
11/21/74 Camden, N.J., Camden Community College
11/22/74 West Chester, Pa., West Chester State College
11/23/74 Salem, Mass., Salem State College
11/29-30/74 Trenton, N.J., War Memorial Building
Great set, including the premiere of Dylan's "I Want You." Incident on 57th Street/Spirit in the Night/Does This Bus Stop at 82nd Street/I Want You/Growin' Up/Saint in the City/E Street Shuffle/Jungleland/Kitty's Back/New York City Serenade/Rosalita/ Sandy/A Love So Fine/Wear My Ring Around Your Neck/Quarter to Three.
12/6/74 New Brunswick, N.J., New Jersey State Theater
12/7/74 Geneva, N.Y., Geneva Theatre, Hobert College
12/8/74 Burlington, Vt., Memorial Auditorium, Univ. of Vermont
12/14/74 New Brunswick, N.J., Rutgers University
Bruce joins Billy Joel onstage for an encore of "Twist and Shout." Earlier in the show, Joel dedicates "The Entertainer" to Springsteen.
2/5/75 Bryn Mawr, Pa., The Main Point
Benefit concert for WMMR radio, Philadelphia. Tremendous 18-song set includes the premiere of "Thunder Road," which at the time was called "Wings for Wheels." Incident on 57th Street/Mountain of Love/Born to Run/E Street Shuffle/Thunder Road/I Want You/Spirit in the Night/She's the One/Growin' Up/Saint in the City/Jungleland/Kitty's Back/New York City Serenade/Rosalita/Sandy/A Love So Fine/For You/Back in the USA.
2/6-7/75 Chester, Pa., Widener College
An enterprising student captures some of the earliest footage of Springsteen on video.
2/18/75 Cleveland, Ohio, John Carroll University
2/19/75 University Park, Pa., Penn State University
2/20/75 Pittsburgh, Pa., University of Pittsburgh
Richie Havens opens.
2/23/75 Westbury, N.Y., Westbury Music Fair
Carola Dibbell in the *Village Voice*: "Clomping more, trucking less, capable of grace but more interested in fun, Springsteen is one of the great rock movers and the only performer I have ever seen who seemed to actually like the Westbury revolving stage, which he rode like a tame Tilt-a-Whirl, walking against the revolution and noting, 'I like this, I stay in one place,' The section of audience in front of the one place cheered." Encores include "Wear My Ring Around Your Neck" and "Quarter to Three." Shows in Syracuse and at SUNY. in upstate New York the first two days of March are cancelled.
3/7/75 Baltimore, Md., Painters Mill Music Fair
3/8-9/75 Washington, D.C., Constitution Hall
Suki Lahav plays her last shows with the E Street Band. Dates stretching into April, including Atlanta and Notre Dame University, are cancelled to allow for more studio time.

· · · · ·

BORN TO RUN TOUR

7/20/75 Providence, R.I., Palace Theater
The *Born to Run* tour opens in Providence, after original opening dates at the Beacon Theater in New York City fall through. Miami Steve Van Zandt plays his first show with the E Street Band. Incident on 57th Street/Spirit in the Night/Tenth Avenue Freeze-out/Growin' Up/Saint in the City/E Street Shuffle/Born to Run/Thunder Road/New York City Serenade/Kitty's Back/Rosalita/Sandy/A Love So Fine/Sha La La/Quarter to Three.
7/22/75 Geneva, N.Y., Geneva Theater
Same set at 7/20/75, but "She's the One" replaces "Thunder Road." Soundcheck includes "Needles and Pins," "You Really Got Me," "Cry to Me," "Let the Four Winds Blow," "Soothe Me," and "Higher and Higher."
7/23/75 Lenox, Mass., The Music Inn
Similar set to the preceding night, with the addition of "Thunder

Road" and Clarence Clemons's "Gimme That Wine," as well as an unknown instrumental. A rare afternoon appearance in front of a huge crowd of over 7,000.

7/25/75 Kutztown, Pa., Keystone Hall
Bruce plays two shows in two days: one in the city, one on campus.

7/26/75 Kutztown, Pa., Kutztown State College

7/28-30/75 Washington, D.C., Carter Barron Amphitheater
Set on 7/28 includes "Sandy," "Carol," and "A Love So Fine" in the encores.

8/1/75 Richmond, Va., The Mosque
Set includes "Up on the Roof" and "Quarter to Three" in the encores. C.A. Bustard in the *Richmond Times-Dispatch*: "Like (Van) Morrison and a number of others, Springsteen can trace his music back to the early '60s, when the rhythm and blues of the Northern ghettos was the best pop music you could find. In most songs, he raises the ghosts of Major Lance, Jan Bradley, early Curtis Mayfield, Etta James; you imagine you are hearing an old tape from the Apollo Theater."

8/2/75 Norfolk, Va., Chrysler Auditorium

8/8/75 Akron, Ohio, Civic Theater
Set includes "Then She Kissed Me," "Up on the Roof" and an encore of "Sandy," "A Love So Fine," "Havin' a Party," "Carol," and "Quarter to Three."

8/9/75 Pittsburgh, Pa., Syria Mosque

8/10/75 Cleveland, Ohio, Allen Theater
Set includes "Up on the Roof." Jane Scott in the *Cleveland Plain Dealer*: "He looked like a cross between a dock hand and a pirate. He stood on the darkened Allen Theater stage last night in black greaser jacket, blue jeans, a gray wool cap pulled over an eye and a gold earring in his left ear. Only a pianist played as he began singing about slums and switchblades in his 'Incident on 57th Street.' His name is Bruce Springsteen. He will be the next superstar."

8/13-17/75 New York, N.Y., The Bottom Line
John Rockwell in the *New York Times*: "The cause of the turmoil was a man who might just be the next Mr. Jagger, a 25-year-old rock 'n' roll poet from New Jersey named Bruce Springsteen. And as his earlier performances here had led one to expect, he had two shows Wednesday that will rank among the great rock experiences of those lucky enough to get in. Mr. Springsteen has it all — he is a great lyricist and songwriter, he is a wonderful singer, guitarist and piano player, he has one of the best rock bands anybody has ever heard, and he is as charismatic as stage figure as rock has ever produced."

Bruce gives five nights of shows, with two shows per night. On 8/14/75, a 14-song set includes "Then She Kissed Me" and the premiere of "Night." The show on 8/15/75 is broadcast live on WNEW radio, New York City. Perhaps the most famous show Bruce ever gave. Tenth Avenue Freeze-out/Spirit in the Night/Then She Kissed Me/Growin' Up/Saint in the City/E Street Shuffle/Every Time You Walk in the Room/She's the One/Born to Run/Thunder Road/Kitty's Back/Rosalita/Sandy/Quarter to Three. On 8/16/75, another great set includes "Then She Kissed Me," "It's Gonna Work Out Fine," "Sha La La," "Every Time You Walk in the Room" and "Up on the Roof." The show on 8/17/75 is the same set as 8/16/75, but without "Sha La La" and "Up on the Roof."

8/21-23/75 Atlanta, Ga., Electric Ballroom
Seventeen-song set on 8/21/75 includes "Does This Bus Stop at 82nd Street" for the first time on the tour.

9/1/75 *Born to Run* is released in the U.S.

9/6/75 New Orleans, La., Theater for the Performing Arts
Sell-out crowd of 2,400. Bruce brings Boz Scaggs onstage for a third and final encore of "Twist and Shout."

9/7/75 New Orleans, La., Ya Ya Lounge

9/12/75 Austin, Tex., Municipal Auditorium
Encores include "Save the Last Dance for Me." A show in Arlington the previous night is cancelled.

9/13-14/75 Houston, Tex., Music Hall
Seventeen-song set on 9/13/85 includes Manfred Mann's "Pretty Flamingo." Incident on 57th Street/Tenth Avenue Freeze-out/Spirit in the Night/Pretty Flamingo/Growin' Up/Saint in the City/E Street Shuffle/She's the One/Born to Run/Thunder Road/Kitty's Back/

Jungleland/Rosalita/Sandy/Quarter to Three/Carol/Lucille.

9/16/75 Dallas, Tex., Convention Center Theatre
Originally scheduled for the Electric Ballroom.

9/17/75 Oklahoma City, Okla., Music Hall

9/20/75 Grinnell, Iowa, Grinnell College

9/21/75 Minneapolis, Minn., Guthrie Theater
Set includes "Pretty Flamingo," "Incident on 57th Street," "Then She Kissed Me" and "Backstreets."

9/23/75 Ann Arbor, Mich., Hill Auditorium, University of Michigan
Nineteen-song set opens with "Thunder Road" and closes with encores of "Detroit Medley," "Sandy," "Quarter to Three," "Carol," and "Twist and Shout."

9/25/75 Chicago, Ill., Auditorium Theatre
Variety Magazine described the show as, "a delirious two-and-a-half hour celebration of what rock music is all about: reckless, rough and tumble stage antics; screamingly evocative vocals and a blistering wall of sound from one of America's best bands. All bathed in an exuberant light show." Set includes "Pretty Flamingo."

9/26/75 Iowa City, Iowa, Hancher Auditorium, University of Iowa
Fifteen-song set opens with "Meeting Across the River," and includes "Kitty's Back" and "Saint in the City."

9/27/75 St. Louis, Mo., Ambassador Theater

9/28/75 Kansas City, Mo., Memorial Hall, University of Missouri

9/30/75 Omaha, Neb., Music Hall
Because of ticket demand, the show is moved from the campus of the University of Nebraska to the 3,000 seat Music Hall.

10/2/75 Milwaukee, Wis., Uptown Theater
Famous "bomb scare" show. "Meeting Across the River" premieres. Seven songs are played before the band leaves the stage because of a bomb threat. Just after midnight, they return after apparently spending most of the time off the stage in a bar, for what can only be described as a very loose second set. Meeting Across the River/Tenth Avenue Freeze-out/Spirit in the Night/Pretty Flamingo/She's the One/Born to Run/Thunder Road/Little Queenie/E Street Shuffle/Saint in the City/Sha La La/Kitty's Back/Jungleland/Rosalita/Detroit Medley/Sandy/Quarter to Three.

10/4/75 Detroit, Mich., Michigan Palace
Six-song encore of "Detroit Medley," "Sandy," "Ain't Too Proud to Beg" (sung for the only time as a duet with Steve), "Quarter to Three," "Little Queenie," and "Twist and Shout." A series of southern dates, including Memphis, Shreveport, Knoxville and Nashville, appear to have been cancelled to move up dates on the West Coast.

10/11/75 Red Bank, N.J., Carlton Theater
Two shows in one night. The theater marquee reads simply "The Homecoming." Early set opens with "Meeting Across the River," and also includes "Pretty Flamingo" and "Sandy." Late set opens with "Incident on 57th Street," and includes "Carol" in the encores.

10/16/75 Los Angeles, Calif., The Roxy
Bruce plays four nights, with two sets per night. Jimmy Iovine is present in the mobile recording truck, documenting every performance. On this evening, one of the sets is open exclusively to *Billboard* magazine staff and guests, prompting Bruce to proclaim with a vengeance during the radio broadcast the following night: "Ain't nobody here from *Billboard* tonight," which becomes the title of a famous bootleg LP of the show. The incident appears to have stuck with him, for when Springsteen returns here in '78, he makes sure that fans are allowed access to the tickets, and comments during the radio broadcast of the July 1978 show, "I don't play no private parties."

10/17/75 Los Angeles, Calif., The Roxy
Early set broadcast live on K-WEST radio, Los Angeles, includes "Pretty Flamingo" and "Goin' Back." Late show includes "It's Gonna Work Out Fine" and "Every Time You Walk in the Room."

10/18/75 Los Angeles, Calif., The Roxy
First show of the night is one of the 16 source concerts for *Live 1975-85*, and is also shot professionally on video, though the footage remains unseen to this day. The opening number, "Thunder Road," is played by Bruce, alone on piano. Thunder Road/Tenth Avenue

Asbury Park, N.J., July 31, 1987. ▶

Freeze-out/Spirit in the Night/E Street Shuffle/Every Time You Walk in the Room/She's the One/Born to Run/Sandy/Backstreets/Kitty's Back/Jungleland/Rosalita/Goin' Back/Carol. Late set includes "Pretty Flamingo."

10/19/75 Los Angeles, Calif., The Roxy

10/25/75 Portland, Ore., Paramount Theater

10/26/75 Seattle, Wash., Paramount Theater
Sixteen-song set includes encores of "Detroit Medley," "For You," "Quarter to Three," "Carol," and "Twist and Shout." A show is scheduled for Eugene, Oregon on 10/28, but it is cancelled.

10/30/75 Sacramento, Calif., Memorial Auditorium
Mark Gerig in *Rock-N-Roll Magazine*: "Bruce Springsteen is from New Jersey, home of Stephen Crane. . . . Bruce Springsteen to music may be what Crane was to literature, since Springsteen describes his slices of life in a related naturalistic impressionism. This style scrutinized artistically is comprised of individual colored dots representing with Springsteen the musically vivid colors of Bo Diddley, the Mar-Keys, and Them with Van Morrison. Springsteen knows how to place these important images so that close together, they seem blurred personalities, but at a distance they mesh into one sound that someday may be his distinctive own."

10/31/75 Oakland, Calif., Paramount Theater
Joel Selvin in the *San Francisco Chronicle*: "The lighting scheme, the heavily rehearsed monologues, the band members' uptown outfits, the overdone theatrics; all these were obvious elements of show business schlock inserted to the detriment of Springsteen coming across like the genuine street-wise, rebel rocker he may very well be."

11/1/75 Santa Barbara, Calif., Robertson Gym, UCSB

11/3-4, 6/75 Tempe, Ariz. Gammage Auditorium, ASU
Bruce's biggest-paying gigs to date, playing to over 6,000 people in three nights.

11/10/75 Tampa, Fla., Jai Alai Fronton
Fifteen-song set includes "Growin' Up."

11/11/75 Miami, Fla., Jai Alai Fronton

11/18/75 London, England, Hammersmith Odeon
Bruce's first European show ever includes "Lost in the Flood" for the first time since 10/74.

11/21/75 Stockholm, Sweden, Konserthuset
A reviewer in the Swedish paper *Aftonbladet* declares: "This half hour after the concert I am still a bit shaken. For once in my life I found myself standing up in the seat screaming for more. . . . It is good to be exhausted and happy after a rock concert."

11/23/75 Amsterdam, The Netherlands, R.A.I. Center

11/24/75 London, England, Hammersmith Odeon
Michael Watts in *Melody Maker*: "There are a few, I believe, though in a minority, who have expressed doubts about Bruce Springsteen's first London performance at the Hammersmith Odeon last Tuesday. Perhaps it was not surprising. It's hard to be the future of rock and roll every night, especially in a country where practically no one has ever seen you play before. Springsteen, who is no faker, was cast down by a response that was less magnanimous than he usually receives. 'Two cold,' said his manager Mike Appel. 'Too cynical.' His comments would appear to have been invalidated by his artist's second performance on Monday at the same venue. The facts are that Springsteen played three-quarters of an hour over time, returned to the stage five times and did ten encores in all. . . . It was a night on which one's emotions were completely exhausted."

The twenty-two song set is Bruce's longest to date. Footage from this show is later included in the BBC's "Glory Days" special in 1987. The show was described by Peter Gabriel as the second greatest concert he had ever seen, second only to Otis Redding. In attendance is film director Milos Forman, who attempted to woo Springsteen to Hollywood two weeks earlier for a screen test. Thunder Road/Tenth Avenue Freeze-out/Spirit in the Night/Lost in the Flood/She's the One/Born to Run/Growin' Up/Saint in the City/Pretty Flamingo/ Backstreets/Sha La La/Jungleland/Rosalita/Sandy/Wear My Ring Around Your Neck/Detroit Medley/For You/Every Time You Walk in the Room/Quarter to Three/Twist and Shout/Carol/Little Queenie.

12/2-3/75 Boston, Mass., Music Hall
Set on 12/2/75 includes "Lost in the Flood," "Santa Claus," and "Party Lights." "Pretty Flamingo" and "For You" are both included in the 12/3/75 set.

12/5-7/75 Washington, D.C., McDonough Gym, Georgetown University
Thanks to Bruce's improving "rock star" status, requests for backstage refreshments through contract riders are now being met, including 66 cans of Hawaiian Punch at these shows.

12/10/75 Lewisburg, Pa., Bucknell University, Davis Gym

12/11/75 South Orange, N.J., Walsh Gym, Seton Hall University
A hot eight-song encore includes "Party Lights," "Santa Claus," "Wear My Ring Around Your Neck," and "Twist and Shout."

12/12/75 Greenvale, N.Y., The Dome, C.W. Post College
The show is recorded for potential use on a live album, though only one track is ever used. Set includes "It's My Life," "For You," "Sha La La," and "Santa Claus" which will later be released on the *In Harmony II* LP and as the B-side of "My Hometown."

12/16/75 Oswego, N.Y., State University of New York

12/17/75 Buffalo, N.Y., Kleinhaus Music Hall

12/19/75 Montreal, Quebec, Place des Artes

12/20/75 Ottawa, Ontario, National Arts Centre

12/21/75 Toronto, Ontario, Field House, Seneca College

12/27-28/75 Philadelphia, Pa., Tower Theater
A triumphant homecoming, as Bruce closes the year with four sold-out shows at the Tower Theater. Eighteen-song set on the 28th opens with "Tenth Avenue Freeze-out" in a slowed-down piano version, and also includes "Sha La La."

12/30-31/75 Philadelphia, Pa., Tower Theater
Show opens for the first time with "Night." 12/30/75 set: Night/Tenth Avenue Freeze-out/Spirit in the Night/Does This Bus Stop at 82nd Street/It's My Life/She's the One/Born to Run/It's Gonna Work Out Fine/Growin' Up/Saint in the City/Backstreets/ Mountain of Love/Jungleland/Rosalita/Sandy/Detroit Medley/Thunder Road/ Wear My Ring Around Your Neck/Quarter to Three/For You/Twist and Shout. A similar set on 12/31/75 includes "Pretty Flamingo."

3/21/76 Asbury Park, N.J., Stone Pony
Tour rehearsal in front of 300 invited guests. First performance of "Raise Your Hand."

3/25/76 Columbia, S.C., Township Auditorium
First show of the "Chicken Scratch" tour, named for the unorthodox itinerary the tour follows.

3/26/76 Atlanta, Ga., Fox Theater

3/28/76 Durham, N.C., Duke University
Bruce's largest indoor venue to date as a headliner is the school's 6,000-seat basketball arena.

3/29/76 Charlotte, N.C., Oven's Auditorium

4/1/76 Athens, Ohio, Ohio University

4/2/76 Louisville, Ky., McCouly Hall

4/4/76 East Lansing, Mich., Michigan State University
Eighteen-song set includes "Frankie," which will be recorded for both *Darkness* and *Born in the USA* but not released on either album. Night/Tenth Avenue Freeze-out/Spirit in the Night/It's My Life/ Thunder Road/She's the One/Born to Run/Frankie/Meeting Across the River/Backstreets/Growin' Up/Saint in the City/Jungleland/Rosalita/Raise Your Hand/Sandy/Detroit Medley/Quarter to Three.

4/5/76 Columbus, Ohio, Ohio Theater

4/7-8/76 Cleveland, Ohio, Allen Theater
Same set as 4/4/76, but "Incident on 57th Street" replaces "Meeting Across the River," and Bruce adds "Blinded by the Light" for the first time since 4/74. Set on 4/8/76 includes the last known performance of "Every Time You Walk in the Room."

4/9/76 Syracuse, N.Y., Colgate University
Identical set to 4/7/76.

4/10/76 Wallingford, Conn., Paul Mellon Arts Center, Choate School
Bruce speaks fondly of John Hammond before playing "Growin' Up" at this show, which is played at Hammond's request. Set includes "Pretty Flamingo."

4/12/76 Johnstown, Pa., Memorial Auditorium

Rehearsal at the Hammersmith Odeon, London, England, November 24, 1975.

4/13/76 University Park, Pa., Recreation Hall, Penn State Univ.
Encores include "Raise Your Hand," "Quarter to Three" and "Twist and Shout."
4/15/76 Pittsburgh, Pa., Syria Mosque
4/16/76 Alleghany, N.Y., Allegheny College
4/17/76 Rochester, N.Y., University of Rochester
4/20/76 Johnson City, Tenn., Freedom Hall
4/21/76 Knoxville, Tenn., Civic Auditorium
4/22/76 Blacksburg, Va., Burrus Auditorium
4/24/76 Boone, N.C., Appalachian State University
4/25/76 Greensboro, N.C.
4/26/76 Chattanooga, Tenn., Tivoli Theater
4/28/76 Nashville, Tenn., Grand Ol' Opry House
Springsteen and the E Street Band become the first "hard" rock act to play the Opry house.
4/29/76 Memphis, Tenn., Ellis Auditorium
Eddie Floyd guests on "Knock on Wood" "Yum Yum I Want Some" and "Raise Your Hand." It is after this show that Bruce and Steve take a cab to Graceland, and Bruce jumps the fence in an attempt to meet Elvis Presley.
4/30/76 Birmingham, Ala., Municipal Auditorium
5/3/76 Little Rock, Ark., Robinson Auditorium
Paul Johnson in the *Arkansas Gazette*: "The Doubting Thomases, who had been put off by a super hype last year that had Springsteen on the covers of *Time* and *Newsweek* the same week and had heralded him as the hottest thing in rock since Dylan and the Beatles, must have come away convinced that Springsteen is indeed the best rock musician now performing. . . . The intensity, the sexual power, the sheer energy of the young man cannot be communicated from his records alone; to

see him live is to see a young man so dynamic he makes James Brown look like a sluggard." Set opens with "Tenth Avenue Freeze-out."
5/4/76 Jackson, Miss., Municipal Auditorium
5/6/76 Shreveport, La., Municipal Auditorium
5/8/76 Baton Rouge, La., LSU Assembly Center
5/9-10/76 Mobile, Ala., Municipal Auditorium
5/11/76 Auburn, Ala., Memorial Coliseum, Auburn University
A show in Montgomery the following night cannot be confirmed.
5/13/76 New Orleans, La., Municipal Auditorium
Set includes Gary U.S. Bonds's "New Orleans."
5/26/76 New York, N.Y., Beacon Theatre
Bruce joins Carole King for one song.
5/27/76 West Point, N.Y., Eisenhower Hall, U.S. Military Academy
Bruce mounts a brief two-show tour of the country's military academies.
5/28/76 Annapolis, Md., Halsey Fieldhouse, U.S. Naval Academy
Set includes "Sea Cruise."
5/30/76 Asbury Park, N.J., Stone Pony
Bruce guests with Southside on "Havin' a Party." Some discussions are held to schedule a Springsteen performance for athletes at the Olympic Village in Montreal, but the show does not materialize.
8/1-3/76 Red Bank, N.J., Monmouth Arts Center
Bruce and the E Street Band are joined by the Miami Horns (Rick Gazda, Earl Gardner, Bob Malarch, Bill Zacagni, and Louis Parente) for this second tour of '76 and the '77 tour. They will regularly play on "Tenth Avenue Freeze-out," "Raise Your Hand," and "You Can't Sit Down." Sixteen-song set on 8/1/76 includes the premieres of "Something in the Night" and "Rendezvous." Night/Rendezvous/Spirit in the Night/It's My Life/Thunder Road/She's the One/Born to Run/

Something in the Night/Backstreets/Tenth Avenue Freeze-out/Jungleland/Rosalita/Raise Your Hand/Sandy/She's Sure the Girl I Love/You Can't Sit Down. The 8/2/76 set is the same as 8/1/76, but without "She's Sure the Girl I Love." A 15-song set on 8/3/76 includes "The Promise" for the first time.

8/5-7/76 Red Bank, N.J., Monmouth Arts Center
Same as 8/2/76, with the addition on 8/7/76 of "Growin' Up" and "Quarter to Three."

8/21/76 Waterbury, Conn., Palace Theater
Same set as 8/2/76.

9/4/76 Asbury Park, N.J., Stone Pony
Bruce guests with Southside Johnny on "Havin' a Party."

9/26/76 Phoenix, Ariz., Veterans Memorial Coliseum
Bart Bull in *Sounds*: "Okay, I'll be honest. I'll come clean: as far as I'm concerned, when you're talking about Brucie and the E Streeters, it's not a question of whether or not they're terrific or not, it's just a matter of deciding *how* terrific they were compared to the last time and the time before that and the . . . So much for objectivity. Anyway, this time around they were . . . yep, you guessed it, terrific . . . but maybe not *quite* as terrific as the time when. . . . More attention was given to two new originals that were unveiled, 'Rendezvous' and 'Something in the Night.' Both were interesting, well-formed pieces but the latter stood out as one of the concert's high points. The band moved offstage and Springsteen faced the mike, accompanied only by Roy Bittan's bittersweet piano." Not surprisingly, Phoenix becomes the first city in which Springsteen headlines a sports arena. "Growin' Up" is added in the encores, expanding the standard 8/2/76 set to 16 songs.

9/29-30/76 Santa Monica, Calif., Santa Monica Civic Auditorium
Ricardo Forrest in the U.S.C. *Daily Trojan*: "'Remember,' he whispers before he leaves. 'Remember.' His words echo back 2,000 years to a phrase a certain prophet once uttered. 'Do this in remembrance of me,' he said. Fame is fleeting, I've heard, and the Midas touch is golden until you recollect what happened to Midas. Perhaps Springsteen's words show he is feeling the pressures of rock 'n' roll fame and 'the clock that waits so patiently on your song' that David Bowie spoke so eloquently of. Perhaps we should 'remember' as Springsteen asks us to. The crucifixion may not be that far away." On 9/29/76 "The Promise" replaces "Growin' Up" in the encores, and "Born to Run" closes the show, replacing "You Can't Sit Down" in a 15-song set. "Growin' Up" is added in a 16-song set on 9/30/76. The same set will be played for the next nine shows.

10/2/76 Oakland, Calif., Paramount Theater
Evan Hosie in the *Berkeley Gazette*: "There were some noticeable differences this time around, however. Springsteen's moves, the dramatic lighting, and his comments to the crowd all seemed more calculated — more timed for effect. Although he may be more polished, Springsteen is still inarticulate onstage. A story about a beer, his father, and a screen door was supposedly interrelated, although frustratingly obscure." Joel Selvin in the *San Francisco Chronicle*: "His two-hour concert was as powerful and exciting as rock music gets — in stark contrast to his uneven performance last year. . . . With apparently less on the line than at his last Paramount show, Springsteen opened up and showed some of the stuff that has been knocking East Coast audiences — and critics — on their ears for several years now."

10/3/76 Santa Clara, Calif., Santa Clara University
10/5/76 Santa Barbara, Calif., County Bowl
10/9/76 South Bend, Ind., Notre Dame University
10/10/76 Oxford, Ohio, Miami University
10/12/76 New Brunswick, N.J., Rutgers University
10/13/76 Union, N.J., Wilkins Theater, Kean College
10/16/76 Williamsburg, Va., William and Mary University
10/17-18/76 Washington, D.C., Georgetown University
"You Can't Sit Down" is included in the encores.

10/25/76 Philadelphia, Pa., The Spectrum
Bruce's first headlining arena date on the East Coast, but only after a two-hour-plus soundcheck. Night/Rendezvous/Spirit in the Night/It's My Life/Thunder Road/She's the One/Something in the Night/Backstreets/Growin' Up/Tenth Avenue Freeze-out/Jungleland/Rosalita/Sandy/A Fine, Fine Girl/Raise Your Hand/The Promise/Born to Run.

10/27/76 Philadelphia, Pa., The Spectrum
This show was originally scheduled for 10/26, but Clarence was involved in filming for his cameo in *New York, New York*. Set includes both "Incident on 57th Street" and "A Fine, Fine Girl."

10/28-30/76 New York, N.Y., The Palladium
On 10/29/76, "Quarter to Three" with special guest Gary U.S. Bonds replaces "A Fine, Fine Girl." The set on 10/30/76 is the same as 10/25/76, with special guest Patti Smith on "Rosalita."

11/2/76 New York, N.Y., The Palladium
11/3-4/76 New York, N.Y., The Palladium
"Mona" is played for the first time on 11/3/76 as an intro to "She's the One." The Beach Boys' "Be True to Your School" is transformed by Bruce into "Be True To Your Band" as a segue to "Rosalita." "Twist and Shout" includes "Farmer John" and "A Fine, Fine Girl" is also included in a 15-song set. The set on 11/4/76 is broadcast on WCOZ radio, Boston, at a later date. Bruce and the E Street Band are joined for this set by Ronnie Spector, who sings on "Baby I Love You," "Walking in the Rain," and "Be My Baby." First known version of the Animals' "We Gotta Get Outta This Place" by Springsteen and the E Street Band.

With the tour over, and the lawsuit still pending, Springsteen's immediate plans are unclear. The November 20, 1976 issue of *New Musical Express* reports that Springsteen and Bob Marley will tour the U.S. and Europe on a co-headlining tour beginning in April 1977, followed by dates in Europe. Though the paper states that contracts had already been signed, the tour never materializes.

11/26/76 New York, N.Y., The Bottom Line
Bruce guests with Patti Smith on piano and guitar, during her early and late shows. Both sets include "Gloria" and "My Generation."

2/7/77 Albany, N.Y., Palace Theater
2/8/77 Rochester, N.Y., Auditorium Theater
Show opens for the first time with "Something in the Night." Soundcheck includes first ever version of "Don't Look Back" as well as another new song, "Action in the Streets," played later that evening and featuring the Miami Horns. "Action in the Streets" belongs to the family of very similar songs that also includes "A Love So Fine" and later "Paradise by the C." All share the same basic style and melody. Something in the Night/Rendezvous/Spirit in the Night/It's My Life/Thunder Road/Mona/She's the One/Tenth Avenue Freeze-out/Action in the Streets/Backstreets/Jungleland/Rosalita/Sandy/Raise Your Hand/The Promise/Born to Run.

2/9/77 Buffalo, N.Y., Kleinhaus Music Hall
2/10/77 Utica, N.Y., Memorial Auditorium
2/12/77 Ottawa, Ontario, Civic Centre
This show also opens with "Something in the Night."

2/13/77 Toronto, Ontario, Maple Leaf Gardens Concert Bowl
"Night" opens the show, and "Something in the Night" is moved to the middle of the set. "The Promise" and "Sandy" are taken out of the encores, and "Growin' Up" is added to the set.

2/15/77 Detroit, Mich., Masonic Temple Auditorium
Show again opens with "Something in the Night." "Raise Your Hand" and "Growin' Up" are left out of the set.

2/16/77 Columbus, Ohio, Franklin County Veterans Memorial Auditorium
2/17/77 Cleveland, Ohio, Richfield Coliseum
Ronnie Spector and Flo and Eddie guest on "Baby, I Love You," "Walking in the Rain," "Say Goodbye to Hollywood," and "Be My Baby." Ronnie Spector later records "Say Goodbye to Hollywood" with the E Street Band. This 17-song set also includes the first 1977 appearance of "Quarter to Three."

2/19/77 St. Paul, Minn., Civic Centre
Short and standard 13-song set.

2/20/77 Madison, Wisc., Dane County Coliseum
2/22/77 Milwaukee, Wisc., Milwaukee Arena
Fourteen-song set.

2/23/77 Chicago, Ill., Auditorium Theater
"The Promise" and "Quarter to Three" are played in the encores.

Austin, Tex., November 9, 1980. ▶

2/25/77 Lafayette, Ind., Purdue University
2/26/77 Indianapolis, Ind., Convention Center
A 13-song set.
2/27/77 Cincinnati, Ohio
2/28/77 St. Louis, Mo., Fox Theater
Standard 14-song set.
3/2/77 Atlanta, Ga., Civic Center
3/4/77 Jacksonville, Fla., Auditorium
3/5/77 Orlando, Fla., Jai Alai Fronton
"Sandy" returns to the encores.
3/6/77 Miami, Fla., Jai Alai Fronton
3/10/77 Toledo, Ohio, Centennial Arena
First in-concert performance of "Don't Look Back," which replaces "Rendezvous." "Growin' Up" is also included in a 14-song set.
3/11/77 Latrobe, Pa., St. Vincent's College
"Sandy" and "Rendezvous" both return to a 15-song set that closes with "Twist and Shout."
3/13/77 Baltimore, Md., Towson State College
"Don't Look Back" replaces "Rendezvous," as it will for the remainder of the '77 tour. "Something in the Night" is left out of the set.
3/14/77 Poughkeepsie, N.Y., Mid-Hudson Civic Center
"Something in the Night" replaces "It's My Life" in a 13-song set.
3/15/77 Binghampton, N.Y., Broome County Veterans Arena
"It's My Life" replaces "Something in the Night."
3/18/77 New Haven, Conn., Veterans Memorial Coliseum
3/19/77 Lewiston, Maine, Central Maine Youth Center
3/20/77 Providence, R.I., Alumni Hall, Providence College
3/22-25/77 Boston, Mass., Music Hall
Bruce brings back "The Promise" and "You Can't Sit Down" in a 16-song set on the first night of four that many consider to be among the finest shows of his career. The second night is another excellent 15-song set that includes "Growin' Up," "Incident on 57th Street," and "Little Latin Lupe Lu" which is played for the first time. On 3/24/77, surprises continue as Bruce brings back "Saint in the City" for the first time since 5/27/76. The 17-song set closes with a terrific cover of Jackie Wilson's "Higher and Higher," previously played only in a soundcheck on 7/22/75. The final night is another candidate for greatest show ever. The Miami Horns play on "Tenth Avenue Freeze-out," "Rosalita," and the final four songs of the encores. The set list speaks for itself: Night/Don't Look Back/Spirit in the Night/Incident on 57th Street/Thunder Road/Mona/She's the One/Tenth Avenue Freeze-out/Action in the Streets/Saint in the City/Backstreets/Jungleland/Rosalita/ Born to Run/Quarter to Three/Little Latin Lupe Lu/You Can't Sit Down/Higher and Higher.
4/17/77 Asbury Park, N.J., Stone Pony
Bruce guests with Southside Johnny.
5/12-13/77 Red Bank, N.J., Monmouth Arts Center
Bruce, Steve Van Zandt and Ronnie Spector front the Asbury All-Star Revue. On 5/12/77 Bruce backs up Steve, taking vocals on "The Fever" and sharing vocals on "I Don't Wanna Go Home" and "Havin' a Party." The E Street Band and Bruce play "Thunder Road," "Rendezvous," "Backstreets," and "Born to Run." At the early show on 5/13/77, Bruce and the E Street Band play "Thunder Road." At the late show they perform "Thunder Road" and "Higher and Higher." Bruce also sings "Amen" with Miami Steve and duets with Ronnie Spector on "You Mean So Much to Me."
9/4/77 Asbury Park, N.J., Stone Pony
Bruce joins the Shots onstage, playing guitar on "Funky Broadway" and "Further on Up the Road."
9/13/77 Asbury Park, N.J., Stone Pony
Bruce guests with Southside Johnny and then brings out the E Street Band for "Thunder Road," "Mona," "She's the One," and "Born to Run."
10/13/77 Asbury Park, N.J., Stone Pony
Bruce guests with Southside Johnny for a five-song set of "Down in the Valley," "Ain't Too Proud to Beg," "Soothe Me," "Let the Good Times Roll," "Carol."
12/2/77 New York, N.Y., NYU Loeb Student Center
Bruce joins Robert Gordon and Link Wray for "Heartbreak Hotel."

12/30/77 New York, N.Y., CBGB's
Bruce joins Patti Smith on "Because the Night."
12/31/77 Passaic, N.J., Capitol Theater
Bruce first joins Southside Johnny and the Jukes for "Havin' a Party," "Higher and Higher," "Little Latin Lupe Lu," and "You Can't Sit Down." Later he brings on the E Street Band for "Backstreets," "Born to Run," and "Quarter to Three." "Backstreets" includes for the first time a new song often called "Sad Eyes," which will later evolve into "Drive All Night." The middle section of "Backstreets," including these new lyrics, will become a favorite of fans on the next tour.
5/19/78 Asbury Park, N.J., Paramount Theater
Tour rehearsal includes most of the new set, plus assorted covers including the Rolling Stones' "Satisfaction" and the Yardbirds' "Heart Full of Soul."

. . . . .

DARKNESS ON THE EDGE OF TOWN TOUR

For song counts on this tour, "Mona/Not Fade Away/Gloria/She's the One" will be counted as one song. "Detroit Medley" consists of "Devil With the Blue Dress," "Jenny Take a Ride," "Good Golly Miss Molly," and "C.C. Rider," and will be counted as one song. On the tour, 118 shows are played. Each show now includes an intermission between two sets, designated by "//."

5/23/78 Buffalo, N.Y., Shea Theater
Soundcheck includes "Is That All to the Ball, Mr. Hall." First show of the *Darkness* tour includes nine songs off the new album and four songs not available on any release. "Prove It All Night" features a beautiful instrumental beginning not on the album, which makes this song one of the highlights of this tour. "The Promise" is played in a full band arrangement. Besides songs from the new record, the instrumental "Paradise by the C" and "Fire" premiere here also. Badlands/Night/Something in the Night/For You/Thunder Road/Spirit in the Night/Prove It All Night/Racing in the Street/Candy's Room/Promised Land//Paradise By the C/Fire/Darkness/Streets of Fire/Mona/She's the One/Adam Raised a Cain/Backstreets/Rosalita/The Promise/Born to Run/Tenth Avenue Freeze-out/You Can't Sit Down.
5/24/78 Albany, N.Y., Palace Theater
"Spirit in the Night" is moved to the front of the first set, where it will remain for the rest of the tour. "Streets of Fire" is left out of the set, as is "You Can't Sit Down."
5/26-27/78 Philadelphia, Pa., The Spectrum
During "Spirit in the Night" on 5/26, Bruce not only enters the crowd, but finishes in a seating section on the second level of the Spectrum. Later in the set, Bruce swings from a rope ladder that leads to the overhead lighting rig. "Growin' Up," "Saint in the City," and "You Can't Sit Down" return to the 22-song set. On 5/27/78, "Jungleland" closes the first set, and "Candy's Room" is not played. Soundcheck includes two versions of "Lucille" and "Jungleland."
5/29-31/78 Boston, Mass., Music Hall
On 5/30/78, "Because the Night" is added to the encores, "You Can't Sit Down" is left out. "Candy's Room" also returns. On 5/31/78, "Quarter to Three" closes the show.
6/1/78 Annapolis, Md., U.S. Naval Academy
6/3/78 Uniondale, N.Y., Nassau Coliseum
"Sandy" and "Quarter to Three" close out the encores.
6/5/78 Toledo, Ohio, Centennial Arena
6/6/78 Indianapolis, Ind., Convention Center
6/6/78 *Darkness on the Edge of Town* is released in the U.S.
6/8/78 Madison, Wisc., Dane County Coliseum
"Jungleland" returns, and "Saint in the City" and "The Promise" are left out of a 20-song set.
6/9/78 Milwaukee, Wisc., Milwaukee Arena

Bryn Mawr, Pa., July 6, 1975.

"Darkness" replaces "Something in the Night." The set now looks like this: Badlands/Night/Spirit in the Night/Darkness/For You/Promised Land/Prove It All Night/Racing in the Street/Thunder Road/Jungleland//Paradise by the C/Fire/Adam Raised a Cain/Mona/She's the One/Growin' Up/Backstreets/Rosalita/Born to Run/Tenth Avenue Freeze-out/Quarter to Three.

6/10/78 Bloomington, Minn., Met Center
6/13/78 Iowa City, Iowa, University of Iowa
6/14/78 Omaha, Neb., Music Hall
"The Promise" returns to the encores.
6/16/78 Kansas City, Mo., Municipal Auditorium
6/17/78 St. Louis, Mo., Kiel Auditorium
6/20/78 Morrison, Colo., Red Rocks Amphitheater
Five-song encore of "The Promise," "Born to Run," "Tenth Avenue Freeze-out," "I Fought the Law," and "Quarter to Three."
6/24/78 Portland, Ore., Paramount Theater
Twenty-one song set again includes "The Promise."
6/25/78 Seattle, Wash., Paramount Theater
Twenty-two song set with "I Fought the Law" in the encores.
6/26/78 Vancouver, British Columbia, Queen Elizabeth Theatre
Vaughn Palmer in the *Vancouver Sun*: "Bruce Springsteen is the one. Monday night at the Queen Elizabeth Theatre, in a two and three-quarter hour outburst of rock and roll, he gave what must be one of the finest shows this city has ever experienced. The audience was completely reduced to screaming, rocking frenzy. They were standing, applauding, and demanding more, more, even after over 200 minutes of music. And there, for one night at least, went our town's laid-back reputation."
6/29/78 San Jose, Calif., Performing Arts Center
6/30-7/1/78 Berkeley, Calif., Community Theater
"Darkness" is dedicated to *Mystery Train* author Greil Marcus. "Paradise by the C" and "Prove It All Night" are recorded for "The King Biscuit Flower Hour."

7/5/78 Los Angeles, Calif., The Forum
The 21-song set includes "Because the Night" in the encores.
7/7/78 Los Angeles, Calif., The Roxy
Broadcast live on KMET radio, Los Angeles, this is one of the 16 source concerts for *Live 1975-85*. "Rave On," "Point Blank," "Independence Day," and "Heartbreak Hotel" are all premiered in a devastating set. Rave On/Badlands/Spirit in the Night/Darkness/Candy's Room/For You (included as the live B-side to "Fire" from *Live 1975-85*)/Point Blank/Promised Land/Prove It All Night/Racing in the Street/Thunder Road//Paradise by the C/Adam Raised a Cain/Mona/She's the One/Growin' Up/Saint in the City/Backstreets/Heartbreak Hotel/Rosalita/Independence Day/Born to Run/Because the Night/Raise Your Hand/Twist and Shout.
7/8/78 Phoenix, Ariz., Veterans Memorial Coliseum
"Raise Your Hand" and "Because the Night" are both included in the encores. This show is filmed for promotional use and "Rosalita" is released as a video in 1984.
7/9/78 San Diego, Calif., Sports Arena
First set includes "I Fought the Law" and "Candy's Room." "Mona/Not Fade Away/Gloria" segues into "She's the One."
7/12/78 Dallas, Tex., Convention Center
"The Promise" returns to the encores.
7/14/78 San Antonio, Tex., Municipal Auditorium
"The Fever" makes a surprise appearance for the first time since 3/74. "Candy's Room" and "The Promise" are also included in a 23-song set.
7/15/78 Houston, Tex., Sam Houston Coliseum
"The Fever" is played in the first set and "Candy's Room" in the second set. This is the last known version of "The Promise."
7/16/78 New Orleans, La., The Warehouse
A problem with the P.A. in the first set causes an unplanned break to solve the technical difficulties, during which time, Steve leads the band through an improvised instrumental vamp.

New York, N.Y., November 27, 1980.

7/18/78 Jackson, Miss., Civic Center
Twenty-song set.

7/19/78 Memphis, Tenn., Ellis Auditorium

7/21/78 Nashville, Tenn., Municipal Auditorium
"Factory" premieres. "Saint in the City" returns to the second set.

7/28/78 Miami, Fla., Jai Alai Fronton
Show opens for the first time with "Summertime Blues"; the second set opens with "Heartbreak Hotel" and includes "I Fought the Law."

7/29/78 St. Petersburg, Fla., Bayfront Civic Center Auditorium
Unusual 20-song set includes covers of Buddy Holly's "Oh Boy" and "Around and Around." Oh Boy/Badlands/Spirit in the Night/Darkness/Factory/Promised Land/Prove It All Night/Racing in the Street/Thunder Road/Jungleland//Paradise by the C/Sandy/Around and Around/Not Fade Away/She's the One/Growin' Up/Backstreets/Rosalita/Born to Run/Because the Night/Quarter to Three.

7/31/78 Columbia, S.C., Municipal Auditorium

8/1/78 Charleston, S.C., Municipal Auditorium

8/2/78 Charlotte, N.C., Charlotte Coliseum

8/4/78 Charleston, W.Va., Civic Center
Show again opens with "Oh Boy" and also includes the premiere of "Sherry Darling," which will later be included on *The River.*

8/5/78 Louisville, Ky., Louisville Gardens
"Sweet Little Sixteen" is included in the first set.

8/7/78 Kalamazoo, Mich., Wings Stadium
Surprisingly, Bruce debuts his newest composition "The Ties That Bind," following "For You" to open the second set. He would continue refining the song at the soundchecks in Passaic, before playing it again formally in concert in Princeton, N.J., November 1, 1978. "Point Blank" and "Rendezvous" also appear in an unusual second set.

8/9/78 Cleveland, Ohio, The Agora

Broadcast live on WMMS radio, Cleveland, for its tenth anniversary. Also rebroadcast on some specially selected FM stations not included on any of the '78 tour simulcasts. "Growin' Up" includes the now-famous "I was a teenage werewolf" story. "Summertime Blues" cranks open the 22-song set, which ends with encores of "Raise Your Hand" and "Twist and Shout."

8/10/78 Rochester, N.Y., War Memorial
"Summertime Blues" opens the first set, "Sweet Little Sixteen" opens the second.

8/12/78 Augusta, Maine, Civic Center

8/14/78 Hampton, Va., Hampton Roads Coliseum
"High School Confidential" opens the 21-song set that again includes "Sweet Little Sixteen."

8/15/78 Landover, Md., Capital Centre
"Summertime Blues" opens Springsteen's most famous unauthorized video, recorded from the closed-circuit television system in the Capital Centre's luxury boxes and arena big-screen. The "Sad Eyes" portion of "Backstreets" includes lyrics from "Pretty Flamingo."

8/18-19/78 Philadelphia, Pa., The Spectrum
Strange soundcheck for the 8/18 set includes "The Harder They Come," "Save the Last Dance for Me," and "The Fever," the only song of the three that will be played later in the show. A 22-song set on that date opens with "Summertime Blues" and includes special guest Gary Busey on "Rave On" and "Quarter to Three." On 8/19/78, Gary Busey again joins Bruce for "Rave On." Bruce starts the show for the first time with "Good Rockin' Tonight," in a 23-song set that also includes "Heartbreak Hotel" and "Sweet Little Sixteen."

8/21-23/78 New York, N.Y., Madison Square Garden
The 8/21 set is the same as 8/19/78, but "Summertime Blues" opens the show, and "Paradise By the C" replaces "Rave On" to open the second set. These are Bruce's first shows in Madison Square Garden

as the headliner. On 8/22, "Candy's Room" is played in the second set, and "Streets of Fire" enters the first set following "Badlands," where it will appear in most of the remaining shows on the tour. The final night's 25-song set includes "High School Confidential," "Heartbreak Hotel" and a visit from Bruce's mother in the encores.

8/25/78 New Haven, Conn., Veterans Memorial Coliseum
A 24-song set includes "It's Gonna Work Out Fine."

8/25/78 New Haven, Conn., Toad's Place
Bruce and Clarence guest with Beaver Brown.

8/26/78 Providence, R.I., Civic Center
A 24-song set opens with "Summertime Blues."

8/28-29/78 Pittsburgh, Pa., Stanley Theater
Hank Williams' "I Heard That Lonesome Whistle" is played for the first and only time on 8/29/78, while "The Fever," "Saint in the City" and "Sandy" join the second set.

8/30/78 Cleveland, Ohio, Richfield Coliseum

8/31/78 Cleveland, Ohio, The Agora
Bruce joins Southside Johnny for "The Fever," "I Don't Wanna Go Home," and "Havin' a Party."

9/1/78 Detroit, Mich., Masonic Temple Auditorium
A 23-song set includes the first performance of Bob Dylan's "Chimes of Freedom." This song will reappear ten years later on the European leg of the *Tunnel of Love Express* tour, as well as the Amnesty International Human Rights Now tour. "Lost in the Flood" is also played for the last time to date.

9/3/78 Saginaw, Mich., Civic Center
Another great 25-song set includes the first appearance of "It's My Life" on the *Darkness* tour, as well as the first known version of "I Don't Wanna Hang Up My Rock 'n' Roll Shoes" and "Good Rockin' Tonight." "Santa Claus" opens the second set.

9/5/78 Columbus, Ohio, Veterans Memorial Auditorium
A 22-song set again includes "It's My Life."

9/6/78 Chicago, Ill., Uptown Theater
A 24-song set.

9/9/78 South Bend, Ind., Notre Dame University
A 22-song set includes first performance of the Swinging Medallions' "Double Shot of My Baby's Love" and "Louie, Louie." "Sandy" is also added to the second set.

9/10/78 Cincinnati, Ohio, Riverfront Coliseum

9/12/78 Syracuse, N.Y., War Memorial Auditorium
Typical set for this part of the tour: Badlands/Streets of Fire/Spirit in the Night/Darkness/Heartbreak Hotel/Factory/Promised Land/Prove It All Night/Racing in the Street/Thunder Road/Jungleland//Paradise by the C/Fire/Candy's Room/Saint in the City/Sandy/Not Fade Away/Gloria/She's the One/Backstreets/Rosalita/Born to Run/Because the Night/Quarter to Three.

9/13/78 Springfield, Mass., Civic Center

9/15-17/78 New York, N.Y., The Palladium
Unusual 23-song set on 9/15 includes "Something in the Night," and the last "Adam Raised a Cain" until Worcester 2/25/88. The first set opens the only time with "Darkness," and the second set opens with "Kitty's Back," played for the first time since Philadelphia 12/27/75. "Tenth Avenue Freeze-out" also returns to the encores, and "I Fought the Law" is added to the first set. On 9/16 "Independence Day" is played for the first time since Los Angeles 7/7/78, while "Point Blank" returns for the first time since Kalamazoo 8/7/78. They will be included in the set for the rest of the tour. "Incident on 57th Street" is played for the first time since Boston 3/25/77, and the "Detroit Medley" is also played for the first time on this tour. "You Can't Sit Down" closes the show. On 9/17 a 24-song set includes "Meeting Across the River" for the first time since 1976. 9/17 set: Badlands/Streets of Fire/Spirit in the Night/Darkness/Independence Day/Factory/Promised Land/Prove It All Night/Racing in the Street/Thunder Road/Meeting Across the River/Jungleland//Kitty's Back/

Tacoma, Wash., May 5, 1988.

Fire/Candy's Room/Because the Night/Point Blank/Not Fade Away/ She's the One/Incident on 57th Street/Rosalita/Born to Run/Tenth Avenue Freeze-out/Detroit Medley/Quarter to Three.

9/19/78 Passaic, N.J., Capitol Theater
Show is broadcast live on WNEW radio, New York City. Similar set to 9/17/78, but without "Factory" or "Incident on 57th Street" and the addition of "Sandy" as the first encore. Show closes with "Raise Your Hand" instead of "Quarter to Three."

9/20-21/78 Passaic, N.J., Capitol Theater
Truly remarkable soundcheck before the show on 9/20/78. "The Ties That Bind" is played in a completely different arrangement than the final released version, that will never be played again. Also included is Hank Williams's "Wedding Bells," which will never be performed in concert. The evening show includes "Incident on 57th Street," "Kitty's Back," "Santa Claus," and "It's My Life," played for the final time. Unusual soundcheck on 9/21/78 includes "Wedding Bells," "I Walk the Line," "Guess Things Happen That Way," and two other songs believed to be called "Hey Porter," and "Go Away." The 24-song set includes "Meeting Across the River," "The Fever" and "Incident on 57th Street."

9/25/78 Boston, Mass., Boston Gardens

9/29/78 Birmingham, Ala., Boutwell Auditorium
A 23-song set again includes "The Fever" and closes with the "Detroit Medley." "Paradise by the C" is played for the final time on the 1978 tour.

9/30/78 Atlanta, Ga., Fox Theatre
A 23-song set is broadcast live across the southeast. "Night Train" enters the second set, replacing "Paradise by the C," which won't appear again for ten years, until its surprising revival in Rotterdam, The Netherlands, 8/29/88. The show opens with "Good Rockin' Tonight," "Santa Claus," and closes with "Raise Your Hand." During the break, Springsteen and Landau reportedly mix the Cleveland, 8/9/78 show recording for potential release.

11/1/78 Princeton, N.J., Jadwin Gym, Princeton University
Soundcheck includes "Thunder Road," "Badlands," "Prove It All Night," and "Promised Land." "The Ties That Bind" is played for the first time, as the fourth song of the set. The arrangement is completely different from the Passaic soundchecks of a month earlier, and similar to the final form that will appear on *The River* LP.

11/2/78 Landover, Md., Capital Centre
"The Ties That Bind" and "Detroit Medley" are both included in a 21-song set.

11/4/78 Burlington, Vt., University of Vermont

11/5/78 Durham, N.H., University of New Hampshire

11/7/78 Ithaca, N.Y., Cornell University

11/8/78 Montreal, Quebec, The Forum
A 21-song set.

11/10/78 Olean, N.Y., St. Bonaventure University

11/12/78 Troy, N.Y., Rensselaer Polytechnic Institute
Soundcheck includes "Badlands," "High School Confidential," "I Don't Wanna Hang Up My Rock 'n' Roll Shoes," "Darkness," and "Promised Land." This 23-song set includes "Sandy" in the encores and "Rave On" opens the second set.

11/14/78 Utica, N.Y., Utica Memorial Auditorium
"Rave On" opens the show, "High School Confidential" opens the second set, and "Louie, Louie" is played in the encores.

11/16/78 Toronto, Ontario, Maple Leaf Gardens
A 22-song set opens for the first time with "Ready Teddy." "The Ties That Bind" opens the second set as it will for most of the remaining shows on the tour.

11/17/78 East Lansing, Mich., Michigan State University

11/18/78 Oxford, Ohio, Millet Hall, Miami University

11/20/78 Champaign, Ill., University of Illinois
A 22-song set, typical of this part of the tour: Badlands/Streets of Fire/Spirit in the Night/Darkness/Independence Day/Promised Land/ Prove It All Night/Racing in the Street/Thunder Road/Jungleland// Saint in the City/The Ties That Bind/Fire/Candy's Room/Because the Night/Point Blank/Mona/She's the One/Backstreets/Rosalita/Born to Run/Detroit Medley/Quarter to Three.

11/21/78 Evanston, Ill., Northwestern University
A 22-song set.

11/25/78 St. Louis, Mo., Kiel Opera House
Second set opens with "For You," and "Tenth Avenue Freeze-out" returns to the encores.

11/27/78 Milwaukee, Wisc., Milwaukee Arena
Second set opens with "The Ties That Bind," followed by "Santa Claus." "Santa Claus" will be played at all remaining shows on the tour.

11/28/78 Madison, Wisc., Dane County Coliseum
"High School Confidential" opens a 23-song set.

11/29/78 St. Paul, Minn., Civic Center
"Tenth Avenue Freeze-out" and "Detroit Medley" are in the encores.

12/1/78 Norman, Okla., Lloyd Noble Center, Univ. of Oklahoma
A 24-song set includes "Heartbreak Hotel," "Factory," and "Saint in the City."

12/3/78 Carbondale, Ill., Arena, Southern Illinois University
Show opens with "High School Confidential."

12/5/78 Baton Rouge, La., Louisiana State University

12/7/78 Austin, Tex., University of Texas
"The Fever" returns to the second set.

12/8/78 Houston, Tex., The Summit
"Badlands" kicks off an excellent 25-song set that closes with "You Can't Sit Down."

12/9/78 Dallas, Tex., Convention Center

12/11/78 Boulder, Colo., University of Colorado

12/13/78 Tucson, Ariz., Community Center
Home stretch of the *Darkness* tour is a streak of superb shows, including this 26-song set that closes with "Quarter to Three."

12/15-16/78 San Francisco, Calif., Winterland
Broadcast live on 12/15/78 across the West Coast, a 25-song set includes one of the very best and passionate performances of "Backstreets" ever. "Fire," recorded live here on 12/16/78, is included on *Live 1975-85*. Terrific follow-up show to the previous night's radio broadcast. Set includes "Good Rockin' Tonight," "Rendezvous,", "Santa Claus," and "The Fever."

12/19/78 Portland, Ore., Paramount Theater
A 26-song set includes "Good Rockin' Tonight," "Rendezvous,""Rave On," and "Quarter to Three."

12/20/78 Seattle, Wash., Seattle Center Arena
"Pretty Flamingo" is played in the first set for the first time since 5/27/76. Bruce and the band return to the stage 15 minutes after the show appears to end. The stage is already partly disassembled. Undaunted, Bruce plugs in and plays "Rave On" and "Twist and Shout" for the remaining and duly amazed crowd. Badlands/Streets of Fire/Rendezvous/Spirit in the Night/Darkness/Independence Day/ Promised Land/Prove It All Night/Pretty Flamingo/Thunder Road/ Jungleland//The Ties That Bind/Santa Claus/Fire/Candy's Room/ Because the Night/The Fever/Mona/She's the One/Backstreets/Rosalita/Born to Run/Detroit Medley/Tenth Avenue Freeze-out/Quarter to Three/Rave On/Twist and Shout

12/27-28/78 Pittsburgh, Pa., Stanley Theater
A new song, "Ramrod," opens the 26-song set on the second night, which includes first-set performances of "Sandy" and "Factory," and second-set performances of "Saint in the City" and "Rave On."

12/30/78 Detroit, Mich., Cobo Hall
A 24-song set.

12/31/78-1/1/79 Cleveland, Ohio, Richfield Coliseum
Twenty-eight-song New Year's special includes "Rendezvous," "Pretty Flamingo," "Rave On," "Auld Lang Syne" and "Good Rockin' Tonight." Final night of the *Darkness* tour (1/1/79) is Bruce's longest to date, clocking in at three and a half hours and 31 songs. This will be the final performance to date of "The Fever," "Meeting Across the River," and "Streets of Fire." First ever performance of the Rolling Stones' "The Last Time." Rave On/Badlands/Rendezvous/Spirit in the Night/Darkness/Factory/Streets of Fire/Heartbreak Hotel/Promised Land/Prove It All Night/Racing in the Street/Thunder Road/Meeting Across the River/Jungleland//For You/Saint in the City/Santa Claus/I Fought the Law/The Fever/Fire/Candy's Room/Because the Night/

Outside the Roxy, Los Angeles, Calif., October 1975.

Point Blank/Mona/She's the One/Backstreets/The Last Time/Rosalita/
Born to Run/Detroit Medley/Tenth Avenue Freeze-out/Quarter to
Three.

3/14/79 Asbury Park, N.J., The Fast Lane
Bruce joins Robert Gordon on "Heartbreak Hotel" and "Fire."

4/13/79 Asbury Park, N.J., The Fast Lane
Bruce guests with Beaver Brown.

4/15/79 Asbury Park, N.J., The Fast Lane
Bruce guests with Beaver Brown on four songs.

5/27/79 Asbury Park, N.J., Paramount Theater
Bruce again guests with Robert Gordon on "Fire" and "Heartbreak
Hotel."

9/22-23/79 New York, N.Y., Madison Square Garden
Bruce and the E Street Band perform at the MUSE anti-nuclear ben-
efit concert. Jackson Browne guests both nights on "Stay." Bruce
debuts "The River," which will become the title track of his next
record. The "Detroit Medley" is recorded and later released on the *No
Nukes* soundtrack album. Prove It All Night/Badlands/Promised
Land/The River/Sherry Darling/Thunder Road/Jungleland/Rosalita/
Born to Run/Stay/Detroit Medley/Rave On. Same set on 9/23/79, but
without "Rave On." Footage from this night will be included in the *No
Nukes* film.

10/5-6/79 Asbury Park, N.J., The Fast Lane
Bruce guests with Beaver Brown on "Rosalita" and "Twist and
Shout."

3/1/80 Asbury Park, N.J., The Fast Lane
Bruce guests with David Johansen on "Personality Crisis" and
"Lucille."

·   ·   ·   ·   ·

THE RIVER TOUR

For this tour, the "Detroit Medley" will count as one
song and will consist of "Devil with the Blue Dress,"
"Jenny Take a Ride," "C.C. Rider," "Good Golly Miss
Molly," and "I Hear a Train," after the 10/9/80 Detroit
show. "Here She Comes/I Wanna Marry You" will be
counted as one song. "No Money Down/Cadillac
Ranch" will be counted as one song.

10/3/80 Ann Arbor, Mich., Crisler Arena
First show of *The River* tour. Bruce plays 11 songs from *The River*,
which will not be released for over two weeks. Bob Seger closes the
show with Bruce on "Thunder Road," which had also been played
earlier in the set. Born to Run/Prove It All Night/Tenth Avenue
Freeze-out (with new sax solo)/Wreck on the Highway/Darkness/
Jackson Cage/Promised Land/Out in the Street/Racing in the Street/
The River/Thunder Road/Badlands//Cadillac Ranch/I Wanna Marry
You/Crush on You/Ramrod/Point Blank/Stolen Car/Because the
Night/Backstreets/Rosalita/Jungleland/Detroit Medley/Thunder
Road.

10/4/80 Cincinnati, Ohio, Riverfront Coliseum
A 27-song set opens with "Prove It All Night" and also includes
"Independence Day," "Factory," and "The Ties That Bind."

10/6-7/80 Cleveland, Ohio, Richfield Coliseum
"Two Hearts" is added to the first set on 10/6/80. "You Can Look" is
added to the second set on 10/7/80. "Two Hearts" is left out of an otherwise identical 28-song set.

10/9/80 Detroit, Mich., Cobo Hall

A 27-song set. "Wreck on the Highway" is moved to late in the second set.

10/10-11/80 Chicago, Ill., Uptown Theater
"Stolen Car" returns to a 28-song set on 10/10/80, and a new song "Here She Comes," which can be traced back to the early seventies, is used for the first time to introduce "I Wanna Marry You" on 10/11/80. A 31-song set includes "For You," "Good Rockin' Tonight," "You Can Look," and "Raise Your Hand."

10/13/80 St. Paul, Minn., Civic Centre
A 30-song set.

10/14/80 Milwaukee, Wisc., Milwaukee Arena
Another 30-song set includes "In the Midnight Hour."

10/17/80 *The River* is released in the U.S.

10/17-18/80 St. Louis, Mo., Kiel Opera House
A 33-song set on 10/18/80 including the premieres of "Hungry Heart," "Drive All Night," and "I'm a Rocker." The Kiel Opera House is the smallest venue on the U.S. leg of the *River* tour, at only 3,500 seats. It was in St. Louis and not Denver that Bruce meets a fan while watching Woody Allen's *Stardust Memories* and ends up going home with him to meet his family. Badlands/Out in the Street/Tenth Avenue Freeze-out/Darkness/Factory/Independence Day/Racing in the Street/Two Hearts/Jackson Cage/Promised Land/The River/Prove It All Night/Thunder Road//Good Rockin' Tonight/Cadillac Ranch/Fire/Sherry Darling/Here She Comes/I Wanna Marry You/The Ties That Bind/Wreck on the Highway/Point Blank/Crush on You/Ramrod/Hungry Heart/Drive All Night/Rosalita/Jungleland/Born to Run/I'm a Rocker/Detroit Medley.

10/20/80 Denver, Colo., McNicholls Arena

10/23/80 Seattle, Wash., Old Timer's Cafe
Bruce guests with the Lost Highway Band.

10/24/80 Seattle, Wash., Seattle Center Coliseum
A 29-song set includes a silent "Cadillac Ranch," as Bruce's microphone is dead. "Raise Your Hand" closes the show. "Good Rockin' Tonight" is played to the early arriving crowd who see the last part of the soundcheck. *Backstreets #1* handed out free to the first 10,000 fans.

10/25/80 Portland, Ore., Coliseum
Great set includes the only live performance of "On Top of Old Smokey," played in honor of Mount St. Helens, as well as rare versions of "I'm a Rocker" and "Prove It All Night" as the show opener.

10/27-28/80 Oakland, Calif., Coliseum
A 30-song set on 10/27/80 includes "I'm a Rocker" in the encores. A 32-song set on 10/28/80 opens with "Good Rockin' Tonight." For the first time, the dark trio of "Wreck on the Highway," "Stolen Car," and "Point Blank" are played in sequence.

10/30-11/1/80 Los Angeles, Calif., Sports Arena
A 31-song set on 10/30/80 opens with "Born to Run." The wild Halloween show opens with "Haunted House" and Bruce in a coffin. "The Price You Pay" is debuted in the first set, and the second set includes "Outer Limits" and "No Money Down" as an introduction to "Cadillac Ranch." On 11/1/80, "Prove It All Night" is played with the long introduction for the only time on the tour. "Fade Away" premieres in the second set, and Jackson Browne joins Bruce in the encores for "Sweet Little Sixteen."

11/3/80 Los Angeles, Calif., Sports Arena
"Growin' Up" makes its first appearance on the *River* tour in a 28-song set that again includes "The Price You Pay." The version of "The Price You Pay" performed on the tour includes a new verse not included on the recorded LP track.

11/5/80 Tempe, Ariz., Arizona State University Activities Center
One day after the election of Ronald Reagan for President, Bruce prefaces "Badlands" by saying, "I don't know what you guys think about what happened last night, but I think it's pretty frightening. You guys are young, there's gonna be a lot of people depending on you comin' up, so this is for you." "Badlands" from this night is included in *Live 1975-85*. This set is a good example of the shows on the first leg of the *River* tour. Of note is the inclusion of "Jackson Cage," and "Crush on You," which will be played very infrequently

on the rest of the tour, and the linkage of "Stolen Car," "Wreck on the Highway," and "Point Blank," in what would have to be considered the darkest segment of any Springsteen concert ever. Born to Run/Prove It All Night/Tenth Avenue Freeze-out/Darkness/Independence Day/Factory/Jackson Cage/Two Hearts/Promised Land/Out in the Street/Racing in the Street/The River/Badlands/Thunder Road//No Money Down/Cadillac Ranch/Hungry Heart/Fire/Candy's Room/Sherry Darling/Here She Comes/I Wanna Marry You/The Ties That Bind/Stolen Car/Wreck on the Highway/Point Blank/Crush on You/Ramrod/You Can Look/Drive All Night/Backstreets/Rosalita/I'm a Rocker/Jungleland/Detroit Medley.

11/8/80 Dallas, Tex., Reunion Arena
A 31-song set opens with "Born to Run." Second set opens with "Yellow Rose of Texas."

11/9/80 Austin, Tex., Frank Erwin Center
A 33-song set includes "The Price You Pay," "Waltz Across Texas," and "Yellow Rose of Texas." The show opens with "Prove It All Night," followed by "Two Hearts."

11/11/80 Baton Rouge, La., LSU Assembly Center
A 28-song set with "The Price You Pay."

11/14-15/80 Houston, Tex., The Summit
"In the Midnight Hour" is played fourth in a 30-song set on 11/14/80. A 31-song set on 11/15/80 is marked by the returns of "Fade Away" and "Growin' Up." Badlands/Jackson Cage/Tenth Avenue Freeze-out/Darkness/Independence Day/Factory/Two Hearts/Out in the Street/Promised Land/Racing in the Street/The River/Prove It All Night/Thunder Road//No Money Down/Cadillac Ranch/Hungry Heart/Fire/Candy's Room/Because the Night/Fade Away/Stolen Car-Growin' Up/Wreck on the Highway/Point Blank/The Ties That Bind/Ramrod/Crush on You/Backstreets/Rosalita/Born to Run/Jungleland/Detroit Medley.

11/20/80 Chicago, Ill., Rosemont Horizon
A 29-song set includes "The Price You Pay," "Growin' Up," and "Drive All Night."

11/23-24/80 Landover, Md., Capital Centre
A 29-song set with "I'm a Rocker" in the encores on 11/23/80. "You Can Look" is moved to the first set on 11/24/80 in a 32-song concert that opens with "Prove It All Night." "Fade Away" and "Growin' Up" are both included in the second set.

11/27-28/80 New York, N.Y., Madison Square Garden
A 31-song set on 11/27/80 includes "The Price You Pay." On 11/28/80 a marathon 33-song set includes the first *River* tour performance of "Sandy" in the encores. "Mystery Train" is included in the "Detroit Medley," the only non-Springsteen composition played all night. "Ramrod" includes a few lyrics that will later evolve into "Open All Night." "For You" is played for the first time in 1980.

11/30-12/1/80 Pittsburgh, Pa., Civic Arena
On 11/30/80, "Growin' Up" is included in a 32-song set. On 12/1/80, the first set includes "You Can Look" and "The Price You Pay," while the second set features "Fade Away."

12/2/80 Rochester, N.Y., War Memorial
A 31-song set includes "For You," "Sandy," and "I'm a Rocker."

12/4/80 Buffalo, N.Y., War Memorial Auditorium
A 34-song set includes "The Price You Pay," "I Fought the Law," "For You," "Stolen Car," "Drive All Night," and "Santa Claus."

12/6/80 Philadelphia, Pa., The Spectrum
A 34-song set includes "Sandy," "Point Blank," and "I'm a Rocker."

12/8-9/80 Philadelphia, Pa., The Spectrum
Another 34-song set on 12/8/80 includes "Growin' Up." A 35-song set the night after the murder of John Lennon on 12/9/80. Bruce opens the show with a few comments about Lennon, explaining why he felt he should go on and play that night. "Rendezvous" is played for the first time since 1/1/79. 12/9/80 set: Born to Run/Out in the Street/Tenth Avenue Freeze-out/Darkness/The Price You Pay/Independence Day/Two Hearts/Prove It All Night/Promised Land/Racing in the Street/The River/Badlands/Thunder Road//Cadillac Ranch/Sherry Darling/Hungry Heart/Fire/Candy's Room/Because the Night/Sandy/For You/Stolen Car/Wreck on the Highway/Point Blank/Rendezvous/Ramrod/You Can Look/Drive All Night/Rosalita/Santa

Claus/Jungleland/I'm a Rocker/Detroit Medley/Twist and Shout.

12/11/80 Providence, R.I., Civic Center
Same set as 12/9/80, but "Crush on You" and "Backstreets" replace "You Can Look" and "Drive All Night," and "Twist and Shout" is not played.

12/12/80 Hartford, Conn., Civic Center
"Fade Away" is included in a 33-song set that opens with "Prove It All Night."

12/15-16/80 Boston, Mass., Boston Gardens
A 32-song set on 12/15/80. A great 34-song set on 12/16/80 includes the first *River* tour performance of "Spirit in the Night." Also included are "I Fought the Law," "Sandy," "Growin' Up," "For You," and "Drive All Night." "Crush on You" makes its last appearance to date.

12/18-19/80 New York, N.Y., Madison Square Garden
Bruce returns to New York for two more shows, a month after his first two *River* shows there. "Who'll Stop the Rain" premieres in a 35-song set on 12/18/80 that again includes "I Fought the Law." A 34-song set on 12/19/80 includes "Fade Away" and "Raise Your Hand."

12/28-29/80 Uniondale, N.Y., Nassau Coliseum
Show opens on 12/28/80 with the premiere of "Merry Christmas Baby," the first of many surprises that will occur over these three nights. Flo and Eddie join the band for "Hungry Heart," and that, along with "Because the Night," are the songs from this night included on Live 1975-85. "This Land is Your Land" is credited on *Live 1975-85* liner notes to this night, but it is actually taken from the following night. "Who'll Stop the Rain" and "Santa Claus" are also included in this 33-song set. The show on 12/29/80 is the last to include "Incident on 57th Street," and one of the few shows that links it to "Rosalita" as they appear on the second album. "Incident" becomes one of the two live B-sides from *Live 1975-85*. The show opens with a rare version of "Night," in a 35-song set. "Darkness" and "You Can Look" from this night are included on *Live 1975-85*.

12/31/80 Uniondale, N.Y., Nassau Coliseum
The longest show Springsteen and the E Street Band have ever played, clocking in at four hours and 38 songs, is also one of the best. Rarities include "Night," "Rendezvous," "Fade Away," "The Price You Pay," "Spirit in the Night," "Held Up Without a Gun," "In the Midnight Hour," and "Auld Lang Syne," all done infrequently at best, or never before this show in a few cases. Night/Prove It All Night/Spirit in the Night/Darkness/Independence Day/Who'll Stop the Rain/This Land Is Your Land/Promised Land/Out in the Street/Racing in the Street/The River/Badlands/Thunder Road//Cadillac Ranch/Sherry Darling/Hungry Heart/Merry Christmas Baby/Fire/Candy's Room/Because the Night/Sandy/Rendezvous/Fade Away/The Price You Pay/Wreck on the Highway/Two Hearts/Ramrod/You Can Look/Held Up Without a Gun/In the Midnight Hour/Auld Lang Syne/Rosalita/Santa Claus/Jungleland/Born to Run/Detroit Medley/Twist and Shout/Raise Your Hand.

1/20-21/81 Toronto, Ontario, Maple Leaf Gardens
After almost three weeks off, the *River* tour's second leg opens with a 32-song set that includes "Who'll Stop the Rain," "Sandy," "For You," and "I'm a Rocker." The concert on 1/21/81 is another 32-song set: Night/Out in the Street/Tenth Avenue Freeze-out/Darkness/Independence Day/Who'll Stop the Rain/Prove It All Night/Two Hearts/Promised Land/The Price You Pay/The River/Badlands/Thunder Road//No Money Down/Cadillac Ranch/Sherry Darling/Hungry Heart/Fire/You Can Look/Sandy/Growin' Up/Fade Away/Stolen Car/Wreck on the Highway/Candy's Room/Ramrod/Backstreets/Rosalita/I'm a Rocker/Jungleland/Born to Run/Detroit Medley/Raise Your Hand.

1/23/81 Montreal, Quebec, The Forum
"Night" opens a 31-song set that also includes "Because the Night," "The Ties That Bind" and "Drive All Night" in the second set.

1/24/81 Ottawa, Ontario, Civic Centre
"I Fought the Law" and "Sandy" are included in a 31-song set.

1/26/81 South Bend, Ind., Notre Dame University
"Out in the Street" opens a 32-song set. "Double Shot of My Baby's Love" and "Louie, Louie" are included in the first set.

1/28/81 St. Louis, Mo., Checkerdome
"Night" kicks off a 29-song set including "Fade Away," "The Price You Pay," and "For You."

1/29/81 Ames, Iowa, Hilton Coliseum
"Jackson Cage" is included in the first set.

2/1/81 St. Paul, Minn., Civic Centre

2/2/81 Madison, Wis., Dane County Coliseum
Five-song encore of "I'm a Rocker," "Jungleland," "Born to Run," "Detroit Medley," and "Twist and Shout."

2/4/81 Carbondale, Ill., Arena, Southern Illinois University
A 31-song set includes "Sandy," "For You," "I Fought the Law" and "Who'll Stop the Rain."

2/5/81 Kansas City, Mo., Kemper Arena
"I Fought the Law" and "Because the Night" are played in a 29-song set that features "Kansas City" in the encores.

2/7/81 Champaign, Ill., Assembly Center, University of Illinois
"Here She Comes/I Wanna Marry You" returns to a 30-song set.

2/12/81 Mobile, Ala., Municipal Auditorium
"This Land Is Your Land" is played for the first time since the Nassau Coliseum shows in December.

2/13/81 Starkville, Miss., Mississippi State University
A 28-song set includes "Fade Away," "For You," and "Sandy" in the second set.

2/15-16/81 Lakeland, Fla., Civic Center
Twenty-eight-song sets are played both nights. The set on 2/16/81 includes "Good Rockin' Tonight" and "High School Confidential" in the "Detroit Medley." Show opens with "Born to Run."

2/18/81 Jacksonville, Fla., Memorial Coliseum
"This Land Is Your Land" returns to a 27-song set.

2/20/81 Hollywood, Fla., Sportatorium
Bruce plays a 27-song set that includes "The Price You Pay," "Fade Away," and "Because the Night."

2/22/81 Columbia, S.C., Carolina Coliseum
A 28-song set.

2/23/81 Atlanta, Ga., The Omni
"Fade Away" is included in a 28-song set.

2/25/81 Memphis, Tenn., Mid-South Coliseum

2/26/81 Nashville, Tenn., Municipal Auditorium
A 27-song set.

2/28/81 Greensboro, N.C., Greensboro Coliseum
"Racing in the Street" is played in the second set of a 29-song set.

3/2/81 Hampton, Va., Hampton Roads Coliseum
"Ramrod" opens the second set of a 28-song show that opens with "Prove It All Night."

3/4/81 Lexington, Ky., Rupp Arena
A 12-song first set includes "This Land Is Your Land" and "Who'll Stop the Rain."

3/5/81 Indianapolis, Ind., Market Square Arena
Final show of the second leg of the tour. The band will take a month off before going to Europe for their first extended overseas tour. Prove It All Night/Out in the Street/Tenth Avenue Freeze-out/Darkness/Promised Land/This Land Is Your Land/The River/Badlands/Thunder Road//Cadillac Ranch/Sherry Darling/Hungry Heart/Fire/You Can Look/Fade Away/Because the Night/Stolen Car/Racing in the Street/Candy's Room/Ramrod/Rosalita/I'm a Rocker/Jungleland/Born to Run/Detroit Medley.

4/7/81 Hamburg, West Germany, Congress Centrum
Bruce and the E Street Band kick off their second European tour and play their first show ever in Germany.

4/9/81 West Berlin, Germany, ICC Halle
A 27-song set. Factory/Prove It All Night/Out in the Street/Tenth Avenue Freeze-out/Darkness/Independence Day/Who'll Stop the Rain/Two Hearts/Promised Land/This Land Is Your Land/The River/Badlands//Thunder Road/Cadillac Ranch/Sherry Darling/Hungry Heart/Fire/You Can Look/Wreck on the Highway/Racing in the Street/Backstreets/Ramrod/Rosalita/Born to Run/Detroit Medley/Rockin' All Over the World/ Twist and Shout.

4/11/81 Zurich, Switzerland, Hallenstadion

Cleveland, Ohio, December 31, 1978. ▶

A 26-song set opens again with "Factory." Identical set to the preceding show with the omission of "Twist and Shout."

4/14/81 Frankfurt, West Germany, Festhalle
Another 26-song set, with "Point Blank" replacing "Wreck on the Highway."

4/16/81 Munich, West Germany, Olympiahalle
A 25-song set includes "The Ties That Bind" and "Wreck on the Highway."

4/18-19/81 Paris, France, Palais Des Sports
"Candy's Room" and "I Can't Help Falling in Love" are added to a 27-song set on 4/18/81. The second show opens for the first time with "Follow That Dream," a song originally performed by Elvis Presley and now rewritten by Bruce, incorporating part of Roy Orbison's "In Dreams" and some original lyrics. The 28-song set also includes "Because the Night," "Point Blank," "I Can't Help Falling in Love," and "Sweet Soul Music."

4/21/81 Barcelona, Spain, Palacio de Deportes
"Factory" again opens the show. A 26-song set.

4/24/81 Lyon, France, Palais des Sports
"Follow That Dream" opens a 25-song set.

4/26/81 Brussels, Belgium, Vorst National
Second set of the show includes "Stolen Car" and "Fire."

4/28-29/81 Rotterdam, Holland, Ahoy Sportspaleis
"Candy's Room" and "Point Blank" return to a 27-song set on 4/28/81. Bruce's frightening cover of Creedence Clearwater Revival's "Run Through the Jungle" starts an exceptional show on 4/29/81. The song is the first indication of the kind of material that Bruce will release the following year on the *Nebraska* LP. The arrangement of "Run Through the Jungle" is similar to the 1984 performances of "State Trooper." Run Through the Jungle/Prove It All Night/The Ties That Bind/Darkness/Independence Day/Factory/Who'll Stop the Rain/Two Hearts/Out in the Street/Thunder Road/This Land Is Your Land/The River/Promised Land/Badlands//Cadillac Ranch/Sherry Darling/Hungry Heart/Fire/You Can Look/Wreck on the Highway/Racing in the Street/Backstreets/Candy's Room/Rosalita/Born to Run/Detroit Medley/I'm a Rocker/Rockin' All Over the World.

5/1/81 Copenhagen, Denmark, The Forum
Bruce sings "Hungry Heart" with the Danish group Malurt.

5/2/81 Copenhagen, Denmark, Brondby-Hallen
A 30-song set opens with "Follow That Dream," and also includes "Candy's Room," "Because the Night," and "Point Blank" in the second set.

5/3/81 Gothenberg, Sweden, Scandinavium
"Run Through the Jungle" and "I Can't Help Falling in Love" are included.

5/5/81 Oslo, Norway, Drammenshallen

5/7-8/81 Stockholm, Sweden, Johnanneshovs Isstadion
A 27-song set on 5/7/81 opens with "Follow That Dream." On 5/8/81, a superb 31-song set opens with "Run Through the Jungle," which, regrettably, is not played again. The second set includes "Point Blank," "Wreck on the Highway," and "I Can't Help Falling in Love" in the encores. These two shows become the source for the famous bootlegs *Follow That Dream* and *Teardrops on the City.*

5/11/81 Newcastle, England, Newcastle City Hall
Bruce's first U.K. appearance since 1975.

5/13-14/81 Manchester, England, Apollo Theatre
"Johnny Bye Bye" premieres in the first set of a 29-song show on 5/31/81 that also features the first European performance of "The Price You Pay." The 24-song set on 5/14/81 is the shortest of the European tour.

5/16-17/81 Edinburgh, Scotland, Playhouse Theatre
"The Ties That Bind" opens a 26-song set on 5/17/81 that again includes "Johnny Bye Bye."

5/20/81 Stafford, England, New Bingley Hall
A 27-song set opens with "Prove It All Night."

5/26-27/81 Brighton, England, Brighton Centre
A 26-song set is played on 5/26/81. On 5/27/81, encores include "Jungleland" for the first time on the European tour. "Born to Run" opens the first set, which also includes "The Price You Pay."

5/29-30, 6/1-2/81 London, England, Wembley Arena
On the first night of six in London, Bruce's reworking of Jimmy Cliff's "Trapped" premieres. "Jackson Cage," "Trapped," "Because the Night," and "Jungleland" are included in a 28-song set on 5/30/81. The third show opens with "The Ties That Bind." The 27-song set includes "Follow That Dream," "Johnny Bye Bye," and "Trapped" in sequence in the first set. A 27-song set on 6/2/81 includes "I Fought the Law" in the encores.

6/4-5/81 London, England, Wembley Arena
Final night in London is a 31-song set that includes "Jole Blon" for the first time. Born to Run/Prove It All Night/Out in the Street/Follow That Dream/Darkness/Independence Day/Johnny Bye Bye/Two Hearts/Who'll Stop the Rain/Promised Land/This Land Is Your Land/The River/I Fought the Law/Badlands//Thunder Road/Hungry Heart/You Can Look/Cadillac Ranch/Sherry Darling/Jole Blon/Fire/Because the Night/Here She Comes/I Wanna Marry You/Point Blank/Candy's Room/Ramrod/Rosalita/I'm a Rocker/Jungleland/I Can't Help Falling in Love/Detroit Medley.

6/7-8/81 Birmingham, England, International Arena
Pete Townshend joins Bruce on guitar in the 6/7/81 set for "Born to Run" and the "Detroit Medley." "I Wanna Marry You" is also included in the 27-song set. On 6/8/81, the final 29-song set of the European tour closes with "Rockin' All Over the World."

6/14/81 Los Angeles, Calif., Hollywood Bowl
Bruce joins Jackson Browne and Gary U.S. Bonds for the "Survival Sunday" anti-nuclear benefit. This Land Is Your Land/Promised Land/Jole Blon/Hungry Heart/Brother John Is Gone.

6/15/81 San Francisco, Calif., Old Waldorf
Bruce joins Gary U.S. Bonds at his own show, playing on "Jole Blon," "This Little Girl," "Quarter to Three," "School's Out," and "New Orleans."

7/2-3/81 East Rutherford, N.J., Brendan Byrne Arena
Bruce and the E Street Band open this brand-new arena with a 29-song set. Tom Waits's "Jersey Girl" is played for the first time, and many songs make their U.S. premieres. 7/2/81 set: Born to Run/Prove It All Night/Out in the Street/Darkness/Independence Day/Johnny Bye Bye/Two Hearts/Who'll Stop the Rain/Promised Land/This Land Is Your Land/The River/Badlands/Thunder Road//You Can Look/Cadillac Ranch/Sherry Darling/Jole Blon/Hungry Heart/Wreck on the Highway/Follow That Dream/Racing in the Street/Ramrod/Rosalita/I'm a Rocker/Jungleland/Jersey Girl/I Don't Wanna Go Home/Detroit Medley/Rockin' All Over the World. The 28-song set on 7/3/81 includes a guest appearance from Gary U.S. Bonds on "This Little Girl." "Summertime Blues" is also played in the first set.

7/5-6/81 East Rutherford, N.J., Brendan Byrne Arena
"Sandy" is added to a four-song encore on 7/5/81, in a 28-song set that opens with "Thunder Road." "Independence Day," "Cadillac Ranch" and "Racing in the Street" from 7/6/81 are later included on *Live 1975-85.*

7/8-9/81 East Rutherford, N.J., Brendan Byrne Arena
"Two Hearts" and "Candy's Room" from 7/8/81 are later included on *Live 1975-85.* A four-song encore on 7/8/81 includes "Jersey Girl," which will later appear as the B-side of "Cover Me" and as the closing song on *Live 1975-85.*

7/11/81 Red Bank, N.J., Big Man's West
Bruce and the E Street Band open Clarence's new club. Summertime Blues/Jole Blon/Ramrod/Around and Around/You Can't Sit Down/Cadillac Ranch.

7/13/81 Philadelphia, Pa., The Spectrum
A 27-song set.

7/15-16/81 Philadelphia, Pa., The Spectrum
A 26-song set is played on 7/15/81. The 7/16/81 set consists of 25 songs, with "Hungry Heart" as the second set opener.

7/18-19/81 Philadelphia, Pa., The Spectrum
A 26-song set on 7/18/81 includes "Candy's Room" and "Point Blank." The show of 7/19/81 is the only show of the five at the Spectrum with significant set changes. "Factory," "For You," "I Fought the Law," "Sandy," and "Growin' Up" are all played in a 25-song set.

7/29-30/81 Cleveland, Ohio, Richfield Coliseum

At the Main Point, 1976, visiting former E Streeters David Sancious (left) and Boom Carter (center). Photographer Phil Ceccola says this is the last known picture of Bruce with his beard — the next day he shaved it off and cut his hair.

Southside Johnny guests both nights on "I Don't Wanna Go Home." The 26-song set on 7/29/81 includes "For You." An excellent 28-song set on 7/30/81 opens with "Rockin' All Over the World" and closes with "Twist and Shout."

8/4-5/81 Landover, Md., Capital Centre
The "Detroit Medley" now includes "Spotlight on the Big Man," a tribute to Clarence, to the tune of "Sweet Soul Music." The show on 8/4/81 is a 26-song set. A 27-song set on 8/5/81 opens with "Rockin' All Over the World" and also includes "Jackson Cage," "Wreck on the Highway" and "Twist and Shout."

8/6/81 Washington, D.C., Bayou Club
Bruce jumps onstage with Robbin Thompson's band for "Carol."

8/7/81 Landover, Md., Capital Centre
Final night's 27-song set includes "Summertime Blues," "Sandy," and "Twist and Shout."

8/11-12/81 Detroit Mich., Joe Louis Arena
A 29-song set on 8/11/81 includes "For You." On 8/12/81, Mitch Ryder guests on "Detroit Medley."

8/16-17/81 Morrison, Colo., Red Rocks Amphitheatre
Bruce lets part of the crowd in for a soundcheck of "Hungry Heart," "Prove It All Night" and "Rockin' All Over the World" on 8/16/81. During the show, "Sea Cruise" is played for only the second time. Bruce's first outdoor show since he played here in 1978. On 8/17/81, a 27-song set includes "Summertime Blues" and "For You."

8/20-21/81 Los Angeles, Calif., Sports Arena
The show on 8/20/81 is a benefit for Vietnam veterans. A short speech by Vietnam veteran Bobby Muller is followed by one of Bruce's most passionate sets ever. During "The River," Bruce is overcome with emotion and stops singing. The beautiful "Ballad of Easy Rider" is played for the only time. Who'll Stop the Rain/Prove It All Night/The Ties That Bind/Darkness/Johnny Bye Bye/Independence Day/Trapped/Two Hearts/Out in the Street/Promised Land/The River/This Land is Your Land/Badlands/Thunder Road/Hungry Heart/You Can Look/Cadillac Ranch/Sherry Darling/Jole Blon/Wreck on the Highway/Racing in the Street/Candy's Room/Ramrod/Rosalita/Jungleland/Ballad of Easy Rider/Born to Run/Detroit Medley/Twist and Shout. The set on 8/21/81 consists of 26 songs.

8/23-24/81 Los Angeles, Calif., Sports Arena
A 28-song set on 8/23/81 includes "Stolen Car" and the only *River* tour performance of "Rave On." On 8/24/81, Tom Waits joins Bruce for "Jersey Girl," in a 28-song set that includes "Follow That Dream" and "Growin' Up."

8/27-28/81 Los Angeles, Calif., Sports Arena
The set of 8/27/81 consists of 27 songs. The 28-song final night is another exceptional set. Bruce's only performance of Woody Guthrie's "Deportee (Plane Wreck at Los Gatos)." Also Creedence's "Proud Mary" debuts. Other highlights include "Rockin' All Over the World," "I Fought the Law," and "Quarter to Three."

9/2/81 San Diego, Calif., Sports Arena
A 30-song set again closes with "Quarter to Three," and also includes "Jackson Cage," "Follow That Dream," "Growin' Up," and "I'm a Rocker."

9/5/81 Pasadena, Calif., Perkin's Palace
Bruce joins the Pretenders for an encore of "Higher and Higher."

9/8/81 Chicago, Ill., Rosemont Horizon
A 26-song set.

9/10-11/81 Chicago, Ill., Rosemont Horizon
"Out in the Street" opens a 27-song set on 9/10/81 that includes the only *River* tour appearance of "Mona/She's the One." The song will not be played at all on the *Born in the USA* tour, but will be included in every *Tunnel of Love* tour set. A great 28-song set on 9/11/81 includes "Saint in the City" for the first time since 1/1/79. The set also includes "Jersey Girl," "For You," "I Wanna Marry You," and "Drive All Night," and closes with "Twist and Shout."

9/13-14/81 Cincinnati, Ohio, Riverfront Coliseum
A 27-song set on 9/13/81 ends with "Twist and Shout." The final night of the *River* tour on 9/14/81, is also Miami Steve's final performance as a full-time member of the E Street Band and the band's last show for 33 months. Rockin' All Over the World/Prove It All Night/The Ties That Bind/Darkness/Follow That Dream/Independence Day/Trapped/Two Hearts/Who'll Stop the Rain/Out in the Street/The Promised Land/The River/This Land is Your Land/Badlands/Thunder Road//Hungry Heart/Saint in the City/Cadillac Ranch/Sherry Darling/Proud Mary/Johnny Bye Bye/Racing in the Street/Ramrod/Rosalita/I'm a Rocker/Jungleland/Born to Run/Detroit Medley/Quarter to Three.

· · · · ·

1982 TOUR OF NEW JERSEY

1/5/82 Asbury Park, N.J., Stone Pony
Bruce guests with the Lord Gunner Group on "In the Midnight Hour" and "Jole Blon." This is the first of over 40 guest appearances Bruce will make during 1982.

1/12/82 New Brunswick, N.J., Royal Manor North
Bruce joins Nils Lofgren onstage for "Lucille" and "Carol."

2/20/82 Red Ban, N.J., Big Man's West
Bruce joins Beaver Brown on "Ain't That a Shame," "Money," and "You Can't Sit Down." Over the next six weeks, Bruce convenes the E Street Band for recording sessions of the acoustic material he has just written, that will later be released as the solo *Nebraska* album.

4/9-11/82 Red Bank, N.J., Big Man's West
Bruce guests with Beaver Brown on "Twist and Shout" on 4/9/82, and on "Lucille," "Jersey Girl," "Jole Blon," and "Twist and Shout" on 4/10/82. On 4/11/82, Bruce guests with John Eddie on "Long Tall Sally," "Rockin' All Over the World," "Proud Mary," and "Carol."

4/16/82 Red Bank, N.J., Big Man's West
Bruce joins Clarence and the Red Bank Rockers.

4/25/82 Asbury Park, N.J., Stone Pony
Bruce guests with Cats on a Smooth Surface.

5/2/82 Asbury Park, N.J., Stone Pony
Bruce joins Cats for "Long Tall Sally" and "Twist and Shout."

5/8/82 Asbury Park, N.J., The Fast Lane
Bruce and Beaver Brown perform "Jole Blon," "Jersey Girl," "Lucille," and "Around and Around."

5/16/82 Red Bank, N.J., Big Man's West
Bruce again joins Clarence and the Red Bank Rockers for "Tenth Avenue Freeze-out."

5/23/82 Asbury Park, N.J., The Fast Lane
Bruce joins Cats on "Carol," "Long Tall Sally," and "Twist and Shout."

5/29/82 Red Bank, N.J., Big Man's West
Bruce and Southside join Beaver Brown on "Little Latin Lupe Lu," "Summertime Blues," "Around and Around," and "High School Confidential."

6/6/82 Asbury Park, N.J., Stone Pony
Bruce guests with Cats on a Smooth Surface.

6/12/82 New York, N.Y., Central Park
Bruce joins Jackson Browne for "Promised Land" and "Running on Empty" at the Rally for Disarmament.

6/12/82 Red Bank, N.J., Big Man's West
After playing with Jackson Browne earlier in the day, Bruce drives to Jersey and guests with Sonny Kenn on "Walking the Dog," "Route 66," and "Carol."

Seattle, Wash., October 24, 1980.

6/13/82 Asbury Park, N.J, Stone Pony
Bruce joins Cats on "Heartbreak Hotel," "Around and Around," "Lucille," "Kansas City," and "Twist and Shout."

6/20/82 Asbury Park, N.J., Stone Pony
Bruce again joins Cats for a six-song set. Come On Let's Go/Little Latin Lupe Lu/Sweet Little Sixteen/Around and Around/Lucille/Twist and Shout.

6/26/82 Red Bank, N.J., Big Man's West
Billy Chinnock calls Bruce onstage for "Lucille."

6/27/82 Red Bank, N.J., Big Man's West
Bruce comes onstage for "Tenth Avenue Freeze-out" with Clarence and the Red Bank Rockers.

7/17/82 Red Bank, N.J., Big Man's West
Bruce guests with the Iron City Houserockers on "Mony Mony," "Shout," Chuck Berry's "Johnny Bye Bye" and "Whole Lotta Shakin' Going On."

7/23/82 Freehold, N.J., Monmouth County Fair
Bruce joins Sonny Kenn for "Sweet Little Sixteen," "Long Tall Sally," "Carol," "Shake," and "Land of 1000 Dances."

7/23/82 Asbury Park, N.J., The Fast Lane
Later in the evening, Bruce joins the Stray Cats for "Twenty Flight Rock," "Be Bop a Lula" and "Long Tall Sally."

7/25/82 Asbury Park, N.J., Stone Pony
Eight-song set with Cats on a Smooth Surface includes "From Small Things," written and recorded for *The River* and later given to and recorded by Dave Edmunds. Come On Let's Go/From Small Things/Ramrod/Lucille/Around and Around/The Wanderer/Long Tall Sally/Twist and Shout.

7/31/82 Red Bank, N.J., Big Man's West
Bruce joins Sonny Kenn for "Sweet Little Sixteen," "Ready Teddy," "Rip it Up," "Around and Around," and "Sweet Little Rock 'n' Roller."

◄ *Landover, Md., August 25, 1984.*

8/1/82 Asbury Park, N.J., Stone Pony
Bruce joins Cats for a six-song set: Rip It Up/Come On Over to My Place/Come On Let's Go/Lucille/Around and Around/Twist and Shout.

8/6-7/82 Red Bank, N.J., Big Man's West
Bruce joins Beaver Brown for "Ready Teddy," "Lucille," "Jersey Girl," and "Twist and Shout" on 8/6/82, and for six songs on 8/7/82: Ready Teddy/From Small Things/Jersey Girl/Lucille/Do You Wanna Dance/Twist and Shout.

8/8/82 Asbury Park, N.J., Stone Pony
Bruce plays for the third straight night, this time for eight songs with Cats. Bruce plays a snatch of a new song titled "On the Prowl," which will later evolve into "Downbound Train." Ready Teddy/From Small Things/Come On Let's Go/Come On Over to My Place/Around and Around/Lucille (including "On the Prowl")/Twist and Shout.

8/13/82 Farmingdale, N.J., Tower Recording Studio
Bruce rehearses with Cats for the Pony anniversary show in two days.

8/15/82 Asbury Park, N.J., Stone Pony
Seven-song set with Cats includes a long "Detroit Medley." Ready Teddy/From Small Things/Around and Around/Jersey Girl/You Can Look/Havin' a Party/Detroit Medley (including "Shake" and "Sweet Soul Music").

8/31/82 Wall, N.J., Jon Jon's
Bruce plays with Cats.

9/4/82 Red Bank, N.J., Big Man's West
Bruce joins Beaver Brown on "From Small Things," "Come On Let's Go," and "Lucille."

9/18/82 Red Bank, N.J., Big Man's West
Dave Edmunds calls Bruce onstage for six songs: From Small Things/Johnny B. Goode/Lucille/Let's Talk About Us/Carol/Bama Lama Bama Loo.

9/19/82 Asbury Park, N.J., Stone Pony
Superb 12-song set with Cats: Ready Teddy/From Small Things/Come On Let's Go/Lucille/Come On Over to My Place/Around and Around/Havin' a Party/Jersey Girl/Wooly Bully/Louie, Louie/High-Heeled Sneakers/Twist and Shout.

9/21/82 New York, N.Y., Peppermint Lounge
Bruce again joins Dave Edmunds for "From Small Things."

9/25/82 Asbury Park, N.J., Stone Pony
Six-song set with Cats: Ready Teddy/From Small Things/Come On Over to My Place/Around and Around/Lucille/Twist and Shout.

9/29/82 Westwood, N.J., On Broadway
Bruce guests with Billy Rancher and the Unreal Gods.

10/3/82 Asbury Park, N.J., Stone Pony
Fourteen-song set is probably Bruce's longest guest appearance ever. "Open All Night" premieres, and "On the Prowl" is now a separate, complete song. Bruce and Cats probably had another rehearsal in the days before this show. From Small Things/Come On Let's Go/Around and Around/Open All Night/Jersey Girl/On the Prowl/Do You Wanna Dance/Lucille/Wooly Bully/Louie, Louie/Rock Baby Rock/Come On Over to My Place/Havin' a Party/Twist and Shout.

10/4/82 *Nebraska* is released in the U.S.

11/27/82 Los Angeles, Calif., Club Lingerie
Bruce guests with Jimmy and the Mustangs.

12/3/82 Palo Alto, Calif., The Keystone
Bruce guests with Clarence and the Red Bank Rockers on "Lucille" and "From Small Things."

12/31/82 New York, N.Y., Harkness House
Bruce and others jam following Little Steven's wedding. Jole Blon/I'm a Rocker/Hungry Heart/Save the Last Dance for Me/Rockin' All Over the World/Shout.

1/8/83 Red Bank, N.J., Big Man's West
Closing night of Big Man's West. Bruce plays on "Rockin' All Over the World" and "Lucille."

4/24/83 Asbury Park, N.J., Stone Pony
Bruce joins Cats for "From Small Things," "Around and Around," "Lucille," and "Twist and Shout."

4/27/83 Asbury Park, N.J., Stone Pony
Bruce guests with the Diamonds on "Lucille" and "Long Tall Sally."

6/18/83 Asbury Park, N.J., Stone Pony
Bruce again plays with the Diamonds.

7/10/83 Asbury Park, N.J., Stone Pony
Bruce and Cats play five songs.

7/16/83 Neptune, N.J., The Headliner
Bruce guests with Midnight Thunder.

8/2/83 New York, N.Y., Madison Square Garden
Bruce and Jackson Browne duet on "Stay," "Running on Empty," and "Sweet Little Sixteen."

8/14/83 Asbury Park, N.J., Stone Pony
Bruce plays six songs with the Cats: Ready Teddy/Around and Around/Jersey Girl/Lucille/Twist and Shout/Ain't That Lovin' You Baby.

8/19/83 Long Branch, N.J., Brighton Bar
Bruce joins John Eddie on "Blue Suede Shoes," "Rockin' All Over the World," "Ain't That Lovin' You Baby," "Jersey Girl," and "Carol."

11/6/83 Asbury Park, N.J., Stone Pony
Bruce joins Cats for a late set.

12/28/83 Red Bank, N.J., Monmouth Arts Center
Bruce lends a hand at La Bamba's "Holiday Hurrah" jam session, playing "From Small Things," "Santa Claus," and "Twist and Shout."

1/8/84 Asbury Park, N.J., Stone Pony
After failing to win the early-evening joke contest, Bruce joins Cats for "Lucille" and "Carol."

1/14/84 New Brunswick, N.J., Patrix
Bruce joins John Eddie for five songs, including his first performance of "Boom Boom," which becomes a staple on the European leg of the *Tunnel of Love Express* tour: Rockin' All Over the World/Ain't Too Proud to Beg/Boom Boom/Proud Mary/Twist and Shout.

3/25/84 Asbury Park, N.J., Stone Pony
Bruce plays "I'm Bad, I'm Nationwide" and "Lucille" with Cats.

4/8/84 Asbury Park, N.J., Stone Pony
Another guest appearance with Cats. Bruce plays on "Proud Mary," "Dirty Water," "I'm Bad, I'm Nationwide," and "Lucille."

4/13/84 Philadelphia, Pa., Ripley Music Hall
Bruce joins Clarence and the Red Bank Rockers for "Fire" and "Rockin' All Over the World."

4/21/84 Mount Ivy, N.Y., Expo
Bruce again guests with Clarence and the Red Bank Rockers.

4/22/84 Asbury Park, N.J., Stone Pony
Bruce joins Cats on "I'm Bad, I'm Nationwide," "Little Latin Lupe Lu," and "Jersey Girl."

5/19/84 Asbury Park, N.J., Stone Pony
Bruce jumps onstage with Clarence and his band for four songs: Fire/Midnight Hour/Lucille/Twist and Shout.

5/26/84 Asbury Park, N.J., Xanadu
Bruce premieres "Dancing in the Dark," guesting with Bystander.

6/1/84 Asbury Park, N.J., Stone Pony
Bruce makes another appearance with John Eddie, joining him on "I'm Bad, I'm Nationwide," "Proud Mary," "Bright Lights, Big City," and "Carol."

6/4/84 *Born in the USA* is released in the U.S.

6/8/84 Asbury Park, N.J., Stone Pony
The E Street Band minus Patti, but with Nils, makes a surprise appearance as a warm-up for the upcoming tour. "Darlington County," "Glory Days," "My Hometown" and "Born in the USA" make their live debut. Thunder Road/Out in the Street/Prove It All Night/Glory Days/The River/Darlington County/Dancing in the Dark/Promised Land/My Hometown/Born in the USA/Badlands/Born to Run.

6/10/84 Asbury Park, N.J., Stone Pony
Bruce and Nils guest with Cats on "Gloria," "Boom Boom," "We Gotta Get Outta This Place," "The Last Time" and "Rockin' All Over the World."

6/21/84 Lancaster, Pa., The Village
An abbreviated E Street Band gives one final warm-up performance, which includes Max Weinberg playing on a drum machine during "Dancing in the Dark." Out in the Street/Prove It All Night/Glory Days/Hungry Heart/Dancing in the Dark/Rosalita.

Asbury Park, N.J., May 19, 1984.

BORN IN THE USA TOUR

For this tour, the "Detroit Medley" will be counted as one song. "Travelin' Band" will be counted as one song when it doesn't appear in the "Detroit Medley." "Do You Love Me" will be counted as one song, though it is included in the middle of "Twist and Shout."

6/29/84 St. Paul, Minn., Civic Centre

Bruce and the E Street Band begin their first tour in over two and a half years. Set includes eight songs from *Born in the USA* and five songs from *Nebraska*. Patti Scialfa's first show with the E Street Band. "No Surrender" is played with the full band, and "Dancing in the Dark" is played twice for the filming of the video. The Rolling Stones' "Street Fightin' Man" also debuts. Thunder Road/Prove It All Night/Out in the Street/Johnny 99/Atlantic City/Mansion on the Hill/The River/No Surrender/Glory Days/Promised Land/Used Cars/My Hometown/Born in the USA/Badlands//Hungry Heart/Dancing in the Dark/Cadillac Ranch/Sherry Darling/Highway Patrolman/I'm on Fire/Fire/Working on the Highway/Bobby Jean/Backstreets/Rosalita/I'm a Rocker/Jungleland/Born to Run/Street Fightin' Man/Detroit Medley.

7/1-2/84 St. Paul, Minn., Civic Centre

A 32-song set on 7/1/84 includes the premieres of "Pink Cadillac, "Open All Night," "Reason to Believe," and "Nebraska." Other changes from the first night are "Ramrod" and "Darlington County." The set on 7/2/84 includes the final, full-band version of "No Surrender." Both "Cover Me" and "Downbound Train" premiere here, but, strangely, "Downbound Train" will not be played again for the next 31 shows. "Racing in the Street" and "Twist and Shout" are also played for the first time in 1984. One of the shortest shows of the tour.

7/5-6/84 Cincinnati, Ohio, Riverfront Coliseum

Six songs from *Nebraska* are included in a 28-song set on 7/5/84. "Cover Me" will not be played in the next 19 shows. A 27-song set on 7/6/84 opens with "Thunder Road."

7/8-9/84 Cleveland, Ohio, Richfield Coliseum

"Born in the USA" opens a 28-song set on 7/8/84 that includes "Open All Night," complete with a story about Bruce being pulled over while driving without a license. "Darkness" is included on 7/9/84, along with "Nebraska" and "Racing in the Street" in a 28-song set. "No Surrender" is played acoustically for the first time, as it will be for the rest of the tour. During the first two months of the tour, "Racing in the Street" and "Backstreets" will be interchanged on successive nights.

7/12-13/84 East Troy, Wisc., Alpine Valley Music Theater

"Man at the Top," premieres, with Bruce introducing it as a "song for an election year." It features beautiful, gospel-tinged backup vocals from Clarence, Nils, and Patti. Twenty-seven-song set. On 7/13/84, "Thunder Road" opens a 27-song set with "Darkness" in the first set.

Asbury Park, N.J., September 26, 1991.

7/15/84 Chicago, Ill., Rosemont Horizon
A 28-song set includes "Nebraska," "Open All Night," and "Atlantic City."

7/17-18/84 Chicago, Ill., Rosemont Horizon
"Born in the USA" opens the show on 7/17/84 and is followed by "Tenth Avenue Freeze-out" for the first time in 1984. "Because the Night" is also included in the second set. On 7/18/84, "Thunder Road" opens the show for the last time in a 29-song set that ends with "Twist and Shout."

7/21/84 Montreal, Quebec, The Forum
First show to include "Do You Love Me" following "Twist and Shout." Born in the USA/Tenth Avenue Freeze-out/Out in the Street/ Atlantic City/Johnny 99/The River/Prove It All Night/Glory Days/ Promised Land/Used Cars/My Hometown/Badlands/Thunder Road// Hungry Heart/Cadillac Ranch/Dancing in the Dark/Sherry Darling/ No Surrender/Because the Night/Pink Cadillac/Fire/Bobby Jean/ Backstreets/Rosalita/Jungleland/Born to Run/Street Fightin' Man/ Twist and Shout/Do You Love Me/Detroit Medley (including "I Hear a Train").

7/23-24/84 Toronto, Ontario, Exhibition Stadium Grandstand
Twenty-eight-song set on 7/23/84. On 7/24/84, a 26-song set opens with "Badlands" and includes the first 1984 appearance of "Trapped."

7/26/84 Toronto, Ontario, Exhibition Stadium Grandstand
"My Father's House" premieres in a 27-song set. It will be performed infrequently on the rest of the tour. "Who'll Stop the Rain" and "Ramrod" are also included in the show, which opens with "Badlands."

7/27/84 Saratoga Springs, N.Y., Performing Arts Center
Bruce allows much of the crowd in to hear a late soundcheck of "Who'll Stop the Rain" at this rain-soaked outdoor show. The band takes the stage a half hour later, opening the set with "Badlands."

7/30-31/84 Detroit, Mich., Joe Louis Arena
"Born in the USA" becomes the consistent show opener from here on.

◄ *Philadelphia, Pa., September 19, 1988.*

A 29-song set on 7/30/84 includes the first 1984 appearance of "Independence Day." "Trapped" and "Growin' Up" are included in a 28-song set on 7/31/84.

8/5-6/84 East Rutherford, N.J., Brendan Byrne Arena
First nights of ten in New Jersey. "Growin' Up" is again played on 8/5/84, and a five-song encore includes "Jersey Girl" for the first time in 1984. A 30-song set on 8/6/84 includes "Nebraska" and "No Surrender," which will later appear on *Live 1975-85*. "Spirit in the Night" makes its 1984 debut. It will only appear in selected East Coast shows.

8/8-9/84 East Rutherford, N.J., Brendan Byrne Arena
A 30-song set on 8/8/84 again includes "Spirit in the Night" and "Jersey Girl." On 8/9/84, J. T. Bowen guests on "Woman's Got the Power" in a 29-song set.

8/11-12/84 East Rutherford, N.J., Brendan Byrne Arena
"Spirit in the Night" is moved to the second half of a 30-song set on 8/11/84 that also includes "Because the Night." John Entwistle guests on "Twist and Shout." "The River" is included in the first set on 8/12/84. Southside Johnny joins the band for "Twist and Shout."

8/16-17/84 East Rutherford, N.J., Brendan Byrne Arena
A 30-song set on 8/16/84 includes "Johnny Bye Bye" for the first time in 1984. The tempo of the song is increased from the 1981 version. An excellent 31-song set on 8/17/84 includes the premiere of "I'm Goin' Down" and the first 1984 appearance of "Follow That Dream." "Cover Me" also returns in the second set.

8/19-20/84 East Rutherford, N.J., Brendan Byrne Arena
A 31-song set on 8/19/84 includes the rarely played "My Father's House." "Reason to Believe" later appears on *Live 1975-85*. The 33-song set on 8/20/84 is one of the best on the tour. Little Steven and the Miami Horns guest at this final night of ten in New Jersey. The horns lend their support on "Tenth Avenue Freeze-out," which later appears on *Live 1975-85*. Little Steven joins on "Two Hearts," and in the encores everyone combines for one of the highlights of the entire tour, a marvelous cover of Dobie Gray's "Drift Away." Born in the

USA/Out in the Street/Spirit in the Night/Atlantic City/Johnny 99/Highway Patrolman/I'm Goin' Down/Darlington County/Glory Days/Promised Land/My Hometown/Darkness/Badlands/Thunder Road//Hungry Heart/Dancing in the Dark/Cadillac Ranch/Tenth Avenue Freeze-out/No Surrender/Cover Me/Prove It All Night/Pink Cadillac/Growin' Up/Bobby Jean/Backstreets/Rosalita/Jungleland/Two Hearts/Drift Away/Born to Run/Detroit Medley (including "Travelin' Band")/Twist and Shout/Do You Love Me.

8/22/84 Asbury Park, N.J., Stone Pony
Bruce guests with La Bamba and the Hubcaps, returning the favor for their appearance with him as the Miami Horns.

8/23/84 Long Branch, N.J., Brighton Bar
Bruce guests with Mama Tried.

8/25-26/84 Landover, Md., Capital Centre
A 31-song set on 8/25/84 includes "I'm Goin' Down" and "Who'll Stop the Rain." On 8/26/84, at the request of a fan, Bruce plays "Be True" for the first and only time on the *Born in the USA* tour. The song will later become a staple on the U.S. leg of the *Tunnel of Love Express* tour. Also included this night are "Spirit in the Night," "Trapped," and "Growin' Up."

8/28-29/84 Landover, Md., Capital Centre
A 32-song set is played on 8/28/84 during which Bruce forgets the lyrics to "Independence Day." "Wooly Bully" is played for the first time in a five-song encore. The second set on 8/29/84 includes "Follow That Dream," "Because the Night," and "Growin' Up."

9/3/84 Asbury Park, N.J., Stone Pony
Bruce guests with John Eddie on "Travelin' Band," "Proud Mary," "I'm Bad, I'm Nationwide" and "Twist and Shout."

9/4-5/84 Worcester, Mass., The Centrum
A 30-song set on 9/4/84 includes "Trapped" and "I'm Goin' Down." The 29-song set on 9/5/84 includes the first appearance of "Downbound Train" since the third show of the tour.

9/7-8/84 Hartford, Conn., Civic Center
A 31-song set is played on 9/7/84. "Rave On" is performed in the encores, in honor of Buddy Holly's birthday. Born in the USA/Out in the Street/Tenth Avenue Freeze-out/Atlantic City/Johnny 99/Highway Patrolman/I'm Goin' Down/Darlington County/Glory Days/Promised Land/My Hometown/Trapped/Badlands/Thunder Road//Hungry Heart/Dancing in the Dark/Cadillac Ranch/Sherry Darling/Downbound Train/I'm on Fire/Cover Me/Pink Cadillac/Bobby Jean/Racing in the Street/Rosalita/Rave On/Jungleland/Born to Run/Detroit Medley (including "Travelin' Band")/Twist and Shout/Do You Love Me. A 30-song set on 9/8/84 includes "Spirit in the Night" and "State Trooper" in the first set.

9/11-12/84 Philadelphia, Pa., The Spectrum
A 30-song set is played on the first of six nights in Philly, perhaps the best multiple-night stand of the tour. On 9/12/84 another 30-song set includes "Spirit in the Night," "State Trooper," "Nebraska," "Point Blank" (for the first time on the tour), and "Trapped."

9/14-15/84 Philadelphia, Pa., The Spectrum
Soundcheck on 9/14/84 includes "Darkness," "Born in the USA," "Tenth Avenue Freeze-out," and "Working on the Highway." The 31-song set includes "Point Blank," "My Father's House," and "Jersey Girl," as well as a guest appearance by the Miami Horns on "Tenth Avenue Freeze-out," "Detroit Medley" and "Twist and Shout." "I'm Bad, I'm Nationwide" is played on 9/15/84 for the only time with the E Street Band, in a show that includes rare performances of "State Trooper" and "Candy's Room."

9/17-18/84 Philadelphia, Pa., The Spectrum
Soundcheck on 9/17/84 includes "Born in the USA" and "Independence Day." The 30-song set that night includes "Independence Day" and "Candy's Room." Final night set: Born in the USA/Out in the Street/Spirit in the Night/Atlantic City/State Trooper/Reason to Believe/I'm Goin' Down/Darlington County/Glory Days/Promised Land/Point Blank/I Fought the Law/Badlands/Thunder Road//Hungry Heart/Dancing in the Dark/Cadillac Ranch/Candy's Room/I'm on Fire/Cover Me/Growin' Up/Bobby Jean/Jersey Girl/Rosalita/Santa Claus/Jungleland/Born to Run/Detroit Medley/Twist and Shout/Do You Love Me.

9/21-22/84 Pittsburgh, Pa., Civic Arena
A 30-song set on 9/21/84 includes "Reason to Believe" and "Mansion on the Hill." On 9/22/84, a 31-song set includes "Who'll Stop the Rain" and closes with "Santa Claus."

9/24-25/84 Buffalo, N.Y., War Memorial Auditorium
A 29-song set with three songs from *Nebraska* is played on 9/24/84. The final show of the first leg of the tour includes the last 1984 performance of "Spirit in the Night" and "State Trooper."

9/26/84 Morristown, N.J., Morris Community Theatre
Bruce joins Southside for "In the Midnight Hour," "Mustang Sally," and "Twist and Shout."

10/7/84 Asbury Park, N.J., Stone Pony
Five-song set with Cats.

10/15/84 Vancouver, British Columbia, PNE Coliseum
Bruce stops the set to calm an unruly crowd that has rushed the stage.

10/17/84 Tacoma, Wash., Tacoma Dome
A 31-song set includes "Follow That Dream" in a six-song encore.

10/19/84 Tacoma, Wash., Tacoma Dome
Energetic 32-song set following a one-day delay due to Bruce's bout with the flu. "Rosalita" is not played for the first time since 1974; instead, "Born to Run" closes the second set. "Wooly Bully" and "Santa Claus" are included in the encores. Born in the USA/Out in the Street/Darlington County/Atlantic City/Johnny 99/Highway Patrolman/Prove It All Night/Who'll Stop the Rain/Glory Days/Promised Land/My Hometown/Point Blank/Badlands/Thunder Road//Sherry Darling/Hungry Heart/Dancing in the Dark/Cadillac Ranch/No Surrender/I'm on Fire/Cover Me/Growin' Up/Bobby Jean/Backstreets/Born to Run/I'm a Rocker/Street Fightin' Man/Wooly Bully/Follow That Dream/Detroit Medley (including "Travelin' Band")/Twist and Shout/Do You Love Me.

10/21-22/84 Oakland, Calif., Coliseum
A 34-song set on 10/21/84 includes five songs from *Nebraska*: "Atlantic City," "Johnny 99," "Reason to Believe," "Mansion on the Hill," and "State Trooper." "Rosalita" returns to the set. "Shut Out the Light" premieres in a stark acoustic arrangement during a 33-song set on 10/22/84 that also includes "Stolen Car," "Growin' Up," and "Darkness." "Stolen Car" is played for the first time since 1981. Show closes with "Santa Claus."

10/25-26/84 Los Angeles, Calif., Sports Arena
Seven-concert series opens with a 34-song set with an eight-song encore. Second night (10/26/84) is a 32-song set.

10/28-29/84 Los Angeles, Calif., Sports Arena
A 33-song set is played on 10/28/84, with "Badlands" as the second song of the first set. The concert on 10/29/84 is the only 1984 appearance of "Night," in a 30-song set that also includes "Candy's Room" and does not include "Rosalita."

10/31/84 Los Angeles, Calif., Sports Arena
Halloween special opens with "High School Confidential." "My Father's House" and "I Fought the Law" are also part of a 32-song set.

11/2/84 Los Angeles, Calif., Sports Arena
"Johnny Bye Bye" and "Stolen Car" are played in a 30-song set.

11/4/84 Los Angeles, Calif., Sports Arena
Final night's 31-song set ends with "Santa Claus."

11/8/84 Tempe, Ariz., Arizona State University Activities Center
Thirty-song set includes "Stolen Car." "Shake" and "Sweet Soul Music" make a rare appearance in the "Detroit Medley."

11/11-12/84 Denver, Colo., McNicholls Arena
Without "Rosalita," the second set now closes with "Racing in the Street." A 28-song set on 11/11/84 includes "State Trooper" and "Johnny Bye Bye."

11/15/84 St. Louis, Mo., St. Louis Arena
A 29-song set.

11/16/84 Ames, Iowa, Hilton Coliseum
A 30-song set includes the premiere of "Sugarland," a song written for possible inclusion on the *Born in the USA* album. The song deals with the plight of a farmer who, under economic strain, contemplates burning his grain field.

Dallas, Tex., November 8, 1980. ▶

11/18/84 Lincoln, Neb., Bob Devaney Sports Center
"Sugarland" is played for the last time.

11/19/84 Kansas City, Mo., Kemper Arena
A 30-song set includes "Kansas City" in the "Detroit Medley."

11/23/84 Austin, Tex., Frank Erwin Center
A 29-song set includes "Stolen Car."

11/25-26/84 Dallas, Tex., Reunion Arena
A 29-song set on 11/25/84 includes "Atlantic City" and "Johnny Bye Bye." Unusual 28-song set on 11/26/84 includes the first *Born in the USA* tour performance of "Factory." Born in the USA/Out in the Street/Prove It All Night/Darkness/Factory/Johnny 99/Reason to Believe/Mansion on the Hill/I'm Goin' Down/Glory Days/Promised Land/My Hometown/Badlands/Thunder Road//Cover Me/Dancing in the Dark/Hungry Heart/Cadillac Ranch/No Surrender/Because the Night/Growin' Up/Bobby Jean/Racing in the Street/Jungleland/Born to Run/Detroit Medley (including "Travelin' Band" and "I Hear a Train")/Twist and Shout/Do You Love Me.

11/29-30/84 Houston, Tex., The Summit
"Factory" is played for the final time on 11/29/84. A 30-song set on 11/30/84 includes "Because the Night" and "The River."

12/2/84 Baton Rouge, La., LSU Assembly Center
A 29-song set. "New Orleans" is included in the "Detroit Medley."

12/6/84 Birmingham, Ala., Jefferson Civic Center
A 28-song set.

12/7/84 Tallahassee, Fla., Civic Center
A 30-song set again includes "Because the Night."

12/9/84 Murfreesboro, Tenn., James T. Murphy Center
A 28-song set.

12/11/84 Lexington, Ky., Rupp Arena
A 28-song set.

12/13-14/84 Memphis, Tenn., Mid-South Coliseum
A 27-song set is played the first night. Little Steven joins the band for the encores on 12/14/84, including "Drift Away" and "Two Hearts," in a 30-song set.

12/16-17/84 Atlanta, Ga., The Omni
Little Steven again joins in encores both nights that include "Two Hearts" and "Ramrod." A 29-song set on 12/16/84. The following night is the final show of the second leg of the tour. Born in the USA/Badlands/Darlington County/Johnny 99/Darkness/Reason to Believe/Shut Out the Light/Johnny Bye Bye/Out in the Street/Glory Days/Promised Land/My Hometown/Prove It All Night/Thunder Road//Cover Me/Dancing in the Dark/Hungry Heart/Cadillac Ranch/Because the Night/I'm on Fire/Growin' Up/Bobby Jean/Racing in the Street/Two Hearts/Ramrod/Born to Run/Detroit Medley (including "Travelin' Band")/Twist and Shout/Do You Love Me/Santa Claus.

1/4-5/85 Hampton, Va., Hampton Roads Coliseum
Third leg of the tour opens with a 28-song set that ends with "Santa Claus." Soundcheck on 1/5/85 includes a rare performance of "Bad

The Main Point, Bryn Mawr, Pa., 1975.

Moon Rising." "Because the Night" is played in the second set.

1/7-8/85 Indianapolis, Ind., Market Square Arena
A 27-song set is played on 1/7/85. Another 27-song set the following night includes "Growin' Up," "Shut Out the Light," and the first *Born in the USA* tour appearance of "I Can't Help Falling in Love."

1/10/85 Louisville, Ky., Freedom Hall Arena
"I Can't Help Falling in Love" is the first encore in a 29-song set.

1/13/85 Columbia, S.C., Carolina Coliseum
"Johnny 99" is introduced by Bruce, who makes reference to South Carolina's first legal execution in many years, which had occurred just days before.

1/15-16/85 Charlotte, N.C., Charlotte Coliseum
A 28-song set is played on 1/15/85. A 29-song set on 1/16/85 ends with "Ramrod."

1/17/85 Greensboro, N.C., Rhinoceros Club
Bruce guests with the Del Fuegos for rousing versions of "Hang on Sloopy" and "Stand By Me."

1/18-19/85 Greensboro, N.C., Greensboro Coliseum
Bruce brings Gary U.S. Bonds and Robbin Thompson onstage on 1/18/85 for "Twist and Shout." A 29-song set again closes with "Ramrod." "Santa Claus" is back in the set on 1/19/85, 24 days after Christmas. The 29-song set includes "Darkness," "Trapped," and "Growin' Up."

1/23-24/85 Providence, R.I., Civic Center
A 28-song set on 1/23/85 includes "Shut Out the Light" and "I Can't Help Falling in Love." "Working on the Highway" finally re-enters the set on 1/24/85, after not having been played since the first night of the tour. It will appear in the set consistently during the rest of the tour. The final two encores are played ten minutes after the taped music begins and the band has apparently left the stage for good. Probably the best show of the third leg. Born in the USA/Prove It All Night/Working on the Highway/Johnny 99/Darkness/Reason to Believe/Mansion on the Hill/Johnny Bye Bye/Out in the Street/Glory Days/Promised Land/My Hometown/Trapped/Badlands//Cover Me/Dancing in the Dark/Hungry Heart/Cadillac Ranch/No Surrender/I'm on Fire/Growin' Up/Bobby Jean/Racing in the Street/I Can't Help Falling in Love/Born to Run/I'm a Rocker/Ramrod/Thunder Road/Wooly Bully/Santa Claus.

1/26-27/85 Syracuse, N.Y., Carrier Dome
Springsteen's first true stadium show is a 30-song set with "Thunder Road" in the encores is played on 1/26/85. Another 30-song set the following night closes the third leg of the tour. Born in the USA/Prove It All Night/Darlington County/Working on the Highway/Johnny 99/Darkness/Reason to Believe/The River/Trapped/Out in the Street/Glory Days/Promised Land/My Hometown/Badlands//Cover Me/Dancing in the Dark/Hungry Heart/Cadillac Ranch/Because the Night/I'm on Fire/Growin' Up/Bobby Jean/Racing in the Street/I Can't Help Falling in Love/Born to Run/I'm a Rocker/Ramrod/Thunder Road/Rockin' All Over the World.

3/21/85 Sydney, Australia, Entertainment Centre
Bruce's first show ever in Australia.

3/23-24/85 Sydney, Australia, Entertainment Centre
A 29-song set on 3/23/85 includes the return of "Rosalita" and a first set inclusion of "Darkness." A 28-song set on 3/24/85 includes "Point Blank."

3/27-28/85 Sydney, Australia, Entertainment Centre
"The River" is included in the first set on 3/27/85. A very unusual 32-song set on 3/28/85 as "Wreck on the Highway" makes its only appearance on the *Born in the USA* tour. Many songs this night have not been played since much earlier in the tour. Born in the USA/Darlington County/Out in the Street/Working on the Highway/Johnny 99/Atlantic City/My Father's House/The River/Prove It All Night/Glory Days/Promised Land/My Hometown/Badlands/Thunder Road//Cover Me/Dancing in the Dark/Hungry Heart/Cadillac Ranch/Wreck on the Highway/I'm on Fire/Pink Cadillac/Bobby Jean/Backstreets//Jungleland/I Can't Help Falling in Love/Born to Run/Ramrod/Twist and Shout/Do You Love Me/Santa Claus/Wooly Bully/Detroit Medley (including "I Hear a Train").

3/31/85 Brisbane, Australia, QE2 Stadium

Patti Scialfa and Bruce Springsteen, Rumson, N.J., 1988.

4/3-4/85 Melbourne, Australia, Royal Melbourne Showgrounds
Final Australian show includes "Working on the Highway," "Open All Night," "Darkness," "Shut Out the Light," "Point Blank," "No Surrender," and "Rockin' All Over the World."

4/10-11/85 Tokyo, Japan, Yoyogi Olympic Pool
Springsteen's first tour of Japan. A 27-song set on 4/10/85 includes "Rockin' All Over the World" and "Ramrod." The Japanese shows are limited to under three hours by government regulation. "Darkness" and "Trapped" are included in the first set on 4/11/85, which begins with "Born in the USA" followed by "Darlington County."

4/13/85 Tokyo, Japan, Yoyogi Olympic Pool
4/15-16/85 Tokyo, Japan, Yoyogi Olympic Pool
A 26-song set on 4/15/85 includes "Point Blank" and "Rosalita." "Because the Night" and "No Surrender" are included in a 26-song set on 4/16/85.

4/19/85 Kyoto, Japan, Furitsu Taiikukan
"The River" is played in the first set.

4/21-22/85 Osaka, Japan, Castle Hall
A 25-song set ends the Japanese tour: Born in the USA/Out in the Street/Darlington County/Atlantic City/Darkness/Point Blank/Working on the Highway/Prove It All Night/Glory Days/Promised Land/My Hometown/Badlands/Thunder Road//Cover Me/Dancing in the Dark/Hungry Heart/Cadillac Ranch/Sherry Darling/No Surrender/Backstreets/Rosalita/Bobby Jean/Born to Run/I Can't Help Falling in Love/Twist and Shout/Do You Love Me.

6/1/85 Dublin, Ireland, Slane Castle
Bruce's first European show in nearly four years. The 27-song set includes the only performance of the Beach Boys' "When I Grow Up to Be a Man." "Rosalita" closes the second set.

6/4-5/85 Newcastle, England, St. James Park
A 27-song set on 6/4/85 includes "Trapped," "The River," and "Bobby Jean," now in the encores. The set on 6/5/85 includes "Shut Out the Light," "Because the Night," and "Darkness."

6/8/-9/85 Gothenberg, Sweden, Ullevi Stadium
"Sherry Darling" appears in the encores on 6/9/85.

6/12-13/85 Rotterdam, The Netherlands, Stadion Feynoord
The 28-song set on 6/12/85 is typical of most shows on the 1985 European tour: Born in the USA/Badlands/Out in the Street/Darlington County/Johnny 99/Atlantic City/The River/Trapped/Working on the Highway/Prove It All Night/Glory Days/The Promised Land/My Hometown/Thunder Road//Cover Me/Dancing in the Dark/Hungry Heart/Cadillac Ranch/Downbound Train/I'm on Fire/Because the Night/Rosalita/I Can't Help Falling in Love/Bobby Jean/Born to Run/Ramrod/Twist and Shout/Do You Love Me. The set on 6/13/85 includes "Darkness," "Shut Out the Light," and "Trapped."

6/15/85 Frankfurt, West Germany, Waldstadion
A 28-song set.

6/18/85 Munich, West Germany, Olympic Stadium
6/21/85 Milan, Italy, San Siro Stadium
One of the better shows on the European tour. A 29-song set includes "Backstreets" and closes with "Rockin' All Over the World."

6/23/85 Montpellier, France, Stade Richter
6/25/85 St. Etienne, France, Stade Geoffrey Guichard
"No Surrender" is included in a 28-song set.

6/29-30/85 Paris, France, La Courneuve
A 27-song set on 6/30/85 includes a rare European performance of "Point Blank."

7/3-4/85 London, England, Wembley Stadium
Bruce debuts a new song called "Seeds" in a 27-song set on 7/3/85. An exceptional 30-song July Fourth set opens with an acoustic version of "Independence Day." "Seeds" is again included in the first set, and Little Steven joins the band in the encores, including "Two Hearts."

7/6/85 London, England, Wembley Stadium
Final night in London includes "Street Fightin' Man" in the encores.
A 30-song set also includes "Highway Patrolman," "Because the
Night," and "Two Hearts" with Little Steven.

7/7/85 Leeds, England, Roundhay Park
Final show of the European tour is a 30-song set that includes "Rac-
ing in the Street," "Follow That Dream," "Two Hearts" with Little
Steven, and closes with "Rockin' All Over the World."

8/5/85 Washington, D.C., R.F.K. Stadium
Second performance ever of "Man at the Top," now with slightly different lyrics. The 29-song set list is very similar to the final English
shows. Most of the shows of the 1985 stadium tour have nearly identical set lists, usually varying by only a song or two. The West Coast
shows change a little more dramatically.

8/7/85 Cleveland, Ohio, Municipal Stadium
A 28-song set includes "This Land Is Your Land" and closes with
"Sherry Darling." Born in the USA/Badlands/Out in the Street/
Johnny 99/Seeds/Atlantic City/The River/Working on the Highway/
Trapped/Darlington County/Glory Days/Promised Land/My Home-
town/Thunder Road//Cover Me/Dancing in the Dark/Hungry Heart/
Cadillac Ranch/Downbound Train/I'm on Fire/Pink Cadillac/Bobby
Jean/This Land Is Your Land/Born to Run/Ramrod/Twist and
Shout/Do You Love Me/Sherry Darling.

8/9/85 Chicago, Ill., Soldier Field
A 28-song standard set.

8/11/85 Pittsburgh, Pa., Three Rivers Stadium
Identical 28-song set.

8/14-15/85 Philadelphia, Pa., Veterans Stadium
Again, an identical 28-song set on 8/14/85. "Darkness," "I'm Goin'
Down," and "Jersey Girl" are added to the set on 8/15/85.

8/18-19/85 East Rutherford, N.J., Giants Stadium
A 29-song set on 8/18/85 is the first of six New Jersey stadium shows;
"Jersey Girl" is added to the standard set. "Darkness" replaces
"Atlantic City," and "I'm Goin' Down" replaces "Darlington County"
in a 29-song set on 8/19/85.

8/21-22/85 East Rutherford, N.J., Giants Stadium
"Growin' Up" replaces "Pink Cadillac" in a 27-song set on 8/21/85.
Little Steven guests with the band on 8/22/85 for encores of "Two
Hearts," "Ramrod," "Twist and Shout," and "Do You Love Me."

8/26-27/85 Toronto, Ontario, CNE Grandstand
"I Can't Help Falling in Love" replaces "This Land Is Your Land" on
8/26/85 in a 28-song set that also includes "I'm Goin' Down." A 28-
song set on 8/27/85 includes "Growin' Up."

8/31-9/1/85 East Rutherford, N.J., Giants Stadium
"Growin' Up" is again included on 8/31/85 and Little Steven guests on
a nine-song encore that includes the premiere of "Stand on It." The
final night includes "Darkness," "I'm Goin' Down," and "This Land Is
Your Land," and the only stadium tour performances of "Fire" and
first stadium appearance of "Santa Claus."

9/4/85 Detroit, Mich., Silverdome
"Detroit Medley" makes its only appearance on the 1985 stadium
tour.

9/6/85 Indianapolis, Ind., Hoosier Dome
Set again includes "Santa Claus."

9/9-10/85 Miami, Fla., Orange Bowl

9/13-14/85 Dallas, Tex., Cotton Bowl
"Travelin' Band" is played on 9/13/85 in response to a man in the sec-
ond row who throws his artificial leg onstage during the encores.
"Growin' Up" is added to a 29-song set on 9/14/85 that ends with
"Travelin' Band."

9/18-19/85 Oakland, Calif., Oakland Stadium
"Stolen Car" is played on 9/18/85 for the only time on the 1985 stadium tour. The show on 9/19/85 includes rare performances of "Used
Cars," with Roy Bittan on accordion, and "Highway Patrolman," featuring Clarence Clemons on harmonica.

9/23-24/85 Denver, Colo., Mile High Stadium
A 29-song set is played on 9/23/85. A very cold outdoor show. A 30-

◄ *Brooklyn, N.Y., 1984.*

song set is played the following night, with "Because the Night" and a
rare appearance of "High School Confidential" linked with "Travelin'
Band" in the encores.

9/27/85 Los Angeles, Calif., Coliseum
A 31-song set includes the only performance of "Janey, Don't You
Lose Heart." Edwin Starr's "War" is played for the first time, with
Bruce reading the lyrics from a piece of paper strapped to his forearm.

9/29-30/85 Los Angeles, Calif., Coliseum
A 30-song set is played on 9/29/85, and a 32-song set the following
night.

10/2/85 Los Angeles, Calif., Coliseum
The 33-song final show of the *Born in the USA* tour includes the first
U.S. stadium performance of "Rosalita." Soundcheck includes "I
Don't Wanna Go Home" and "Blinded by the Light." All four Los
Angeles shows are professionally shot by Springsteen for potential
future release. Videos of "War," "My Hometown," and "This Land Is
Your Land" (shown on ABC's "20/20") are culled from this footage.
Born in the USA/Badlands/Out in the Street/Johnny 99/Seeds/Dark-
ness/The River/War/Working on the Highway/Trapped/I'm Goin'
Down/Prove It All Night/Promised Land/My Hometown/Thunder
Road//Cover Me/Dancing in the Dark/Hungry Heart/Cadillac Ranch/
No Surrender/I'm on Fire/Growin' Up/Rosalita/This Land Is Your
Land/Born to Run/Bobby Jean/Ramrod/Twist and Shout/Do You
Love Me/Stand on It/Travelin' Band/Rockin' All Over the World/
Glory Days (with Jon Landau on guitar).

1/19/86 Asbury Park, N.J., Stone Pony
Bruce and the E Street Band minus Nils and Roy play at a benefit for
workers at the 3M plant in Freehold, which is being closed down.
Unfortunately, the plant closes in spite of the efforts to save it. Part of
the 40-minute set is filmed by ABC, and airs the following week on
"20/20": My Hometown/Promised Land/Badlands/Darkness/ Stand
on It/Ramrod/Twist and Shout.

3/2/86 Asbury Park, N.J., Stone Pony
Bruce calls this show "the E Street Band sneak attack." The band,
minus Roy, tears through a loose nine-song set: Stand on It/Working
on the Highway/Darlington County/Promised Land/Darkness/I'm
Goin' Down/My Hometown/Cadillac Ranch/Glory Days.

10/13/86 Mountain View, Calif., Shoreline Amphitheater
Bruce, with help from Nils and Danny, turns in a magnificent acoustic set at Neil Young's Bridge Benefit Concert. The show is Springsteen's first all-acoustic set since the early 1970s. Bruce and Nils first
appear onstage joining Neil Young on "Helpless." Bruce opens his
own set with an accapella version of "You Can Look," followed by a
stunning solo arrangement of "Born in the USA," before being joined
by Nils on guitar and Danny on accordion. Helpless (with Neil
Young)/You Can Look/Born in the USA/Seeds/Darlington County/
Mansion on the Hill/Fire/Dancing in the Dark/Glory Days/Follow
That Dream/Hungry Heart (with Crosby, Stills, Nash, and Young)/
Teach Your Children (all performers).

11/4/86 *Live 1975-85* is released in the U.S.

11/5/86 Paris, France
Bruce and Bob Geldof join Huey Lewis and the News for an encore
of "Barefootin'."

1/21/87 New York, N.Y., Waldorf-Astoria Hotel
Bruce gives the speech inducting Roy Orbison into the Rock 'n' Roll
Hall of Fame. Bruce sings on "Stand By Me" and "Oh, Pretty
Woman."

4/12/87 Asbury Park, N.J., Stone Pony
Bruce and an abbreviated E Street Band (Roy, Patti, Max, and
Garry) make a surprise Pony appearance, their first in over a year.
"Light of Day" debuts, opening the ten-song set. Jon Bon Jovi joins
the band onstage for "Kansas City." Light of Day/Stand on It/Dar-
lington County/My Hometown/Around and Around/Twist and Shout/
Wooly Bully/Lucille/Cadillac Ranch/Kansas City.

7/29/87 Belmar, N.J., Key Largo
Bruce joins reggae band Jah Love onstage for reggae versions of
"Born in the USA" and "My Hometown." One of the most surprising
live appearances Bruce has ever made. He will play three of the next
four nights in Jersey clubs.

7/30/87 Neptune, N.J., Green Parrot
Bruce again joins Jah Love, this night for "One Love, One Heart," and again reggae versions of "Born in the USA" and "My Hometown."

7/31/87 Asbury Park, N.J., Stone Pony
After midnight, actually early the morning of 8/1/87, Bruce joins Marshall Crenshaw onstage for "You Can't Sit Down," a humorous "La Bamba," and "Twist and Shout."

8/2/87 Asbury Park, N.J., Stone Pony
Again, actually in the wee hours of 8/3/87, Bruce and the E Street Band (minus Nils) hit the stage for their longest show since the *Born in the USA* tour, a mix of Bruce's own material and some long-unplayed covers. Light of Day/I'm Bad, I'm Nationwide/Come On Let's Go/ Gloria/I'm on Fire/Ruby Ruby/Sweet Little Sixteen/Proud Mary/Money/Jersey Girl/Around and Around/Glory Days/Havin' a Party/Twist and Shout.

8/9/87 Asbury Park, N.J., Stone Pony
Just after midnight, Bruce and the E Street Band are back for more, turning in another outstanding ten-song set to an overjoyed crowd. "I Don't Wanna Hang Up My Rock 'n' Roll Shoes" is played for the first time since 1978. Light of Day/Darlington County/I'm Bad, I'm Nationwide/Fortunate Son/Ruby Ruby/Stand By Me/I Don't Wanna Hang Up My Rock 'n' Roll Shoes/Glory Days/Havin' a Party/Twist and Shout.

8/14/87 Asbury Park, N.J., Stone Pony
Bruce joins former E Street Band member Ernest Carter and his new band, the Fairlanes. The set includes "Savin' Up," a Springsteen original Bruce had given to Clarence Clemons for his first record with the Red Bank Rockers.

8/21/87 Asbury Park, N.J., Stone Pony
During Little Steven's show, Bruce comes onstage, and the two sing "Native American" and "Sun City."

8/22/87 Asbury Park, N.J., Stone Pony
Bruce joins Levon Helm's All-Stars, including Max Weinberg, for "Lucille" and "Up on Cripple Creek."

8/26/87 Belmar, N.J., Key Largo
Bruce again joins Jah Love for three songs: "Jersey Girl," "My Hometown" and "Born in the USA." Later that same night, Bruce arrives at the Columns, in Avon, N.J., and joins the Cherubs on "Lucille" and "Stand By Me."

8/27/87 Sea Bright, N.J., The Tradewinds
Bruce joins Cats onstage for rousing versions of "Light of Day," "Proud Mary," "Fortunate Son," "I'll Be There," "Around and Around," and "Lucille."

9/25/87 Philadelphia, Pa., J.F.K. Stadium
Bruce joins U2 for "Stand By Me."

9/30/87 Los Angeles, Calif., Coconut Grove
Bruce becomes Roy Orbison's rhythm guitarist for the filming of the Cinemax special "Roy Orbison and Friends: A Black and White Night." Bruce is just one member of an all-star band that also includes Elvis Costello, Tom Waits, James Burton, k.d. lang, and Jackson Browne.

10/6/87 *Tunnel of Love* is released in the U.S.

10/8/87 New York, N.Y., The Ritz
Bruce again joins Little Steven for "Native American" and "Sun City."

10/22/87 New York, N.Y., St. Peter's Church
At the memorial service for John Hammond, Bruce performs an acoustic version of Bob Dylan's "Forever Young."

10/31/87 Sea Bright, N.J., McLoone's Rumrunner
Bruce and the E Street Band (minus Nils and Clarence) make a surprise Halloween appearance, dressed from head to toe in black, wearing hangman's masks, which they wear for the first song. The show includes the full-band debuts of "Brilliant Disguise," "Tougher Than the Rest," and "Two Faces," along with the first acoustic version of "Born to Run." Stand on It/Glory Days/Bad Moon Rising/Around and Around/Brilliant Disguise/Tougher Than the Rest/Light of Day/Born to Run/Fortunate Son/Two Faces/Lucille/Twist and Shout.

◄ Asbury Park, N.J., August 9, 1987.

11/6/87 Rumson, N.J., Rumson County Day School
Bruce shows up for a benefit at the school across the street from his house in Rumson. He joins the Fabulous Grease Band for "Carol," "Lucille," "Twist and Shout," and "Stand By Me." At one point during the show, Bruce says, "Keep it down, my wife's asleep across the street."

11/20/87 Asbury Park, N.J., Stone Pony
Bruce joins Bobby Bandiera for "Little Latin Lupe Lu," "Stand by Me," and "Carol."

12/5/87 Asbury Park, N.J., Stone Pony
Bruce guests with Cats on "Carol," "Stand by Me," "Wooly Bully," "Around and Around," "Little Latin Lupe Lu," and "Twist and Shout."

12/7/87 New York, N.Y., Carnegie Hall
Bruce joins numerous other artists in a tribute to Harry Chapin. He gives a short speech and plays an acoustic version of Chapin's "Remember When the Music."

12/13/87 New York, N.Y., Madison Square Garden
At the request of Paul Simon, Bruce joins this all-star benefit show for New York's homeless. Bruce sings backup to Dion on "Teenager in Love," and performs three other songs: an acoustic version of "Born to Run," "Glory Days" (with David Letterman's band), and the finale of "Rock and Roll Music."

1/88 Oceanport, N.J., Fort Monmouth
Rehearsals for the upcoming tour commence in various locations, reportedly including this old armory site. All members of the E Street Band are present, as well as the *Tunnel of Love* horn section (Mario Cruz, Ed Manion, Mike Spengler, Mark Pender, and Richie "La Bamba" Rosenberg). During the rehearsals, the basic set list and stories for the show are created, though a number of songs are rehearsed for the tour that will not be included at any show, among them "For You," "Candy's Room," "When You're Alone" and "Valentine's Day." Even more surprising are horn-highlighting attempts at "Protection," (the *Born in the USA* sessions outtake given to Donna Summer in 1982) and the Four Tops' "Something About You."

1/20/88 New York, N.Y., Waldorf-Astoria Hotel
Bruce gives the speech inducting Bob Dylan at the Rock and Roll Hall of Fame Awards. He also sings with others on "I Saw Her Standing There," "Born on the Bayou," and "Satisfaction." Max, Patti, Roy, Danny, and Garry are among the performers in the massed band.

· · · · ·

TUNNEL OF LOVE EXPRESS TOUR

For song counts "Detroit Medley" will be counted as one song. "Who Do You Love," "Ain't Got You" and "She's the One" are counted as separate songs. "Land of 1000 Dances" and "Born to Be Wild," included in the midst of "Light of Day," will be counted as separate songs.

2/25/88 Worcester, Mass., The Centrum
Bruce and the E Street Band, joined by the *Tunnel of Love* horns, return to the stage for their first tour in over two years. The 190-minute show includes eight songs from the *Tunnel of Love* LP and four other previously unplayed songs, not counting "Be True," which the band has played only once before (Landover, Md., 8/26/84). "Adam Raised a Cain" is played for the first time since September 1978, and "She's the One" is played for the first time since September 1981. "Born to Run" is played acoustically, a version that debuted at the surprise Halloween show 10/31/87. New songs include "Part Man, Part Monkey," a song about the evolution/creationism battle, and "I'm a Coward," a tune about the perils of love loosely based on Gino Washington's early sixties hit, "Gino is a Coward."

The basic set will remain through most of the tour, not changing significantly until the tour hits the West Coast in late April: Tunnel of

Love/Be True/Adam Raised a Cain/Two Faces/All That Heaven Will Allow/Seeds/Roulette/Cover Me/Brilliant Disguise/Spare Parts/War/ Born in the USA//Tougher Than the Rest/She's the One/You Can Look/I'm a Coward/I'm on Fire/One Step Up/Part Man, Part Monkey/Walk Like a Man/Dancing in the Dark/Light of Day/Born to Run/Hungry Heart/Glory Days/I Can't Help Falling in Love/ Rosalita/Detroit Medley (including "Shake" and "Sweet Soul Music").

2/28-29/88 Worcester, Mass., The Centrum
"Tenth Avenue Freeze-out" is added to the second encore on 2/28/88. "Tenth Avenue Freeze-out" is not played on 2/29/88, but Presley's "Love Me Tender" is premiered, replacing "Can't Help Falling in Love." The beautiful keyboard introduction to "Walk Like a Man" is dropped following this show.

3/3-4/88 Chapel Hill, N.C., Dean Smith Center
"I Can't Help Falling in Love" replaces "Love Me Tender" on 3/4/88. Soundchecks from the two shows include "I Shall Be Released," "Mr.Tambourine Man," and "Just Like a Woman." Though the show set list doesn't vary much from night to night, the soundchecks on the tour are constantly changing and include numerous cover songs. Toward the end of the U.S. dates, Springsteen begins to consistently allow a few hundred fans in early to hear parts of these fascinating soundchecks.

3/8-9/88 Philadelphia, Pa., The Spectrum
"Love Me Tender" replaces "I Can't Help Falling in Love" on 3/8/88. Soundcheck includes "Stolen Car" and the only known live version of "When You're Alone." "Raise Your Hand" is played on 3/9/88 for the first time since the *River* tour. "Shake" leaves the "Detroit Medley."

3/13-14/88 Cleveland, Ohio, Richfield Coliseum

3/16-17/88 Chicago, Ill., Rosemont Horizon
The first notable changes in the set are made on 3/17/88 with "Darkness" replacing "Seeds," and "Backstreets" replacing "Walk Like a Man." Bruce does an Irish jig during "Rosalita" to celebrate St. Patrick's Day.

3/20/88 Pittsburgh, Pa., Civic Arena
"Seeds" returns instead of "Darkness." Joe Grushecky, formerly of the Iron City Houserockers, joins Bruce onstage for "Raise Your Hand."

3/22-23/88 Atlanta, Ga., The Omni
"Darkness" replaces "Seeds"; "Walk Like a Man" returns for "Backstreets" on 3/22/88. Bruce also adds part of "Who Do You Love" as an intro to "She's the One." The standard set returns on 3/23/88, including both "Seeds" and "Walk Like a Man." Spectacular soundchecks here include Ry Cooder's "Across the Borderline," "Crazy Love," "Pretty Flamingo," and "Tupelo Honey" among over fifteen other songs experimented with.

3/26/88 Lexington, Ky., Rupp Arena
Bruce adds one verse of "Ain't Got You" as an introduction to "She's the One."

3/28-29/88 Detroit, Mich., Joe Louis Arena
MTV cameras are present to film footage for a half-hour special that airs a month later. Bruce is interviewed for MTV by Kurt Loder."Ain't Got You" is expanded to two verses. The show is digitally recorded, and a live version of "Be True" later appears on the "Chimes of Freedom"/"Tougher Than the Rest" live EPs. On 3/29/88, "Darkness" and "Backstreets" are both back in the set, for the last time until the West Coast.

4/1-2/88 Uniondale, N.Y., Nassau Coliseum
A standard set is played on 4/1/88 with "Seeds" and "Walk Like a Man." This marks the first of ten shows with identical set lists, not counting songs left out of the set and not replaced. This represents the first time in Springsteen's career when the set stays the very same for so long. "Ain't Got You" is deleted the following night. Bruce begins adding the line "It's just a kiss away," from the Rolling Stones' "Gimme Shelter," to "Cover Me."

4/4-5/88 Landover, Md., Capital Centre
"Ain't Got You" is back in on 4/4/88.

◄ *Greensboro, N.C., January 19, 1985.*

4/12-13/88 Houston, Tex., The Summit
"Love Me Tender" is taken out of the set from here on until Europe. Tunnel of Love/Be True/Adam Raised a Cain/Two Faces/All That Heaven Will Allow/Seeds/Roulette/Cover Me/Brilliant Disguise/ Spare Parts/War/Born in the USA//Tougher Than the Rest/Ain't Got You/She's the One/You Can Look/I'm a Coward/I'm on Fire/One Step Up/Part Man, Part Monkey/Walk Like a Man/Dancing in the Dark/Light of Day/Born to Run/Hungry Heart/Glory Days/Rosalita/ Detroit Medley/Raise Your Hand.

4/15/88 Austin, Tex., Frank Erwin Center
Soundcheck includes "Follow That Dream."

4/17/88 St. Louis, Mo., St. Louis Arena
Enthusiastic crowd here produces perhaps the best of the standard-set shows.

4/20/88 Denver, Colo., McNicholls Arena
"Sweet Soul Music" is played as a separate song from here on.

4/22-23/88 Los Angeles, Calif., Sports Arena
With Roy Orbison in attendance, celebrating his birthday on 4/23/88, Bruce begins a series of small set changes that will continue throughout the rest of the U.S. tour. "Backstreets" returns in place of "Walk Like a Man." The encore begins with Bruce leading the crowd in singing "Happy Birthday" to Orbison. Bruce had rehearsed Orbison's "Crying" in the soundcheck, but unfortunately it is not played. The "Detroit Medley" is given a much-needed rest and is replaced by "Have Love, Will Travel," "Tenth Avenue Freeze-out," and "Sweet Soul Music." "Have Love, Will Travel" is a cover of a song by the Northwest band The Sonics. "Tenth Avenue Freeze-out" returns after being played just once on the second date of the tour. Tunnel of Love/Be True/Adam Raised a Cain/Two Faces/All That Heaven Will Allow/Seeds/Roulette/Cover Me/Brilliant Disguise/Spare Parts/War/ Born in the USA//Tougher Than the Rest/Ain't Got You/She's the One/You Can Look/I'm a Coward/I'm on Fire/One Step Up/Part Man, Part Monkey/Backstreets/Dancing in the Dark/Light of Day/ Born to Run/Hungry Heart/Glory Days/Rosalita/Have Love, Will Travel/Tenth Avenue Freeze-out/Sweet Soul Music/Raise Your Hand.

4/25/88 Los Angeles, Calif., Sports Arena
Same set as on 4/23/88.

4/27-28/88 Los Angeles, Calif., Sports Arena
Ry Cooder's "Across the Borderline," played in soundchecks for weeks, is premiered on 4/27/88, replacing "Backstreets." This show and the following night's are filmed for use in the "Tougher Than the Rest" and "Born to Run (acoustic)" videos. The entire show is also audio-recorded, and live versions of "Tougher Than the Rest" and "Born to Run" later appear on the "Chimes"/"Tougher" live EPs. The same set is played the following night.

5/2-3/88 Mountain View, Calif., Shoreline Amphitheater
On 5/2/88, "Walk Like a Man" replaces "Across the Borderline," and is dedicated by Bruce to his father, who is in attendance. For the first time since the *River* tour, Bruce not only enters the crowd, but climbs on top of a chair to sing "Hungry Heart" while the crowd gently holds him up. During "Glory Days," Bruce, Nils, Patti, Clarence, and the horn section all climb off the stage into the crowd, dancing across the front row. First outdoor show of the tour. On 5/3/88, "Backstreets" replaces "Walk Like a Man." "Little Latin Lupe Lu" is played with the band for the first time since 1977, after "Raise Your Hand," and is followed by "Twist and Shout," played for the first time in 1988. This is the longest show on the U.S. leg of the *Tunnel* tour. These impromptu additions are clearly a surprise to the band, who end "Twist and Shout" by themselves after Bruce leaves the stage. The terrific show is highlighted by Bruce dancing with his mother during "Dancing in the Dark." Perhaps the best show of the entire U.S. tour. Soundcheck includes Roy playing part of "Jungleland" and Nils singing "Man at the Top." Bruce allows part of the crowd in to hear "I'm So Lonesome I Could Cry" and "Crying."

5/5-6/88 Tacoma, Wash., Tacoma Dome
Same set as 5/2/88 is played on 5/5/88. Soundcheck includes "I'm So Lonesome I Could Cry," "Crying," and Jackie Wilson's "Lonely Teardrops." Steppenwolf's "Born to Be Wild" is played for the first

time with the E Street Band on 5/6/88, in the middle of "Light of Day." "Darkness" also returns for the first time since Detroit, this time replacing "Roulette." "Backstreets" replaces "Walk Like a Man," and "Twist and Shout" is again added after "Raise Your Hand." Soundcheck includes "Big Boss Man," "Let It Be Me," "Cathy's Clown," "Crying in the Rain," "Rock 'n' Roll Music" and "Sweet Little Sixteen." This is the first show in four years that doesn't include "Dancing in the Dark." Second longest show of the tour, and one of the best.

5/9-10/88 Bloomington, Minn., Met Center
Same set as 5/2/88 is played on 5/9/88. On 5/10/88, Bruce premieres John Lee Hooker's "Boom Boom," which will be included in the set from here on. "Cautious Man" is played for the first and only time, replacing the story before "Spare Parts." The song is rehearsed numerous times during the day's soundcheck. Tunnel of Love/Boom Boom/Adam Raised a Cain/Two Faces/All That Heaven Will Allow/Seeds/Cover Me/Brilliant Disguise/Cautious Man/Spare Parts/War/Born in the USA//Tougher Than the Rest/Ain't Got You/She's the One/You Can Look/I'm on Fire/One Step Up/Part Man, Part Monkey/Backstreets/Dancing in the Dark/Light of Day/Born to Run/Hungry Heart/Glory Days/Rosalita/Have Love, Will Travel/Tenth Avenue Freeze-out/Sweet Soul Music/Raise Your Hand/Twist and Shout.

5/11/88 New Orleans, La., Maple Leaf Club
Bruce flies the band and much of the crew to New Orleans for a brief mid-tour respite. Despite the vacation theme, Springsteen ends up sitting in with the local band, the New Orleans Blues Department, for five songs including "Boom Boom."

5/13/88 Indianapolis, Ind., Market Square Arena
"Cautious Man" is out of the set. "Across the Borderline" replaces "Backstreets."

5/16/88 New York, N.Y., Madison Square Garden
"Crying" is added to the set after weeks of appearances in soundchecks. Tickets to the five New York shows were impossible to get as Bruce and the band make their first Madison Square Garden appearances since December 1980, with scalpers selling high-quality counterfeit tickets. The band closes the show with a brief snatch of "New York, New York." Tunnel of Love/Boom Boom/Be True/Adam Raised a Cain/Two Faces/All That Heaven Will Allow/Seeds/Roulette/Cover Me/Brilliant Disguise/Spare Parts/War/Born in the USA//Tougher Than the Rest/Ain't Got You/She's the One/You Can Look/I'm a Coward/I'm on Fire/One Step Up/Part Man, Part Monkey/Walk Like a Man/Dancing in the Dark/Light of Day/Born to Run/Hungry Heart/Glory Days/Crying/Have Love, Will Travel/Tenth Avenue Freeze-out/Sweet Soul Music/Raise Your Hand.

5/18-19/88 New York, N.Y., Madison Square Garden
Sets are the same as 5/16/88, but "Backstreets" replaces "Walk Like a Man" on 5/18/88, and on 5/19/88 "Vigilante Man" is premiered and replaces "Roulette"; "Dancing in the Dark" is left out of the set.

5/22-23/88 New York, N.Y., Madison Square Garden
Set on 5/22/88 is the same as 5/19/88, but "Across the Borderline" replaces "Backstreets." "Born to Be Wild" is included in "Light of Day." Jackie Wilson's "Lonely Teardrops" is premiered, replacing "Crying." The final show of the U.S. tour is the same as the preceding night, but "Backstreets" replaces "Across the Borderline." Jon Landau joins the band onstage, strumming guitar during the encores, while Barbara Carr goes onstage for "You Can Look."

5/26/88 Irvine, Calif., Irvine Meadows
Bruce joins John Mellencamp onstage for "Like a Rolling Stone."

6/11/88 Turin, Italy, Stadio Comunale
Fifty-five thousand fans greet Bruce, the E Street Band, and the *Tunnel of Love* Horns for their first European show in nearly three years. Ticket sales across the European tour are varied; as a second show here is canceled owing to poor ticket sales, but shows in Oslo and Copenhagen sell out immediately. This is the first stadium show on the *Tunnel* tour. "Because the Night" makes its *Tunnel* tour debut in the place of "Part Man, Part Monkey." Tunnel of Love/Boom Boom/

◄ *Chicago, Ill., July 17, 1984.*

Be True/Adam Raised a Cain/Two Faces/All That Heaven Will Allow/Seeds/Cover Me/Brilliant Disguise/Spare Parts/War/Born in the USA//Tougher Than the Rest/Ain't Got You/She's the One/You Can Look/I'm a Coward/I'm on Fire/One Step Up/Because the Night/Backstreets/Dancing in the Dark/Light of Day/Born to Be Wild/Born to Run/Hungry Heart/Glory Days/Have Love, Will Travel/Tenth Avenue Freeze-out/Sweet Soul Music/Raise Your Hand/Twist and Shout.

6/13/88 Rome, Italy, Piaza di Spagna
Bruce meets some street musicians and plays acoustic versions of "I'm on Fire" and "The River" on a borrowed guitar, for an audience of fifteen.

6/15-16/88 Rome, Italy, Stadio Flamminio
"Bobby Jean" is played on 6/15/88 for the first time on the *Tunnel* tour, in the place of "Have Love, Will Travel." The horns and Patti do not play on the song. "The River" makes its first *Tunnel* tour appearance on 6/16/88, replacing "Two Faces" in a 30-song set that includes a handful of other set changes and adjustments. Tunnel of Love/Boom Boom/Adam Raised a Cain/The River/All That Heaven Will Allow/Seeds/Cover Me/Brilliant Disguise/Spare Parts/War/Born in the USA//Tougher Than the Rest/Who Do You Love/She's the One/You Can Look/I'm a Coward/I'm on Fire/Because the Night/Backstreets/Dancing in the Dark/Light of Day/Born to Run/Hungry Heart/Glory Days/Can't Help Falling in Love/Bobby Jean/Tenth Avenue Freeze-out/Sweet Soul Music/Raise Your Hand/Twist and Shout.

6/18/88 Paris, France, Chateau De Vincennes
Bruce and Clarence make a surprise appearance at the "SOS Racism" anti-racism benefit. The four-song acoustic set is broadcast live on French TV and includes Creedence's "Bad Moon Rising" and, for the first time, Dylan's "Blowin' in the Wind." Promised Land/My Hometown/Blowin' in the Wind/Bad Moon Rising.

6/19/88 Paris, France, Hippodromes De Vincennes
Same as 6/16/88, but "Born to Be Wild" is added to "Light of Day." Bruce begins adding lyrics from Muddy Waters's "Mannish Boy" to the end of "Adam Raised a Cain."

6/21-22/88 Birmingham, England, Aston Villa Football Ground
A 32-song set is played on 6/21/88 with more fine tuning. Tunnel of Love/Boom Boom/Adam Raised a Cain/Two Faces/All That Heaven Will Allow/The River/Seeds/Vigilante Man/Cover Me/Brilliant Disguise/Spare Parts/War/Born in the USA//Tougher Than the Rest/Ain't Got You/She's the One/You Can Look/I'm a Coward/I'm on Fire/One Step Up/Because the Night/Backstreets/Dancing in the Dark/Light of Day/Born to Run/Hungry Heart/Glory Days/Bobby Jean/Tenth Avenue Freeze-out/Sweet Soul Music/Raise Your Hand/Twist and Shout. The following night's set is the same, without "Vigilante Man." "Born to Be Wild" is added to "Light of Day," "Have Love, Will Travel" is added after "Sweet Soul Music," and "Who Do You Love" replaces "Ain't Got You." Bruce is joined onstage by Edwin Starr for "War."

6/25/88 London, England, Wembley Stadium
Same as 6/22/88, but "Part Man, Part Monkey" replaces "One Step Up." Neither song will be played again on the European tour. "Ain't Got You" is back in for "Who Do You Love," and "Have Love, Will Travel" is now played before "Sweet Soul Music." Bruce adds "Love Me Tender" to the second encore as "something special for London." Edwin Starr again joins Bruce for "War."

6/28-29/88 Rotterdam, The Netherlands, Stadion Feynoord
The set on 6/28/88 is the same as 6/22/88, but "Have Love, Will Travel" follows "Sweet Soul Music." Jon Landau joins the band onstage for "Glory Days." An outstanding second show, on 6/29/88, includes many surprises and changes. The park-bench story before "All That Heaven Will Allow" is dropped completely, and there is no introduction before "Spare Parts." After "Born in the USA," the band remains onstage and instead closes the set with Dylan's "Chimes of Freedom," played only once before, in Detroit on 9/1/78. During the intermission, new set lists are placed onstage. The second set opens with the long-lost instrumental "Paradise by the C," played for the first time since mid-*Darkness* tour. The *Tunnel* tour, as a whole, shares a lot of similarities with the *Darkness* tour; adding "Paradise" to the set further

cements the comparison. This show also premieres the "Don't You Touch That Thing" song/story that introduces "You Can Look." The story is really a song in itself and sounds not unlike "From Small Things (Big Things One Day Come)."

7/2-3/88 Stockholm, Sweden, Stockholms Stadion
The 7/2/88 set is the same as 6/29/88, but "All That Heaven Will Allow" and "The River" switch places. "Can't Help Falling in Love" and "Have Love, Will Travel" are not played, but "Cadillac Ranch" is added after "Bobby Jean" for the first time on the *Tunnel* tour. The first set on 7/3/88 is broadcast live via satellite to 15 countries around the world; it is Bruce's first live radio broadcast since the *Darkness* tour. The entire 35-song set is one of the longest ever. Bruce rearranges the first set to make it a full 90 minutes, and announces that he will be joining the Amnesty International Human Rights Now! tour, before he sings "Chimes of Freedom." "Roulette" is played for the first time on the European tour. "Downbound Train" also makes its *Tunnel* tour debut. Over the next four weeks, nearly all of the *Born in the USA* tour staples will reenter the set for at least one show. "Quarter to Three" makes a surprise appearance for the first time since 8/81. One of the best shows on the 1988 tour, though patients at a hospital next to the stadium don't see it that way and are issued ear plugs. Tunnel of Love/Boom Boom/Adam Raised a Cain/The River/All That Heaven Will Allow/Seeds/Roulette/Cover Me/Brilliant Disguise/Tougher Than the Rest/Spare Parts/War/Born in the USA/Chimes of Freedom//Paradise by the C/Who Do You Love/She's the One/You Can Look/I'm a Coward/I'm on Fire/Downbound Train/Because the Night/Dancing in the Dark/Light of Day/Born to Be Wild/Born to Run/Hungry Heart/Glory Days/I Can't Help Falling in Love/Bobby Jean/Cadillac Ranch/Tenth Avenue Freeze-out/Sweet Soul Music/Raise Your Hand/Quarter to Three/Twist and Shout.

7/7/88 Dublin, Ireland, RDS Jumping Enclosure
Same as 7/3/88, but "Downbound Train" is moved up to the first set, replacing "Roulette." Both "Quarter to Three" and "Can't Help Falling in Love" are not included. "Seeds" and "All That Heaven Will Allow" switch places, and Wilson Pickett's "Land of 1,000 Dances" is included for the first time in the middle of "Light of Day."

7/9-10/88 Sheffield, England, Bramall Lane Stadium
A 33-song set is played on 7/9/88, same set list as Dublin, but the order is rearranged. This show is recorded, and "Spare Parts" is later issued as a live B-side. On 7/10/88, Jackie Wilson's "Lonely Teardrops" is played for the first time on the European tour, during a superb eleven-song encore. Bruce continues to rearrange the set order, as he did the previous night. Tunnel of Love/Boom Boom/Adam Raised a Cain/Downbound Train/All That Heaven Will Allow/The River/Seeds/Roulette/Cover Me/Brilliant Disguise/War/Born in the USA/Chimes of Freedom//Tougher Than the Rest/Who Do You Love/She's the One/You Can Look/I'm a Coward/I'm on Fire/Spare Parts/Because the Night/Dancing in the Dark/Light of Day/Land of 1,000 Dances/Born to Run/Hungry Heart/Glory Days/I Can't Help Falling in Love/Bobby Jean/Cadillac Ranch/Tenth Avenue Freeze-out/Sweet Soul Music/Raise Your Hand/Lonely Teardrops/Twist and Shout.

7/12/88 Frankfurt, West Germany, Waldstadion
Still more rearranging in a 33-song set: Tunnel of Love/Boom Boom/Adam Raised a Cain/Downbound Train/All That Heaven Will Allow/The River/Seeds/Cover Me/Brilliant Disguise/Spare Parts/War/Born in the USA/Chimes of Freedom//Paradise by the C/Who Do You Love/She's the One/You Can Look/I'm a Coward/I'm on Fire/Tougher Than the Rest/Because the Night/Dancing in the Dark/Light of Day/Land of 1,000 Dances/Born to Run/Hungry Heart/Glory Days/Bobby Jean/Cadillac Ranch/Tenth Avenue Freeze-out/Sweet Soul Music/Raise Your Hand/Twist and Shout.

7/14/88 Basel, Switzerland, St. Jakob Stadion
"Follow That Dream" is played following "Glory Days" for the first and only time on the *Tunnel* tour, at the request of a fan before the show. "Roulette" is also played instead of "Seeds" in an excellent 34-song set.

◄ East Rutherford, N.J., September 1, 1985.

7/17/88 Munich, West Germany, Olympia Riding Stadium
"Badlands" replaces "Roulette," as it will for the rest of the European tour. Also added here and remaining for the rest of the tour is "Havin' a Party" following "Twist and Shout." Bruce also throws in a verse and chorus from "Do You Love Me," for its only *Tunnel* tour appearance. Onstage set lists confirm that "Badlands" and "Havin' a Party" were planned additions, but "Do You Love Me" was called out by Bruce to the band. "Havin' a Party" is played for the first time in years outside of club dates.

7/19/88 East Berlin, East Germany, Weissensee Cycling Track
The largest show ever held in East Germany draws more than 160,000 people, and is also the largest show Bruce has ever played, and one of the largest rock concerts ever. DT64, the East German radio station, broadcasts most of the show on a two-hour delay. The East German television network broadcasts the entire show minus six songs later the same night and in a further edited version the next day. This is the only show on the tour that does not include "Tunnel of Love" in the set, and is the first show so far not to open with this song. "Badlands" opens a show for the first time in four years. "Out in the Street" is played for the first and only time on the *Tunnel* tour, and "Promised Land" also makes its 1988 tour premiere. For the first time on the tour, "Born to Run" is not played acoustically, but with the full band. Bruce is inspired, and he shows it in an excellent, government-sanctioned, 180-minute concert. Badlands/Out in the Street/Boom Boom/Adam Raised a Cain/All That Heaven Will Allow/The River/Cover Me/Brilliant Disguise/Promised Land/Spare Parts/War/Born in the USA/Chimes of Freedom//Paradise by the C//Who Do You Love/She's the One/You Can Look/I'm a Coward/I'm on Fire/Downbound Train/Because the Night/Dancing in the Dark/Light of Day/Land of 1,000 Dances/Born to Run/Hungry Heart/Glory Days/I Can't Help Falling in Love/Bobby Jean/Cadillac Ranch/Tenth Avenue Freeze-out/Sweet Soul Music/Twist and Shout/Havin' a Party.

7/22/88 West Berlin, West Germany, Walbuehne Amphitheater
Show opens with "Badlands." "Tunnel of Love" is the second show in another inspired 35-song set. During the next few shows Springsteen includes lyrics from "Tears of a Clown" in the end of "Tunnel of Love." Badlands/Tunnel of Love/Boom Boom/Adam Raised a Cain/All That Heaven Will Allow/The River/Promised Land/Cover Me/Brilliant Disguise/Spare Parts/War/Born in the USA/Chimes of Freedom//Tougher Than the Rest/Who Do You Love/She's the One/You Can Look/I'm a Coward/I'm on Fire/Downbound Train/Because the Night/Dancing in the Dark/Light of Day/Land of 1,000 Dances/Born to Run (acoustic)/Hungry Heart/Glory Days/I Can't Help Falling in Love/Bobby Jean/Cadillac Ranch/Tenth Avenue Freeze-out/Sweet Soul Music/Raise Your Hand/Twist and Shout/Havin' a Party.

7/23/88 Copenhagen, Denmark
Bruce joins street musician John Magnusson on acoustic guitar for a three-song set before a gathered crowd of around 100 on a street in Copenhagen. I'm on Fire/The River/Dancing in the Dark. The performance is filmed by a tourist with a camcorder, and part of the footage is shown later on Danish TV.

7/25/88 Copenhagen, Denmark, Idraetspark
Same as 7/12/88, but "Badlands" replaces "Seeds," "Tenth Avenue Freeze-out" is left out, and "Havin' a Party" closes the show.

7/27/88 Oslo, Norway, Valle Hovin Stadion
Same as 7/25/88, but "Thunder Road" makes its first *Tunnel* tour appearance, replacing "Paradise by the C."

7/31/88 Bremen, West Germany, Weser Stadion
Same as 7/25/88, but "Working on the Highway" replaces "Because the Night," its first Tunnel tour appearance. "Can't Help Falling in Love" is added before "Bobby Jean." "Born to Run" is played with the full band, as it will be for the rest of the tour.

8/2/88 Madrid, Spain, Vicente Calderon Stadium
Same as 7/25/88, but "Born to Run" is played with the full band.

8/3/88 Barcelona, Spain, Camp Nou Stadium
Over 80,000 people are in attendance at this final show of the *Tunnel of Love Express* tour. Springsteen had started the tour off in Worcester, Massachusetts, playing eight tunes from *Tunnel of Love* and five from

Born in the USA. By Barcelona, those numbers were reversed. Tunnel of Love/Boom Boom/Adam Raised a Cain/Downbound Train/All That Heaven Will Allow/The River/Badlands/Cover Me/Brilliant Disguise/Spare Parts/War/Born in the USA/Chimes of Freedom//Thunder Road/Who Do You Love/She's the One/You Can Look/I'm a Coward/I'm on Fire/Tougher Than the Rest/Working on the Highway/Dancing in the Dark/Light of Day/Land of 1,000 Dances/Born to Run/Hungry Heart/Glory Days/I Can't Help Falling in Love/Bobby Jean/Cadillac Ranch/Sweet Soul Music/Raise Your Hand/Twist and Shout/Havin' a Party.

8/21/88 Asbury Park, N.J., Stone Pony
Bruce guests with Cats on "Stand by Me" and "Around and Around."

8/25/88 New York City, N.Y., Madison Square Garden
Just a week before the start of the Amnesty tour, Bruce joins Sting onstage for an acoustic "The River" and "Message in a Bottle."

. . . . .

HUMAN RIGHTS NOW! TOUR

9/2/88 London, England, Wembley Stadium
First show of the Amnesty International Human Rights Now! tour, a multi-artist concert that will tour the entire world during the next three months. Springsteen and the E Street Band are joined on the tour by Youssou N'Dour, Tracy Chapman, Sting, Peter Gabriel, and indigenous artists in each country. Ticket prices vary across the globe according to the average income of each region, ranging from over $35.00 in Japan to less than $5.00 in Harare and San Jose. Press conferences are held before most shows, involving Springsteen with the press on an everyday basis for the first time in many years. Springsteen and the E Street Band close the shows in most cities.

The concerts begin with all five performers onstage singing Bob Marley's "Get Up, Stand Up." After Springsteen's set, all five performers regroup for "Chimes of Freedom" and a reprise of "Get Up, Stand Up," this time backed by the E Street Band. Springsteen's set at a majority of the shows consists mostly of greatest hits, with few introductions and most songs segueing one into the next with no break between them. The result is a hasty, but satisfying set, which varies slightly over the course of the tour. All the artists on the tour give exemplary performances throughout, but in most cities (outside the Southern Hemisphere) the crowd is there primarily to see Springsteen. Born in the USA/Promised Land/Cover Me/Cadillac Ranch/The River/Spare Parts/War/My Hometown/Thunder Road/She's the One/Glory Days/Light of Day/Land of 1,000 Dances/Born to Run/Chimes of Freedom/Get Up, Stand Up.

9/4-5/88 Paris, France, Palais Omnisports Bercy
One of only two cities on this tour to host arena-sized shows. For the first time on the tour, Sting joins Springsteen for a duet on "The River." They will sing it together at every show on the tour in which they both perform. There were enthusiastic crowds of 16,500 each night. Born in the USA/Promised Land/Cover Me/Brilliant Disguise/The River/Cadillac Ranch/War/My Hometown/Thunder Road/Bobby Jean/Glory Days/Born to Run/Raise Your Hand/Chimes of Freedom/Get Up, Stand Up. On 9/5/88 Springsteen performs the same set as the previous night, but replaces "Bobby Jean" with "Because the Night."

9/6/88 Budapest, Hungary, Nepstadion
Springsteen's second concert in an Eastern-Bloc country and the first Western group of artists allowed to perform together in Hungary. The show's only restriction is a ban on the sale of souvenir T-shirts and programs. Amnesty officials hope that this show will pave the way for a performance in Moscow, but it cannot be arranged. During both "Thunder Road" and "Hungry Heart," Springsteen urges the crowd to sing along in the places that are usually familiar to fans, but the crowd in Budapest does not know the lyrics and is largely silent. Born in the USA/Promised Land/Cover Me/Working on the Highway/The River/Cadillac Ranch/War/My Hometown/Thunder Road/Hungry Heart/Glory Days/Raise Your Hand/Chimes of Freedom/Get Up, Stand Up.

9/8/88 Turin, Italy, Stadio Comunale
A very vocal crowd of 60,000 turns out to see Springsteen, singing along from the very first notes of "Born in the USA." The set is the same as on 9/6/88.

9/10/88 Barcelona, Spain, Camp Nou Stadium
The set is the same as 9/5/88. Branford Marsalis lends his saxophone talent to "Raise Your Hand."

9/13/88 San Jose, Costa Rica, Estadio Nacional
Again the set is the one of 9/5/88 but played during a heavy rainstorm. Church and parent groups in this country that see few rock 'n' roll programs are worried that the show will have ill effects on the nation's youth. One parent group issues a statement calling rock 'n' roll music "subversive energy with erotic overtones, in an environment of base passions and evil." Bruce's first-ever show in Central America.

9/15/88 Toronto, Canada, Maple Leaf Gardens
The same set as 9/4/88, except that "Dancing in the Dark" replaces "Bobby Jean." The final arena show of the tour will always be memorable if only for "Dancing in the Dark," during which Springsteen chose, and danced spiritedly with, a male partner. This was Springsteen's first indoor show in Toronto since 1981 and his first show there since 1985, as the *Tunnel* tour did not include Canada.

9/17/88 Montreal, Quebec, Olympic Stadium
For the first time Bruce joins Sting for a duet of "Every Breath You Take," with which the two continue to close Sting's set throughout the remainder of the tour. Born in the USA/Promised Land/Cover Me/Brilliant Disguise/The River/Cadillac Ranch/War/My Hometown/Thunder Road/Glory Days/Born to Run/Twist and Shout/Chimes of Freedom/Get Up, Stand Up.

9/19/88 Philadelphia, Pa., J.F.K. Stadium
This first U.S. show of the tour also brings a big surprise in Springsteen's set. "Jungleland" returns for the first time since 1985, in a superb version that highlights Clarence Clemons on saxophone, as much of the tour abroad has done. Gabriel's violin player, L. Shankar, adds strings to "The River." Same set as 9/17/88, except for the addition of "Jungleland" after "My Hometown."

Another surprise of this performance was the guest appearance of David Sancious on keyboards in "Glory Days." Bruce introduced him as "E Street Alumni." Sancious, who currently plays in Gabriel's band, hadn't sat in with the E Street Band in more than ten years. The band was also joined by the *Tunnel of Love* horn section on "Cover Me," "War," "Glory Days," and "Raise Your Hand."

9/21/88 Los Angeles, Calif., Coliseum
The same set as 9/19/88. Joan Baez opens the show, as she does at all three U.S. performances of the tour. U2's Bono joins the artists in encores of "Chimes of Freedom" and "Get Up, Stand Up," and receives a warm welcome from the crowd.

9/23/88 Oakland, Calif., Oakland Stadium
Bruce's 39th birthday means a special show. Roy Orbison flies in to surprise Bruce backstage, something Bruce did for Roy a few months earlier. To open the show, Joan Baez leads the crowd in singing "Happy Birthday" to Bruce, who then joins her onstage for a duet of "Blowin' in the Wind." Because Sting does not perform in either this or the Tokyo show, Gabriel's and Bruce's sets are extended. Gabriel introduces Bruce by leading the crowd once again in "Happy Birthday." Bruce and the band turn in a fourteen-song set that includes the only Amnesty tour performance of "Tunnel of Love." The arrangement of the song is slightly different, opening directly into the verse and leaving out the familiar introduction of the *Tunnel* tour performances. Bruce also plays a superb acoustic version of "I Ain't Got No Home" for the first time in concert. Because of the length of the show and the special occasion, this is probably the best show of the Amnesty tour. War/Born in the USA/Promised Land/Tunnel of Love/Brilliant Disguise/The River/I Ain't Got No Home/Cover Me/Cadillac Ranch/My Hometown/Thunder Road/Glory Days/Born to Run/Raise Your Hand/Chimes of Freedom/Get Up, Stand Up.

9/27/88 Tokyo, Japan, Tokyo Dome (The Big Egg)
Strangely this show does not receive much attention in Japan, and as a result it does not come close to selling out. "I'm on Fire" is performed for the first time in the Amnesty tour. This concert is Bruce's

first in Japan since his triumphant shows there in April of 1985. Born in the USA/Promised Land/Cover Me/Brilliant Disguise/The River/Cadillac Ranch/War/My Hometown/Thunder Road/Dancing in the Dark/I'm on Fire/Glory Days/Born to Run/ Chimes of Freedom/Get Up, Stand Up.

9/30/88 New Delhi, India, Jawaharlal Nehru Stadium
This show is somewhat shrouded in controversy owing to the down-playing of the concert's human rights aspect by the show's sponsor, the newspaper, *The Times* of India. "Working on the Highway" and "Dancing in the Dark" are included in a 15-song set. Gabriel's violinist L. Shankar opens the show and Springsteen joins him on harmonica for one song.

10/3/88 Athens, Greece, New Olympic Stadium
Fourteen-song set without "Thunder Road." The Athens show is added in place of performances planned for Moscow which could not be arranged.

10/7/88 Harare, Zimbabwe, National Sports Stadium
Bruce's first-ever performance in Africa. This show is attended by approximately 20,000 South Africans, and the subject of Apartheid is present in the sets of all the artists. Portions of "War" and "My Hometown," along with Gabriel's "Biko" are broadcast to South Africa via the independent Capitol Radio. Born in the USA/Promised Land/Cover Me/I'm on Fire/The River/Cadillac Ranch/War/My Hometown/Dancing in the Dark/Glory Days/Born to Run/Twist and Shout/Chimes of Freedom/Get Up, Stand Up.

10/9/88 Abidjan, Cote D'Ivoire, Houphouet-Boigny Stadium
The same set as 10/7/88. This is the first show of the tour in which Bruce is not the final performer. All artists on the tour relinquish the closing spot to the immensely popular African artist Johnny Clegg.

10/12/88 São Paulo, Brazil, Palmeiras Stadium
The set for this concert is the same as 10/7/88.

10/14/88 Mendoza, Argentina, Estadio Mundialista Mendoza
The crowd includes thousands of people who crossed the nearby border from Chile. As in Zimbabwe, part of this show is broadcast to Chile.

10/15/88 Buenos Aires, Argentina, River Plate Stadium
The same set as 10/14/88. This final night of the world tour is broadcast on radio around the world and in the U.S. with highly questionable results — fans felt the broadcast did not feature enough music. The show is also filmed and is televised worldwide on December 10, 1988, the 40th anniversary of the United Nations Declarations of Human Rights. All four other artists join Bruce for "Twist and Shout," and David Sancious again sits in on "Cadillac Ranch." Sting and Gabriel are decked out in matching Jersey attire, parodying Bruce's familiar garb. Born in the USA/Promised Land/Cover Me/I'm on Fire/The River/Cadillac Ranch/War/My Hometown/Dancing in the Dark/Glory Days/Raise Your Hand/Twist and Shout/Chimes of Freedom/Get Up, Stand Up.

All totaled, the Amnesty tour covered 20 cities, many of which had never before been visited by Springsteen and the E Street Band, nor by other Western rock music of any kind.

11/12/88 Tarrytown, N.Y., Music Hall
Bruce joins John Prine onstage for a performance of Prine's "Paradise." Patti Scialfa attends the show but does not play. Bruce, Patti and Prine pose for photographers backstage.

11/26/88 San Francisco, Calif., The Stone
For the first time in four years Bruce joins Southside Johnny and the Jukes for a rollicking four-song set that starts at 1:40 a.m. In the Midnight Hour/Hearts of Stone/Keep a Knockin'/Little Queenie.

12/18/88 Asbury Park, N.J., Stone Pony
Bruce attends a Christmas party organized by Jersey Artists for Mankind for seriously ill and mentally retarded children in the area.

Tacoma, Wash., May 5, 1988.

He signs autographs, poses for photos and performs "Santa Claus is Coming to Town" with a group of local musicians.

6/3/89 New York, N.Y., Hotel Carlyle
Bruce sings "Lovin' You," at friend Denise Rubin's wedding.

6/20/89 Pt. Pleasant Beach, N.J., Martells
Bruce climbs onstage early in the evening with Bobby Bandiera for a version of "Kansas City." This show kicks off the summer club tour of '89. As he did previously in 1982 and 1987, Springsteen plays a series of unannounced guest appearances over the next two months.

6/24/89 Asbury Park, N.J., Stone Pony
The summer tour hits full stride as Bruce joins Bobby Bandiera for a three-song set. It features the debut of "Hound Dog," a slow version of "Under the Boardwalk," and a long version of "Glory Days."

6/29/89 Neptune, N.J., Headliner
Bruce joins the Fabulous Greaseband for a 20-minute version of "Twist and Shout."

6/30/89 Atlantic City, N.J., Bally's Grandstand Under the Stars
For the first time since 1982, Bruce joins Jackson Browne on "Stay," "Sweet Little Sixteen," and "Running on Empty." This marks Bruce's first performance in Atlantic City since his Steel Mill days.

7/1/89 Asbury Park, N.J., Stone Pony
Bruce performs the final encore, "Long Tall Sally," with La Bamba and his Big Band.

7/3/89 Long Branch, N.J., Cafe Bar
Bruce joins Gary U.S. Bonds for the first time in many years in his longest appearance of the summer. This Little Girl/Angelyne/Bony Moronie/Your Love/Dedication/New Orleans/Quarter to Three.

7/9/89 Asbury Park, N.J., Stone Pony
Bruce joins Cats on "Travelin' Band."

7/12/89 Pennsauken, N.J.
Bruce reportedly joins Gary U.S. Bonds again at a club in this small town just outside of Philadelphia.

7/15/89 Asbury Park, N.J., T-Birds Cafe
Bruce guests with X-Men on "Little Sister" and "Gloria."

7/22/89 Sea Bright, N.J., McLoone's Rumrunner
Peter Hartung and the Remakes invite Bruce onstage for a four-song set that includes "Twist and Shout" and "Glory Days."

7/23/89 Asbury Park, N.J., Stone Pony
In a wild show, Bruce arrives early with Patti and other family members. After dancing with many in the crowd, Bruce grabs the microphone from Cats and finishes the vocal on "Old Time Rock 'n' Roll" from the middle of the dance floor. He eventually makes it to the stage for a long and loose set that includes "Hound Dog," "From Small Things," "Under the Boardwalk," "Sweet Little Sixteen," "Glory Days," and an eleven-minute version of "Carol" that ended long after 2 a.m.

7/27/89 Neptune, N.J., Headliner
In another wild set, Bruce joins the Fabulous Greaseband for a four-song set. Long Tall Sally/Under the Boardwalk/Sweet Little Sixteen/Glory Days.

8/2/89 Long Branch, N.J., Cheers
In a bar that holds barely 100 people, Bruce joins Bobby Bandiera for "Willie and the Hand Jive."

8/11/89 Holmdel, N.J., Garden State Arts Center
Bruce and nearly all the members of the E Street Band join Ringo Starr and friends onstage. Bruce sings on "Get Back," "Long Tall Sally," "Photograph," and "With a Little Help From My Friends."

8/16/89 Long Branch, N.J., Cheers
Bruce joins Bobby Bandiera during his regular Wednesday night set for a 45-minute set. Highlights include "From Small Things" and "Keep a Knockin'."

9/22/89 Asbury Park, N.J., Stone Pony
Bruce begins his 40th birthday weekend by joining Jimmy Cliff on "Trapped."

9/23/89 Sea Bright, N.J., McLoone's Rumrunner
Bruce is joined at his 40th birthday bash by his mother, Steve Van Zandt, Garry Tallent, Roy Bittan, Patti Scialfa, and others. This abbreviated E Street Band takes the stage with members of the Atlantic Coast Band for an eight-song set that includes "Around and

Around," "Glory Days," "Twist and Shout," "Havin' a Party," "What'd I Say," "Sweet Little Sixteen," and "Stand By Me," sung by Steve Van Zandt while Bruce danced with his mother.

9/29/89 Prescott, Ariz., Matt's Saloon
Rolling into town on a motorcycle, Bruce and his biker entourage pull into this whiskey bar in search of "biker girls." In addition to dancing with the few he found, Bruce also takes the stage with the Mile High Band for a set that begins with "I'm on Fire" and also includes "Don't Be Cruel," "Route 66," and "Sweet Little Sixteen." The band asks Springsteen to sing "Pink Cadillac," but Bruce tells them he could not remember all the words.

12/17/89 Ventura, Calif., Ventura Theatre
In a surprise move after announcing that he won't be using the E Street Band for his next album, Bruce joins Clarence Clemons for a three-song encore of "Glory Days," "Cadillac Ranch," and "Sweet Little Sixteen." Jackson Browne joins the pair for the last two songs after having sung "You're a Friend of Mine" with Clarence earlier in the set.

1/17/90 New York, N.Y., Waldorf-Astoria Hotel
Bruce attends his fourth Rock 'n' Roll Hall of Fame induction dinner and leads the all-star band through "Long Tall Sally" with John Fogerty. Jon Landau introduces Holland-Dozier-Holland.

2/12/90 Beverly Hills, Calif., Ted and Suzie Fields's Backyard
Bruce participates in the "Evening in Brazil" concert, put together by Sting to benefit the preservation of the Amazon rain forests. With ticket prices ranging from $1,000 to $50,000, the event raises over one million dollars. Bruce sings "The River" and lends a hand on other tunes in the short set, notably harmony vocals with Don Henley on Paul Simon's "Slip Slidin' Away" and "Every Breath You Take" with Sting.

2/12/90 Hollywood, Calif., The China Club
After the "Evening in Brazil" benefit, the major participants turn in a 45-minute jam, which includes Bruce leading on "In the Midnight Hour" and "Around and Around."

3/1/90 Los Angeles, Calif., The Forum
Bruce follows Bob Dylan on stage in the encore of a Tom Petty and the Heartbreakers show. Dylan and Petty do "Rainy Day Women" before calling out another friend. Bruce arrives and the trio roll though "Travelin' Band." Bruce remains on stage for one verse of the Animals "I'm Cryin'."

10/29/90 Encino, Calif., Tom Petty's House
Bruce joins Tom Petty for his 40th birthday party with Roger McGuinn, Jeff Lynne, and assorted Heartbreakers in a six-song set. Little Red Rooster/Roll Over Beethoven/Mr. Tambourine Man/Great Balls of Fire/Wipeout/Pipeline.

11/16-17/90 Los Angeles, Calif., Shrine Auditorium
In a benefit concert for the Christic Institute, Springsteen plays two of the most important and dramatic concerts of his career. These shows represent his first announced concert performance since his departure from the E Street Band. Following sets by Jackson Browne and Bonnie Raitt, Springsteen plays solo and acoustic, and this concert reveals more about him than the shows on the previous three tours. The concert begins with a straight ahead acoustic rendition of "Brilliant Disguise," not performed this way since his video clip, and is followed by a new first-time-ever acoustic interpretation of "Darkness on the Edge of Town," that stunned the audience. "Darkness" had not been played since 5/6/88, and had never been done without a band. "Reason to Believe" had not been played since a Tokyo show on 4/13/85. "My Father's House" had last been performed in Australia on 2/28/85. Springsteen played a slow, acoustic version of "Tenth Avenue Freezeout," which had not been performed this way since 1975 at Philadelphia's Tower Theater. The last performance of "Atlantic City" had been in Los Angeles on 9/29/85, while "Nebraska" had not been performed since 8/21/85. Most surprising was the rendition of "Wild Billy's Circus Story," which had not been performed since 4/11/74. Springsteen's version of "Thunder Road" was similar to the style he performed in 1975 and he even forgot the words the first night. The

Asbury Park, N.J., August 21, 1988. ▶

11/16/90 show marks the premieres of several songs including "Red-Headed Woman," "57 Channels," "When the Lights Go Out," and "Real World." Bonnie Raitt and Jackson Browne join Bruce for the encores of "Highway 61" and "Across the Borderline." Brilliant Disguise/Darkness/Mansion on the Hill/Reason to Believe/Red-Headed Woman/57 Channels/My Father's House/Tenth Avenue Freeze-out/Atlantic City/Wild Billy's Circus Story/Nebraska/When the Lights Go Out/Thunder Road/My Hometown/Real World/Highway 61/Across the Borderline.

On 11/17/90, Bruce plays a similar set and debuts two new songs, "The Wish," a song about his mother, and "Soul Driver," along with the first-ever solo piano version of "Tougher Than the Rest." Of the six new songs premiered over the two nights, "57 Channels," "Real World" and "Soul Driver" are later recorded and released on *Human Touch*. Brilliant Disguise/Darkness/Mansion on the Hill/Reason to Believe/Red-Headed Woman/57 Channels/The Wish/Tougher Than the Rest/Tenth Avenue Freeze-out/Soul Driver/State Trooper/Nebraska/When the Lights Go Out/Thunder Road/My Hometown/Real World/Highway 61/Across the Borderline.

1/16/91 New York, N.Y., Waldorf-Astoria Hotel
Bruce makes his annual appearance at the Rock 'n' Roll Hall of Fame dinner and guests on "People Get Ready," "Mustang Sally," and "In the Midnight Hour" with John Fogerty, Jackson Browne, Roger McGuinn, and many others.

1/20/91 Sea Bright, N.J., McLoone's Rumrunner
In a benefit for shore singer Jim Faulkner, Bruce joins a band that includes club proprietor Tim McLoone and Max Weinberg. "Ready Teddy," "Tobacco Road," "Under the Boardwalk," "Jersey Girl" and "Glory Days" are included in the set. Former Upstage proprietor Margaret Potter joins Bruce onstage.

2/17/91 Malibu, Calif.
In a tent set up on the beach, Bruce joins a mixed bag of party guests including Stephen Stills and John McEnroe on "C.C. Rider."

7/12/91 Sea Bright, N.J., McLoone's Rumrunner
Bruce joins Bobby Bandiera for a five-song set. From Small Things/ Jersey Girl/Boom Boom/Travelin' Band/Glory Days.

8/4/91 Long Branch, N.J., Cheers
With the Outcry, Bruce performs another five-song set, consisting of "Ain't That a Shame," "People Get Ready," "Not Fade Away," "Stand by Me," and "Travelin' Band."

9/26/91 Asbury Park, N.J., Stone Pony
Bruce, Little Steven, Bon Jovi, and a host of others come together for a Southside Johnny and the Asbury Jukes concert filmed for television. Bruce sings on three performances of "It's Been a Long Time," as well as "Havin' a Party" and "Talk to Me." It marks the only time that the four favorite sons of the Jersey Shore play together. The footage is later released on home video.

1/30/92 New Orleans, La., Tipitina's
Bruce and Jon Landau host a special party for Sony Music executives and guests to hear *Human Touch* and *Lucky Town*. Landau tells the assembled crowd that Springsteen had told him he planned to record one more song for *Human Touch*, but he suspected Bruce might record more material, and delayed turning in the tapes of the album. Ten songs later, Bruce had *Lucky Town* and a second record to release. The listening party moves from Tipitina's to Arnaud's, where Springsteen himself attends and is greeted with a standing ovation from the record company executives. Bruce visits with the crowd and gives a short speech, expressing how pleased he was with the two records and how eager he was to return to the road, a sentiment repeated in a quote on the official press release announcing the new records: "I'm excited about being finished and am looking forward to being on the road."

2/02/92 New Orleans, La., The Maple Leaf
Introduced as "Louie La Scala," Bruce guests on three songs with the Iguanas during their regular Sunday night set. Afterwards, the band presents Bruce with an Iguanas t-shirt and he poses with them for photos. Ain't That a Shame/Save the Last Dance for Me/Betty Jean.

Remember all the Movies: Washington, D.C., 1985.

RESOURCES
· · · · · · · · · ·

Hiding on the Backstreets

BRUCE SPRINGSTEEN: You can write to Bruce Springsteen care of Columbia Records, Sony Music, 1801 Century Park West, Los Angeles, Calif. 90067.

THUNDER ROAD: *Thunder Road* was the original Bruce Springsteen fanzine and one that provided part of the idea and inspiration for *Backstreets*. Though the magazine stopped publishing in 1982, some back issues are still available and can be obtained by writing Backstreet Records, P.O. Box 51219, Seattle, Wash., 98115-9966. If you write and send a self-addressed-stamped-envelope, we'll send you a list of all currently published fanzines for Bruce Springsteen, Little Steven and Southside Johnny.

CORRECTIONS AND ADDITIONS: If you have any corrections and additions to the material listed in this book, please write us so we can update any future editions.

BACKSTREETS MAGAZINE: If you'd like more information on subscribing to *Backstreets* magazine, rates are currently $15 a year, $25 for two years, or $32 for three years in the U.S. and Canada. Rates for overseas airmail service are $20 a year, or $35 for two years (payable in U.S. funds). Over 40 issues are in print. Some back issues are available and if you send a self-addressed-stamped-envelope, we'll send you a current list of available issues. A sample packet of five selected back issues is $20 postpaid in the U.S. and Canada ($25 overseas). You can fax orders to us at (206) 728-8827 or write us. *Backstreets'* address is P.O. Box 51225, Department P, Seattle, Wash. 98115-9966.

PHOTO CREDITS
· · · · · · · · · ·

Walking in the Sights

Thanks to diligent work by all contributing photographers and researchers; we've attempted to indicate date and location on most photographs. Special thanks for their research efforts go to Kitty O'Niell, Barbara Y.E. Pyle, Phil Ceccola, Debra L. Rothenberg, Ken Viola, Erik Flannigan, Steve Smollen, and the Asbury Park Rock 'n' Roll Museum. Credits: Jeff Albertson/Stock, Boston (64); Mary Alfieri (5,151,152); Asbury Park Rock 'n' Roll Museum (33,37,38); Art Aubry (1); Joel Bernstein/LGI (76); Larry Busacca (200); Watt M. Casey, Jr. (78,182,203, 224); Phil Ceccola (24,30,31,60,61,66,70,74,90,96,113,127,140,145,149,156,185,195,204,220); Mike D'Adamo (164); Ron Delany (190); David Denenberg (19,85,91,95,132,196,200,212); John C. DeSantis/Asbury Park Rock 'n' Roll Museum (22); David DuBois (8,40,43,94,130,166, 187,197,217); David Gahr (20,27,82,104-105,135,142,206); Lynn Goldsmith/LGI (13,54,172); Chuck Jackson/LGI (138,139); Joanne Jefferson (199); Brooks Kraft (2,186,210); Pete Kuhns (106); Kathie Maniaci (45,47,48); Eric Meola/Contact Press (63); Robert Minkin (81); Jim O'Loughlin (170); A.J. Pantsios (44,193); Peter J. Philbin (114,117,123,129,181,189); Barbara Y.E. Pyle/Contact Press (56,69,72,175); Barbara Y.E. Pyle (103,111,119,125,155); Debra L. Rothenberg (49,51,52,86,158,179,208,214,219); Rex Rystedt (10,14,58,79,92,137); Robert Santelli (53); James Shive (59,73,176); Bob "Zimmy" Zimmerman (89,222); Steve Zuckerman (16); Vinnie Zuffante/Starfile (205).

Austin, Tex., November 9, 1980. ▶